PROSECUTING NOBEL SCIENCE

Robert A. Bloomer, Jr.

"Pay a lot of attention to what they're trying to keep you from knowing...Once you know it, you'll be marginalized by society, by newspapers and some of your friends."

> --Grace Paley (author, activist, teacher, and Vermont poet laureate 2003-2007) from her commencement address at Williams College, 1998.

"[Political corruption] is a serious problem...We have a real problem in Vermont. We haven't had a Governor go to prison. We haven't had legislators tearfully apologizing for having taken bribes, facing an indictment the next day. But we have got a problem in Vermont."

> --William Sorrell, Vermont Attorney General during oral arguments before the U.S. Supreme Court in <u>Randall v. Sorrell</u>, 548 U.S. 230 (2006)

1

August 11, 1990. It was an ordinary, small-town Saturday morning when the police began to gather in the parking lot of the West Rutland, Vermont, Grand Union supermarket. Before nine o'clock there were few shoppers, and the overcast sky made it a good day to sleep in. Most of the two-dozen assembled police officers knew only that they were to execute a search warrant. Secrecy had been tight as the target of the warrant, Robert Bloomer, Jr., was from a prominent political family and was himself a candidate for the Vermont House of Representatives.

The officers were briefed that the Bloomer house at 96 Clarendon Ave. was believed to contain a clandestine methamphetamine laboratory. They were to expect an armed confrontation, and were to be on the lookout for booby traps. A fire truck and ambulance were standing by.

After receiving their briefing the officers drove around the corner and down Clarendon Ave., a tree-lined street of white, two-story colonial houses. The cars drew up in front of number ninety-six, and parked in the street. The officers crouched behind their cars, weapons extended across the hoods and trunk lids, and a voice on a bullhorn ordered the occupants of the house to come out with their hands up. No one emerged. After a couple of minutes a masked, black-clad entry team equipped with M-16 assault rifles broke down the side door of the residence and entered. What they found was an unoccupied home undergoing substantial renovations. The upstairs had been almost completely gutted, along with a downstairs bedroom and the home's only bathroom. Local residents monitoring the police frequency on their scanners reported a frantic radio message from the entry team: "There's nothing here!!"

While the police were breaking into my house I was sleeping late 15 miles away at the family camp on Lake Bomoseen. I heard the phone ringing at about nine o'clock, but I did not answer although the caller was persistent, allowing perhaps 20 rings before giving up. I should have rolled out of bed an hour earlier, as a friend was on his way down from Burlington, some seventy miles away, to help me cut firewood, and surely expected that I would be waiting for him when he arrived at the house in West Rutland.

My girlfriend Katrina stirred slightly at my side. She had never liked to get up, and there was no reason to do it now since her daughter, Lindsay, was visiting relatives on the West Coast. After a respite of a few minutes, the phone began to ring again. Thinking it might have been my friend from Burlington, I answered; it was my father.

"What's going on at your house in West Rutland?"

"I don't know," I answered, confused.

"There're a lot of cops there. Do you have any idea why?"

"No."

"Stay there. I'll see what I can find out and call you back."

Perhaps half an hour passed, and the phone rang again. Again it was my father.

"It's some kind of drug raid."

"Well, they won't find anything," I answered. "There's nothing to find."

My brother Rick came on the line.

"The cops love to pull this stuff on weekends. There's no judge or magistrate available to set bail on the weekend. If there's an arrest warrant for you, you'll go to jail until Monday. Do you have someplace you can go?"

"Yes," I replied.

"OK. Don't call anybody. Just go where you're going. Call me Monday morning, and I'll know what's happening. If there's a warrant, you can turn yourself in then and we can get an immediate bail hearing."

I put down the phone and turned to Katrina.

"We'll be leaving for a couple of days. Pack what you need."

Agreeable as always she packed a small bag, and within minutes we were on the road to Burlington, an hour and a half away, to stay with friends.

As we were driving the police were wreaking considerable havoc on my house. There had been no need to break down the side door, as the downstairs front door had been unlocked, and a second-story window just above the front porch roof had been completely removed from its frame. The police showed the same lack of restraint in the rest of the house. They spent the day tracking construction debris over the white bedroom carpet, destroying it; there were black handprints on the suspended ceiling in the bedroom; rubber gloves and acid-bearing drug test kits were abandoned at the scene; even a box of carburetor parts had been dumped on the floor of the garage so the police could use the cardboard box that once contained them. (The box was dutifully logged in the inventory as having been seized by Detective Sgt. James Baker.)

Although much would be said later about strict protocols and procedures, few were in evidence at the search scene. Shortly after the entry team secured the unoccupied premises, the ambulance and fire truck were brought to the site. Uniformed police were posted around the property, and a carnival atmosphere soon developed with a crowd

2

gathering on the sidewalk and cars driving up and down in front of the house. Off-duty police officers showed up - at least one in shorts and t-shirt - and were admitted to the search scene. Around lunchtime a woman in a car handed Detective Raymond LaMoria, Jr. a brown paper bag that was not searched by anyone prior to his reentry to my house. Det. LaMoria and DEA chemist Jack Fasanello left and returned some time later, again entering without being checked by anyone.

No such deference was shown to my brother, Rick, or the neighbors. Rick had attempted to gain entrance to the search scene as my attorney to be sure that no evidence was planted or altered, but Assistant Attorney General Gary Shattuck denied him after consultation with Det. LaMoria. A State Trooper even threatened my northerly neighbor, Rick Prenevost, with arrest for standing on his own lawn.

The carnival atmosphere was in no way diminished by the arrival of a large box truck bearing the name of Pollution Solutions of Vermont. Men in full protective suits - but minus gas masks - carried containers from my house to the Pollution Solutions truck parked in the driveway. A dump truck had also been backed across the front lawn up to the front porch, and various items were being loaded into the back through the upstairs window that I had previously removed. The police finished their work about 5 o'clock and left with their booty.

After a fitful night at a friend's in Burlington, I arose early Sunday morning. Curiosity overcame good judgment, and I called my father from a pay phone. Neither he nor any of my brothers had heard anything from the police meaning that if they were looking for me, they weren't looking very hard. I decided to see what the cops had done to my house, and saw little reason to wait, so Katrina and I said our thank yous and goodbyes and drove to West Rutland. We did take the precaution of having Katrina's sister, Anne, and a friend of mine, Bob Firpo, meet us at the house. Anne had the foresight to bring a camera and several rolls of film.

Having no way to secure the broken door to my house, the police had merely pulled it shut. They had done the same with the garage door, also broken. Mysteriously almost every light in the house had been left on, although the police had left during daylight. A copy of the search warrant had thoughtfully been left on my kitchen table, with an attached nine-page inventory of the articles that had been taken. Not inventoried but missing were several pieces of Katrina's jewelry, a nice set of cased mechanical drawing instruments, handgun ammunition, Katrina's original gynecology records, and $50.00 of saved allowance from a folder bearing a child's handwritten inscription, "Lindsay's Money". Also missing was

3

the page from the search warrant itemizing which items the police had been authorized by the court to seize.

The authorities had a window of opportunity of several days to make an apology and make restitution for the missing articles and damage to my home. They chose not to do so. The train of justice was leaving the station with some important and high-profile passengers, a few of whom thought they could get off at the next stop, but the truth was that everyone would be aboard until the end of the line. No one knew where the end of the line was, but it was going to be a long ride.

2

In one sense nothing in my life had prepared me for the ordeal that was to come. But in another sense with a good education and a varied life experience I was as well prepared as anyone might have been, although lingering notions that there was some integrity and basic fairness in the court system served me poorly.

I was born just before midnight on July 3, 1948. Although my parents lived in Rutland, Vermont my mother wanted to have her first baby while attended by her old family physician, so the delivery took place in Burlington. Shortly afterwards the new arrival was taken to the family home, a small single-family cape in a typical residential neighborhood convenient to both an elementary school and the high school.

Dad had been a lackluster college student, but a year of dodging antiaircraft fire in the skies over Germany had made up his mind about what he wanted to do. As soon as he was discharged from the service in 1946 he enrolled in Boston University law school and married his college sweetheart. After Dad graduated, Mom willingly (or so she said) gave up her career as an occupational therapist to become a wife and mother. Dad's father immediately made him a full partner in his law firm, which spared the newlyweds any financial anxiety and, while we were hardly wealthy by big city standards we did enjoy advantages that some of my friends did not. Among those advantages was a summer camp at Lake Bomoseen that was purchased when I was six.

I acquired two brothers at two-year intervals, and a third when I was ten. In theory Mom's hands were full, but she had read the postwar childrearing books and tried to indulge my curiosity, a curiosity that ran to things mechanical and electrical, and over the years I accumulated an impressive collection of wires, batteries, Erector Sets and chemistry sets. At the time chemistry sets actually had toxic chemicals and alcohol burners, although such things are now considered too dangerous for

4

children. After a while I outgrew the primitive equipment, so Mom purchased a propane Bunsen burner and some good laboratory glassware through the local high school.

I was encouraged in my experiments by our neighbor at Lake Bomoseen, Dick "Creature" Lamphere, West Rutland's favorite son. He had acquired that nickname from his childhood habit of sleeping on a screened-in porch among his own private zoo of squirrels, raccoons, skunks and other wildlife brought home from the woods. In spite of this unusual beginning Lamphere had gone on to MIT, participated in the original atomic bomb program, and continued his career in nuclear physics at the Oak Ridge National Laboratory. His own son was older than I and was rarely around, so I became Lamphere's fascinated listener. Often he would take an afternoon break on the couch in his large bay window with me sitting cross-legged on the floor, hanging on his every word.

Dick Lamphere gave me more than knowledge and incentive. He gave me my first explosives chemicals and my favorite toy of all time, a Ford Model T spark coil, which was to be the heart of many spark-gap radio transmitters as well as the catalyst for hundreds of high voltage experiments over the years.

In 1957 the Russians had launched Sputnik, the world's first artificial orbiting satellite and, while they could be accused of stealing the secrets of the atomic bomb, Sputnik was a Russian achievement (with a little help from World War II German rocket scientists). Its national pride gravely wounded, this country was swept with rocket fever, and everyone from little old ladies to real rocket scientists were constructing and launching amateur rockets. By the time I was in 7th grade I was ready to participate, and formed a rocket club of my friends. Launchers and fins were made in junior high school metal shop, and nose cones in wood shop.

We had many problems with the consistency of our homemade rocket fuel, and it was during this period I made an exciting discovery. My mother's father was much more than a retired professional soldier - he was an engineer in Army Ordnance with an intimate knowledge of explosives chemistry, artillery ammunition, bombs and rockets. He was able to set us straight on the proper methods of preparing various powders, and the experiments soon expanded to rocket sleds, cannons and small bombs.

A poorly timed explosion in a snow bank in front of our house put a temporary end to such experiments. The device went off just as my father was walking home from work, blowing snow and ice in all directions and rattling the windows in the neighborhood. Mother, however, was more forgiving and would take 5 or 10 of us with batteries, wire, powder and apparatus to a sand pit north of town where we could pursue our investigations to our hearts' content without unduly menacing the neighbors. At the time such activities could be carried on openly, and on various occasions other mothers would take us to the sand pit.

During my teen years I developed a reputation for fireworks, and a large group of young people used to gather at our Lake Bomoseen camp on the 4th of July to see what I had made. It eventually became such a big project that I enlisted the help of other kids at the lake to roll paper tubes, mix powder and load the various devices.

I survived these activities to graduate as valedictorian of the class of 1966, subsequently enrolling in the engineering program at Cornell University, and it was there that I suffered a great crisis of spirit. First, my studies were no longer fun. I discovered that most engineers worked for large corporations and usually concentrated on only a small piece of the puzzle. Although I loved cars, spending months perfecting a door handle didn't sound very exciting. I had already proved to myself that I could compete with the best students in the country academically, and I was no longer interested in where my studies were leading me. Second, the Vietnam War was a hot topic at Cornell. President Johnson had ordered the big troop buildup in Vietnam in 1965, and by the time I entered Cornell in the fall of 1966 there was a large and well-organized antiwar movement. It didn't take much investigation to discover that the government's official version of events was a lie, and there were firsthand accounts of the situation in Viet Nam. Daniel Berrigan, a priest with Cornell religious services, returned from Hanoi with a report that the bombs we were dropping on the city were of the antipersonnel variety, intended only to shred the civilian population while leaving the buildings standing.

The World War II generation continued to believe in the American government, even after the 1968 Tet offensive proved to many that the government had been consistently untruthful about the war. On the one hand there was tremendous pressure to be patriotic. "My country right or wrong" was a popular slogan of the time. On the other hand was my belief that any sacrifice in Vietnam would be for nothing. Amidst these conflicts I lost my bearings and drifted intellectually for several years.

I transferred to Castleton State College and the University of Vermont, changed my major to psychology, but ultimately couldn't resolve my inner conflicts, so when I received a low number in the draft lottery I left school to be drafted. In what may have been the greatest irony of my life, I was found unfit for military service because of psoriasis, a hereditary skin condition of occasional red patches and dandruff. I thought at the

6

time that there would be a horrible karmic price to pay for this bit of good fortune, but for the time being I was more concerned with an income, and when an acquaintance asked me to repair a motorcycle engine I accepted.

That one motorcycle engine soon led to dozens, and I established a small business in a barn in Rutland behind a commercial building owned by my father and uncle. Life became simple. My girlfriend and I spent much of our time working, and the rest riding motorcycles and going to bars. After 3 years I found a new girlfriend, the former Mary Ann Trinci. We moved first to Florida, and then to California where I worked for a Honda motorcycle dealership in Buena Park. Returning to Vermont after a year, I worked briefly as service director for Val Preda Olds-Cadillac in Burlington, and it was there I was reunited with Mark Malmros.

Mark had been a childhood friend from Lake Bomoseen, and his father was an idea man for IBM - above the engineering department - and a man of unquestioned brilliance. Mark and I used to talk for hours about scientific topics, and I had visited him a few times in Binghamton, New York while I was at Cornell. I had even gone to see him once at Lehigh University in Pennsylvania, but we had drifted apart. He was doing some graduate work in biochemistry at the University of Vermont, had seen my picture in the newspaper in one of Val Preda's ads, and had given me a call. We renewed our scientific friendship, but unfortunately he moved to Pennsylvania a few months later, and I was not to see him again for several years. The meeting was nonetheless fateful, as it set into motion a chain of events that would ultimately result in the criminal charges against me.

3

While living in Burlington I decided to settle down, and married my girlfriend, Mary Ann, in 1975. Two years later we bought a house on Clarendon Avenue in West Rutland and, while the house was bargain-priced, it needed a lot of work before we could even move in. Over the next several years I worked on the house, other construction work and an occasional repair job in the large barn behind the house.

Following a brief vacation to Washington, D.C. in 1979 I stopped in Bucks County, Pennsylvania near the New Jersey Turnpike to visit Mark Malmros. I stayed only a few hours, but long enough to learn that Mark was obsessed with an idea for a medical testing device, which was in theory fairly simple. An antibody was to be placed on a piece of special plastic, polyacetylene, and electrical changes in the plastic were to be measured when the antigen was added. According to Mark the device had a wide range of potential applications from thyroid hormone assays to AIDS testing.

Despite Mark's enthusiasm, I had absolutely no interest in the project as neither biology nor biochemistry had ever excited me. However I was interested in visiting with Mark about other scientific topics, and returned to Bucks County several times over the next three years, often spending the weekend. Sometimes my wife would accompany me, doing girl things with Mark's wife while we were engrossed in discussions. Again and again Mark would return to the subject of his testing machine.

Polyacetylene was an experimental material, and was not commercially available. It required specialized equipment to make, which Mark did not have, and consequently he was receiving small quantities of the material from two professors at the University of Pennsylvania. The professors, Alan Heeger and Alan MacDiarmid, would go on to win the 2000 Nobel Prize in chemistry for their polyacetylene research, but at the time Mark's association with them was less than satisfactory. They required a vast amount of paperwork, undoubtedly so that they could incorporate Mark's results into their own, but more importantly the material they were providing was brittle and unsuitable for the test fixtures Mark needed to hold it.

I finally relented to the extent that I agreed to study the methods of polyacetylene manufacture. At the time Mark worked for a major pharmaceutical company, and it was a simple matter for him to retrieve the relevant articles from the company's computerized chemistry library. A quick glance at the literature revealed that the principal ingredient of the catalyst system was triethylaluminum, a substance that would explode when exposed to either air or water, and it could only be handled in an atmosphere of nitrogen or argon, a fact that finally piqued my interest.

The chemical literature described the synthesis of polyacetylene in a small flask, which produced discs only an inch in diameter, but since we were going to need a large quantity of the material, making it in one-inch discs would not be practical. After many discussions Mark and I decided that we were going to need a glove box, which was a large sealed chamber fitted with a window and gloves that could be filled with nitrogen or argon. Although glove boxes were available from the laboratory supply houses, they were expensive, and we decided that I would build most of the equipment we needed.

The first step was to prepare a suitable workshop/laboratory area, and the logical place for it was the second floor kitchen at the rear of my house. The second floor had been an apartment, but had remained vacant

8

for 30 years, lapsing into poor condition, although the kitchen drain piping was intact. I had planned to eventually gut the entire second floor, and soon a friend and I began remodeling the kitchen, pantry and bathroom at the rear of the house to the extent necessary to accommodate the polyacetylene project. Since my friend was studying to become an electrician he insisted on doing a proper job on all the wiring, which suited my plan to complete the renovations and rent the upstairs when the polyacetylene project was over. After we had finished there were three upstairs rooms wired, insulated, covered with sheetrock and heated by electric strip.

I had planned to eventually replace the windows with more efficient units but, needing to conserve heat immediately, cut pieces of white Styrofoam insulation to fit the frames. Over several years the Styrofoam was yellowed by sunlight. Det. LaMoria would claim much later in his search warrant application that "yellow paper covers the windows surrounding the area, blocking any view into this portion of the residence…Through this writer's training and experience, I know that this is consistent with other methamphetamine laboratories or clandestine laboratories where the secrecy of the operation is of uppermost importance."[1]

With a place to work, I began to construct the glove box and the other apparatus to manufacture the polyacetylene, and by the spring of 1982 I had produced the first samples, which were three-inch discs of a purplish-black flexible film. Mark then began to come to Vermont to work on the project, sometimes staying with me, and other times staying with his sister 20 miles away in Benson. We tried various fixtures to mount the polyacetylene for testing; we tried various procedures to synthesize, purify and modify the plastic, and in the process we ordered numerous chemicals, laboratory apparatus and glassware. By the end of the summer it looked as though the technology would work.

Those were heady times, and we thought we might repeat the success of Hewlett and Packard, who started in a garage and ended with a huge corporation. I dragged anyone that was interested – and many that weren't – up the stairs of my home to witness the collection of odd apparatus, wires, tubes and chemicals that comprised the polyacetylene project. There was nothing secret about the laboratory.

Mark's wife had given birth to their second child during the summer, and she was not pleased that he was spending so much time away from home. At her urging, Mark suggested that we move the glove box and much of the polyacetylene manufacturing equipment, to Bucks County. In return Mark promised that he would work on the project full-time, and since I was unable to do so, it seemed at the time to be a good trade. I continued to do some work on the project in Vermont, but the new arrangement required that I travel frequently to Pennsylvania.

After months of experimenting Mark and I could not get consistent results, and our earlier exuberance began to fade. We would punch a number of 3/8-inch circles out of the same 3-inch disc of polyacetylene to use for tests. While theoretically all the small circles were identical - and they did look identical - some gave good results and others did not. It was difficult to explain, as we had no way to sort our test samples except visually. Other researchers investigating polyacetylene had electron microscopes, infrared spectrophotometers and other powerful and very expensive scientific instruments that were unavailable to us, necessitating some kind of partnership with a bigger entity.

Mark had been successful obtaining free monoclonal antibodies by offering the supplier the right of first refusal for the technology if it proved successful, and he decided to try a similar approach with one of his former employers, American Hoechst. It worked, and we were given $60,000 and some supplies to help us along, although we still lacked most of what we wanted. Hoechst was interested in evaluating the technology, but made it quite clear that they wanted us to take a shotgun approach, that is, to pursue the widest variety of experiments in the shortest time. Instead, Mark began to focus more and more exclusively on electronic measurement techniques. In retrospect he may have been on the right track in that the circuits he was designing might have overcome some of our problems with inconsistency in the polyacetylene, but in any event Hoechst apparently learned what it had wanted to learn, as it offered no further financing. The $60,000 did, however, strain the relationship between Mark and myself as I had received very little of the money.

It turned out that Mark's personal finances were in disarray and that he had borrowed considerable sums from his brother-in-law. Mark needed whatever money he could get to stay afloat, and there was still the problem of the debt. His solution was to incorporate the polyacetylene project, giving a large block of stock to his brother-in-law. When I refused to terminate our joint venture agreement in favor of the corporation, Mark sued me in Pennsylvania in 1985. The suit dragged on until 1987 when we settled it for a cash payment to me, but unfortunately legal fees consumed most of the payment.

Mark went on to secure more than $1,000,000 in federal grants for the polyacetylene project and associated the operation with a venture capital group, an enterprise that ended badly. Mark would claim later that I made more money on the project than he did, although that ignored his
10

considerable salary. We would not become friends again until after I was imprisoned.

4

In addition to my successful synthesis of polyacetylene, the year 1982 marked my first real venture into politics, and that experience gave me a first-hand look at the corruption that I would encounter again and again in future years.

Shortly after I had moved to West Rutland in 1977, the town found itself facing bankruptcy. One source of the problem was that the town's leading taxpayer, the Vermont Marble Company, had closed its operations in West Rutland, but the town had, nevertheless, continued to tax it at the previous rate. Although the marble company was paying the taxes into an escrow account during its tax appeal, the town was spending the money. When the tax appeal was decided in favor of the marble company, the town found itself in debt.

That was not the Town's only problem. A horrific bookkeeping system maintained by longtime Town Treasurer Stanley Brzoza kept the Board of Selectmen from knowing the true state of the Town's financial affairs. Outside accountants were brought in, and they determined that the Town's books were in disarray. The bottom line, however, was discernable: the town was in debt for an amount roughly equal to two years' budgets. Amazingly, Brzoza escaped the scandal without a scratch and continued as Town Treasurer, with voters blaming the Board of Selectmen, most of whom were replaced. While some might have thought the town's problems were solved, the reality was that there were other problems brewing just around the corner in the Fire District.

Fire Districts were independent governmental entities authorized by Vermont law to administer municipal water systems and/or fire departments that were intended to serve only a portion of a town, usually the village. West Rutland's Fire District was responsible for both the fire department and water system. The governing body was the Prudential Committee, duly elected by the voters of the District.

The West Rutland Fire District obtained most of its water from a reservoir behind an earthen dam. There was also a backup well with an electric pump near the Clarendon River, but its output was inadequate to meet the demand.   The purpose of the well was only to supplement the reservoir during times of drought or other shortage with any water pumped in excess of that required by the town going into the reservoir.

The federal Safe Drinking Water Act of 1974 required that all water from surface sources, i.e. reservoirs, be treated to remove suspended solids, which meant at the very least that a filtration plant would have to be constructed. Municipalities all over country were dragging their feet because of the high costs of building and operating such a plant, and West Rutland was no exception. The local thinking seemed to be that someone's great-grandfather had drunk the water and had lived to be 95, which was proof that the system was all right the way it was. Under the circumstances it was going to be a hard sell that the taxpayers needed to vote themselves another huge tax increase on top of that already required to pay off the town debt, but the Prudential Committee nevertheless began to plan a new water supply system in 1977.

The final plans for the project were completed by August of 1980, and consisted of a new drilled well, a storage tank, the necessary controls and the associated piping. The reservoir was to be shut off from the system. The project was estimated to cost $1.1 million, all of which was to be borrowed from the Farmers' Home Administration. A vote on the project was held on December 15, 1980, and it was defeated by a margin of more than five to one.

Another problem emerged that was more difficult to ignore. The Army Corps of Engineers had inspected earthen dams throughout New England and West Rutland's had been condemned as unsafe. The Corps' report was discussed at the January 1981, meeting of the Prudential Committee, and the dam had to be either repaired or breached. The Town had had firsthand experience with a ruptured reservoir, as the same dam had broken in 1948, releasing a wall of water into the village. Old-timers remembered steps washed away on Clarendon Avenue, and there were photographs of people boating in the center of town until the water level subsided several hours later.

In 1948 there was only forest and farmland immediately downstream of the dam but in 1981 there was a housing development, and loss of life was probable if the dam broke. Even West Rutland's hardheaded and long-suffering taxpayers realized something would have to be done, although they weren't quite sure what it was. The Prudential Committee's proposed solution to all the problems remained the same and another bond vote was held in March of 1981. It, too, was defeated.

Unfortunately yet another difficulty arose that had immediate consequences. The State Department of Health had determined that West Rutland's water had unacceptably high bacteria counts, and had issued an order that any water for drinking had to be boiled. In this instance one didn't need to be acquainted with the fine points of water system

12

management to understand the problem, as after a heavy rain the water had the appearance of coffee in the sections of town closest to the reservoir. In addition, the Vermont Agency of Environmental Conservation was demanding that the water level in the reservoir be substantially lowered until something could be done about the dam, which would have left the town dangerously short of water in the event of a drought or major fire. While there was much grumbling among the townspeople, they figured that they had no choice, and the Fire District taxpayers voted to bond for the project on the third try in February of 1982.

A small group of citizens had been attending Prudential Committee meetings and, thinking that there were too many unanswered questions, successfully petitioned for a revote of the water project. At this point, I was approached by a couple of my neighbors who had been attending meetings, and both thought something was very wrong with the administration of the Fire District.

I had avoided participation in town politics up to that point as lifelong residents of any small town resented newcomers moving in and telling them how to run things. My grandfather was a legend in West Rutland, and my father had been born and raised there, but I had only lived in town for 5 years - a short time by local standards. While I had attended several meetings about the town's financial problems, I had not taken an active role. Still, my neighbors' request that I attend a few meetings was fair enough and I went to the first in April 1981. I asked for and was loaned the Army Corps of Engineers' report, the preliminary engineering report on the dam and other documents. I also went to visit the Vermont Forestry Department in Rutland and took a tour of the watershed area above the reservoir. A frightening picture emerged.

State law required that the forestry department be involved in any logging of a municipal watershed, but the department stated that it couldn't analyze and mark trees for the entire 450-acre watershed in one year. Two representatives of the Department, Gene Keenan and Gary Salmon, had attended the Prudential Committee meeting of February 24, 1980. They advised that the Committee's proposed logging contract for the watershed differed substantially from their sample contract in three significant aspects: 1) it did not require that the logger post a bond; 2) payment was based upon mill receipts as turned in by the logger rather than stumpage; and, 3) the logger was allowed to cut any trees he wanted. Not mentioned in the minutes of the meeting was the fact that any wood declared by the logger to be firewood was simply to be given to him. The Prudential Committee then announced that it would go ahead with the project anyway as it "needed money". By some accounts Keenan and Salmon were then

13

thrown out of the meeting. The contract was given to a West Rutland resident with no competitive bidding, and the consequences of the Committee's actions were not long in coming.

My own visit to the watershed revealed that roughly 30 of the 450 acres had been clear-cut. In addition, the buffer strips of old-growth trees left to protect the brooks from runoff had been removed. Worst of all, logs had been dragged through the tributaries to the reservoir. It was now readily apparent why the water in the reservoir turned muddy after a rain, but it was not at all apparent what to do to remedy the devastation. In spite of the Prudential Committee's repeated denials of any connection between the logging and the dirty water, it was impossible to ignore the obvious. Angry townspeople claimed that the reservoir had been deliberately sabotaged to force them into approving the water project, and there was little to refute that assertion.

The Prudential Committee now had to backpedal. In an attempt to placate the taxpayers it decided to clean the reservoir, a process that consisted of nearly draining the impoundment and removing the accumulated leaves and silt. Since the real purpose of the cleaning was political, large numbers of local teenagers were hired to help. Virtually everyone in town with heavy equipment was employed at one time or another, and the definition of heavy equipment was stretched to the maximum. One bulldozer used on the job was barely larger than a garden tractor, but its owner was coincidentally on the Board of Selectmen.

Whatever goodwill was generated by the cleaning boondoggle was quickly dissipated by the hard facts. While the logging project had only brought in about $17,000 the reservoir-cleaning bill was more than $26,000. Furthermore, based on figures for the limited logging of an adjoining property, the Fire District should have received more than $60,000 from the timber sale. The Prudential Committee was peppered with questions at its meetings until finally its chairman resigned in July of 1982.

Since I had become the de facto leader of the rebel group of taxpayers, I was urged to apply for the vacancy, and the Board of Selectmen subsequently appointed me. My first meeting was August of 1982, and the remaining two members of the Committee wasted no time in nominating and electing me as chairman. Under the circumstances I thought I would receive little cooperation, but my initial fears turned out to be wrong.

With longtime Committee member and system repairman Joe Skaza as my guide, I quickly discovered that there had been no genuine attempt to fix the existing water system. A brand new chlorination system

14

for the town well still sat in its box at the pump house despite having been purchased months earlier. No maintenance appeared to have been done on the reservoir chlorinator for years, and it was heavily corroded and inoperative. Joe and I repaired the reservoir unit as best we could, and installed the new chlorinator at the pump. For the first time in years we were able to reliably chlorinate West Rutland's water, but still the bacteriological problems did not go away, and the Health Department would not lift the boil water order.

The order was of more than academic significance as West Rutland schools and restaurants had to haul potable water, a considerable headache. The Farmers' Home Administration, the putative lender for the new water project, stopped any mortgage lending in West Rutland because of the persistent water quality problems, and local banks quickly followed suit. The practical effect was that real estate in West Rutland was worthless, and it would remain worthless unless and until something was done about the water.

There was certainly a double standard at work. The neighboring City of Rutland also had a reservoir with persistent water quality problems, but what it did not have was a permanent boil-water order. One year a boil-water order for Rutland had been inconveniently issued during the week of the Vermont State Fair. After men in boats shoveled a large amount of disinfectant powder into Rutland's reservoir, the boil water order was quickly lifted. No such solution was proposed for West Rutland.

Joe Skaza did not have much confidence in the Vermont Health Department, and secretly decided to do an experiment. As he collected a mandatory water sample for the Health Department, he took a second sample for himself and had it analyzed at Biologix, a private laboratory run by a group of nurses in Rutland. After he had done this about a dozen times he shared his secret with me: the private lab could find nothing wrong with samples that the Health Department had declared to be contaminated. I then accompanied Joe several more times as he continued his experiment, and I visited at length with the private lab. It turned out that bacteriological testing of water was very easy to do, special care was given to our samples, and nothing was wrong with them.

I was shocked. It was inescapable that either the Health Department had selectively contaminated West Rutland's samples, or the test results had been falsified, but whichever alternative was correct, it was the result of a deliberate, malicious action. I subsequently called the Health Department and spoke with Chuck Moderesi, explaining the situation and our conclusion. Mr. Moderesi was not particularly helpful,

15

offering only that we should keep on doing what we were doing and hope for the best, but in response to my direct question said that the only way to challenge the Health Department's result was through another certified laboratory.

The West Rutland Sewer Plant already had a laboratory to test its effluent, and was already doing water clarity (turbidity) testing for the Fire District. In theory it should have been a simple matter to purchase the apparatus for drinking water testing and have the lab certified. Since the Town owned the Sewer Plant we, the Prudential Committee, approached the Board of Selectmen with our proposal. Both governing bodies agreed to split the cost of an autoclave, and the Fire District bought the remainder of the necessary equipment. When the time came for the certification inspection of the laboratory, it didn't pass. The Health Department refused to reveal the reason, so we were unable to take any remedial action.

At this point I could only conclude that the corruption in the Department went all the way to the top. I would not be able to confront it from West Rutland, and reluctantly called my father. Dad had been president of the Vermont Senate for years, as well as the chairman of the Senate Judiciary Committee, and with those positions he was one of the most powerful politicians in the state. Dad had no tolerance for corrupt or officious bureaucrats, and had previously threatened to haul agency heads before the Judiciary Committee to be questioned about the performance of their subordinates. Whether he had actually grilled anyone was open to question, but no one wanted to risk his wrath. My grandfather had also been president of the Senate, and had a well-deserved reputation for a very long memory and vindictiveness. While Dad's style was more conciliatory, a call to the Commissioner of Health and Human Services received a prompt response. The problem with the West Rutland Sewer Plant Laboratory amounted to no more than a chip in a glass funnel.

The offending funnel was immediately replaced, and the lab received its provisional certification for drinking water testing. The very day that the lab was certified, a new technician was assigned to test West Rutland's water at the Health Department lab, and from that day forward there were no more than sporadic problems with the water quality.

While the rescission of the boil water order allowed the resumption of real estate transactions in West Rutland, it did not solve all the outstanding problems. The water was still dirty in some parts of town after a hard rain, and the dam in particular had to be dealt with immediately. A study of the dam was made by Wright Engineering at the Prudential Committee's request to determine what, if anything, could be done, but a major obstacle was that no records were kept of the

16

reconstruction of the dam following its failure in 1948, meaning that both the materials and the exact construction were unknown. Under the circumstances no contractor would give a firm bid for the repairs, but rough guesses were in the half-million dollar range. That expense, coupled with the eventual but mandatory construction of a filtration plant, made that option much more expensive that the proposed project of a new well and storage tank. For the long term I realized that there was really no alternative to the original project. The fifth vote for the water project was warned for October 11, 1983.

This time things were different. The Prudential Committee had gained considerable credibility by fighting to have the boil water order lifted; thorough public discussions had been held on the project, and all questions had been answered. The measure passed, and there was no petition for a revote. The project was projected to cost over one million dollars, with 35% coming from a state grant and the rest borrowed through the Farmers' Home Administration.

Since the Vermont Department of Health had done so much to force West Rutland to build a new water system, I expected that it would do everything in its power to expedite construction, but not even a month after the vote the funding itself was in question. The Town of Manchester had suddenly been elevated above West Rutland in the funding priority list, and there were insufficient monies available to fund both projects. I called the Department demanding that our grant be reinstated, but I was refused, and again I had to ask Dad to intercede. Suddenly, money that was not shown to be available for water project grants miraculously appeared. The priority list was to be disregarded. West Rutland's project was to be funded after all.

No sooner had the misunderstanding been rectified with the Health Department than Farmer's Home Administration announced that it would not be lending West Rutland any money. Since nothing had changed with West Rutland's lending status and Farmer's Home had agreed to lend funds in the past, it made no sense that the funding commitment had been withdrawn just as we were going to bid. I contacted U.S. Senator Robert Stafford, who informed me that he was well aware of problems with Farmer's Home, and assured me that the Town would be getting an Economic Development Administration (EDA) grant. It seemed strange to me that while the problem was mismanagement or corruption in the Farmers' Home Administration, the proposed solution was an EDA grant. Even so, the EDA grant was not to be the source of funds for the water project. Actually, it was just the reverse – the Town was using the money for the Fire District's water project as the local matching funds for the grant. I didn't want to anger Sen. Stafford and possibly jeopardize the Town's EDA grant, so I asked nothing more from the good senator. We would somehow solve the financing problem ourselves.

A neighbor related another interesting story about Farmer's Home casting additional doubt on the honesty of its officials. He had applied for a home loan, and had been turned down. A few days later a gentleman from that agency, one of the same gentlemen involved with our water project funding, had stopped by to visit. The house needed repairs, he had said, but if the buyer were to agree to use a contractor from his list of "approved contractors", things might be different - and they certainly were. A few days after selecting an "approved contractor", the man's loan had gone through. At this point I had a pretty good idea what the game was, and I decided I was not going to play.

Funding was available through the state bond bank, but the bond sale was not to be for some time. The Prudential Committee reluctantly agreed that we had to go to bid and gamble on the exact interest rate that would be determined at the bond auction. The project was started in September of 1984 and completed the following spring. Aside from a couple of minor disputes with contractors and routine startup glitches, the project proceeded smoothly and the new water system functioned well.

By 1987 all the Fire District's outstanding problems had been solved. We had had no further problems with water quality, and the District was on a good financial footing. A local CPA had set up a number code bookkeeping system that allowed budgeting and the tracking of expenditures. The water account carried a $70,000 surplus due to investment income. (We had borrowed money at the municipal bond rate, but had invested it at the money market rate until we needed to pay contractors. The difference at the time was substantial and produced the surplus.) The backlog of delinquent water rents had been cleaned up. Even the reservoir problem had been solved: a Connecticut man bought the land around the dam, and wanted the dam itself. At the insistence of its attorney the Fire District made a full disclosure of the situation with the dam, but the buyer wanted it anyway. He was later to regret that decision, but the Fire District taxpayers were off the hook.

There were few challenges left in the Fire District, and my marriage to Mary Ann was beginning to fail. I had accomplished, with considerable help, more than I had set out to accomplish, but I had made some enemies in the process. It was time to retire from the Prudential Committee.

5

Superficially my life was going well. I had done an extensive restoration on the barn next to my house, and it now had a cement floor, heat and insulation. I had accumulated a variety of tools over the years, but had just added the crown jewel – a metal cutting lathe. My overhead was extremely low, and I could easily meet my monthly obligations by doing repair work. I still had a reputation for motorcycle repairs from years before when I had had the small shop in Rutland, and even the dealers would send me an occasional perplexing problem. My plan was to renovate the upstairs of my house and rent it, producing additional income. I would then be free to spend much of my time developing inventions, such as I had done before with Mark Malmros.

My wife, Mary Ann, did not share my enthusiasm. She was dissatisfied with her job as a hairdresser, but wasn't sure exactly what would make her happy. First it was a sports car. Then it was my agreement that we could move back to Florida. Suddenly she hit upon it exactly. She wanted to go back to college, complete her undergraduate work, and continue on to become a psychologist or therapist. Since virtually any job in the field required at least a master's degree, this was not a terribly practical plan, but she went ahead anyway, enrolling in Castleton State College in the fall of 1987.

During all this mental turmoil Mary Ann had been seeing a therapist herself, and had determined the source of her unhappiness: everyone but herself. Her parents and I came in for the harshest criticism, and I became responsible for everything from bad weather to a flat tire. The same flat tire might be brought up months later as if it had happened the same day, and life at home became increasingly difficult.

Normal college events became transformed in Mary Ann's mind into daily crises. I found it best to avoid her whenever possible, and began working in my garage until midnight, drinking beer with whomever might come by to help. Unfortunately she usually waited up until I came in from the garage, launching then into a tirade about the injustice of the day at school, and things clearly could not continue the way they were going.

One day in mid-December my brother, Rick, came to visit me when Mary Ann was in school. He said: "Husbands are always the last to know. Nobody wanted to tell me about my wife when things weren't going well, but I'm going to tell you. Mary Ann has been telling her customers that you're a violent drunk and you beat her up all the time."

"I never touched that woman once in 15 years," I retorted.

"It doesn't make any difference. It sounds like you're being set up for a divorce. All a judge has to see is that there's a drunk involved and you're history. I don't know what Mary Ann has been doing at night, but she tried to arrange a date with my brother-in-law a few weeks ago at the salon. He saw her name tag and turned her down."

We had a long talk about the effects of alcohol, and that I showed several of the indicators for alcoholism. I vowed at the time to get control of my life, and never took another drink since. I made a few inquiries and discovered that Mary Ann had first complained of emotional abuse, but when no one was properly sympathetic the abuse had metamorphosed into beatings.

Mary Ann apparently thought that if I would stop drinking, I would agree with her about everything, but just the opposite happened. Without the anesthesia of alcohol, I had no tolerance for Mary Ann's constant complaining, and at one point she actually urged me to start drinking again, but I had made my decision. I was going to have to make a decision about her, too, and soon. Divorce seemed the only option, but I was reluctant to mention it as Mary Ann was given to violent arguments and fits of screaming, and I couldn't fully imagine the scene if I asked her to move out.

My problem was solved in January of 1987 when Mary Ann announced that she was leaving. The departure seemed to be part of a larger strategy to regain control of the game, because a month later she suggested that we get back together, but I was greatly relieved when she left, and not even slightly tempted to resume any relationship with her. After her initial fury subsided, the situation stabilized at an uneasy calm.

So much had changed already that I decided to change the rest of my lifestyle. It had been many years since I had spent much time at the family camp at Lake Bomoseen, and at least ten since I had been water skiing. As a youth I had been a very good skier, but after such a long lapse I was afraid of injury. I spent a month at a local gym building my strength, and finally was ready to go in the early spring. I foolishly decided to jump off the dock as I had done many years before, left way too much slack in the tow rope, and severely sprained two fingers on takeoff. Injuries not withstanding, I began to spend more and more time at the lake skiing, swimming, boating and just enjoying the area.

A frequent visitor over that summer was Robert Spencer of Rutland who had a reputation for very fast motorcycles. I had built his latest engine in my shop, but partly due to defective parts and partly due to abuse by Spencer, the engine had suffered myriad problems, and during a short but intense association with the motorcycle we became friends. In

20

the spring of 1988 Spencer purchased a boat from Woodard Marine on Lake Bomoseen, and rented a dock space there. Since Woodard's was located in a narrow, weedy part of the lake unsuitable for either touring or water sports, Spencer frequently used my camp as his base of operations.

It was a two-way street as Spencer was almost always willing to give my guests rides in his boat or pull them water skiing. He was about 5-5, grossly overweight, not athletic, and suffered from a bad ankle injured in a motorcycle accident. Consequently Spencer did not participate in any water sports himself except driving the boat. The arrangement suited everyone.

In spite of Spencer's seeming lack of sex appeal he was involved with at least two women at the same time, but by the middle of the summer his longtime live-in, Donna Goodrich, had moved out. Taking Donna's place in Spencer's new trailer was the other woman (and mother of Spencer's child), Debbie Mason. Debbie was very pleasant, and on the surface everything appeared to be tranquil. I was to learn later that the tranquility was only a very thin veneer. I was also to learn later that the rumors of Spencer's drug dealing were true, but at the time I saw no drugs, and there was no discussion of them. My only involvement with Spencer was as his motorcycle mechanic and as a passenger in the boat, and I saw nothing to fear. This was to be a serious error in judgment, but that would not be apparent until two years later.

6

Over the summer of 1988 I dated a couple of girls without provoking any particular reaction from my estranged wife, Mary Ann. I made no inquiry, but mutual friends told me that she was also dating. I deluded myself into thinking that the divorce would proceed relatively smoothly, but by the late fall I had no further illusions in that regard, and I knew I was in for a bitter fight. Perhaps it would have happened anyway or perhaps it was because of a child, Lindsay.

Sometime in the late 60s I had taken a petite but adventuresome blonde, Katrina Carris, to the motorcycle races in Loudon, New Hampshire. The races were universally called "Laconia", for the town 30 miles to the north where they had been held before bikers had rioted some years before, and even in the late 60s, the races were still a raw and undisciplined event. Motorcycle gangs from around the country came for the scene, camping along Route 106, while actual race fans camped at the track. There were few fences and little security, and it was possible to stand on the track close enough to touch the riders as they sped past.

Katrina was 2 years younger than I, and we did not know each other particularly well, but I had seen her on the street, asked her if she wanted to go to the races, and she had accepted. When I picked her up on race day, I realized that she had little conception of the environment at the track as she was wearing a purple miniskirt, but we went anyway

After the races, through a convoluted series of events, we wound up drinking beer with several bikers including a Hell's Angel. Although she weighed less than 100 pounds, Katrina won the undying admiration of the bikers by successfully kick starting a large Harley at the expense of an unsightly burn on her bare leg. While Katrina appeared to be just my kind of girl, something didn't click, and we didn't date again. She married, had a child, divorced and left town.

In the fall of 1988 I had heard that Katrina had recently moved back to Rutland, along with her daughter, Lindsay, age 9, and one crisp day in late September day I stopped by Katrina's house on my motorcycle. We got along well from the outset, and I became a frequent dinner guest at her house. While not enthusiastic about my presence, Lindsay tolerated me at the beginning, but as I spent more time there she started to resent the competition for her mother's attention. She also became used to having me around, and more of her true behavior began to manifest itself. Lindsay was very headstrong and through sheer obstinacy, occasionally supplemented by a spectacular tantrum, she could almost always get her way. While sympathetic to Katrina's dilemma, I was greatly amused by the diminutive rebel.

Mary Ann and I had had no children by choice. I had no affection for them, avoided my nephews, nieces and children of friends whenever possible, and consequently I had little idea of how to conduct a relationship with a child. I brought various things to the house for Lindsay with limited success, but when I brought a basketball, she was genuinely interested. Her school had a hoop on the playground that was unused, but soon Lindsay had organized a group of other children, and began to play daily.

She also began to accompany me when I went shopping or did errands, and soon we were seen together all over Rutland. It was about this time that Mary Ann became unreasonable over the terms of the divorce. Something had clearly changed, as I heard that she had been asked to leave a couple of downtown bars for being drunk and disorderly, although during the marriage she had been a moderate drinker.

My brother, Rick, had represented numerous clients in divorces, and had been through one of his own. He counseled me to be as conciliatory as possible, and to look at the big picture. When Mary Ann demanded a .30-06 deer rifle in which she had never shown the slightest interest, Rick advised me to give it to her, as disputes over five-hundred dollar items could quickly rack up thousands in legal fees. He also counseled me to give Mary Ann virtually unlimited access to the house to remove her personal effects, but by the spring of 1988 that had become an increasing burden. Mary Ann would stop about once a week, supposedly to sort through her property, and would stay for hours. The visits usually ended with her trying to pick a fight, but since most of the supposed sorting was going on in one small room upstairs, I concluded that the real reason for the frequent visits was to provoke me. I was even more convinced when I learned that she had approached the court for a relief from abuse order after one of her orchestrated confrontations. Luckily, the victims' advocate saw the situation for what it was and told her that since she had already moved out such an order was inappropriate.

I wanted no more to do with Mary Ann's games, and went throughout the house rounding up anything that belonged to her. I put it all in one room downstairs, and asked her to come and pick everything up, even offering to help her load. When Mary Ann saw what I had done an incredible fit of shrieking commenced and, while it was obvious that she was displeased, she was unable to articulate why. I surely didn't help the situation by delivering some papers to her a few weeks later with Lindsay accompanying me. That also led to a fit of shrieking with Mary Ann purporting to throw Linds and me out of the shopping mall where she worked. Lindsay did a pretty good imitation afterwards.

Not surprisingly, the divorce negotiations took a turn for the worse. Mary Ann made it clear that she wanted to reduce me to poverty such that I would have to beg for a night shift job at a local factory. She also demanded that I borrow money to pay her a bigger divorce settlement. Her demands were ridiculous, and I told her so, but she then began to make threats. While she was not specific, Mary Ann said that she would cause me serious problems with the police if I didn't pay her. She also was going to file ethics charges against my father in connection with some legal documents that he had prepared for her parents. Mary Ann had dropped out of college to spend as much time as necessary on the contested divorce, and further negotiation seemed fruitless. I informed her that I would not be paying one penny more than the court ordered, and that I was not intimidated by her various threats. "Hit me with your best shot," I invited her. I was soon to learn the truth of the adage that hell hath no fury like a woman scorned.

The divorce hearing finally came in the spring of 1989. Although Mary Ann had brought virtually no assets to the marriage she was awarded half of everything, a typical result in Vermont. I kept the house in West Rutland and my tools. Mary Ann got a large sum in cash and securities. The ordeal was finally over – or so I thought.

7

While my divorce was pending, much of my life was dictated by what the court might think. For that reason I didn't buy a boat that caught my eye, and I postponed travel plans. With the end of the divorce proceedings in sight, Katrina and I began to plan a trip to Guatemala for the summer of 1989. Her parents had been there twice, and I was eager to go after hearing Stanley Orzech's stories.

I first met Stanley around 1985 through his tenants at a property next to his mother's home in West Rutland. Stanley was born and raised there, but developed a wanderlust as a young man, and spent many years in Latin America. He had returned to West Rutland to participate with his half-brother in a project to store electrical energy using the town's abandoned marble quarries, but his heart remained in Latin America.

Ultimately the electricity storage project did not pan out, due primarily to an agreement Vermont's utilities made to import cheap hydropower from Quebec. Stanley was looking for a new endeavor, and had remained in touch with his Guatemalan law partner; I was looking for someplace with a little harder edge than Vermont.

Mary Ann had had absolutely no desire to visit any third-world countries, but Katrina had no such reservations. Lindsay had expressed an interest in summer camp, a longstanding family tradition, and this gave Katrina and me seven weeks for Guatemala. Besides looking around the country, I was interested in learning Spanish, and consequently we spent most of our time in Antigua, a popular tourist destination also famous for inexpensive Spanish schools. There would later be much innuendo about my supposed drug dealing in Guatemala, apparently based on the supposition that no one would go there for any other reason. Given Guatemala's rich Mayan heritage, spectacular views, stunning architecture and exquisite native handicrafts, such ignorance was barely believable.

8

The Guatemala trip drew Katrina and me closer together, and after spending the day working in my shop in West Rutland, I spent almost every night at her house in Rutland. While we were, in fact, living together we were simultaneously maintaining two separate residences. After much discussion we decided that Katrina and Lindsay would move

24

to West Rutland after school was over in the spring of 1990, and the house in Rutland would be sold. Two issues mitigated in favor of the move. One was that I had a substantial amount of tools and machinery in place in West Rutland. The second was that Lindsay was doing well in school after a rocky period. Katrina felt that she would do better in a small school system like West Rutland's, especially after hearing about the wild extracurricular activities of students in the Rutland Middle School.

Unfortunately for me, the proposed move would require a significant upgrade of my house. When Mary Ann and I had first moved in 13 years before, I had immediately remodeled the downstairs kitchen and two other rooms. Subsequently we had redone the bedroom, and I had started on the upstairs to facilitate the polyacetylene project. This left more than half the house with cracked plaster and peeling wallpaper, including the bathroom and what was to be Lindsay's bedroom. The bathroom in particular needed a total overhaul, along with the drain plumbing. Since any upstairs plumbing would have to pass through the downstairs to the basement, I had to decide on exactly what renovations I was going to make there to turn it into an apartment, and under the circumstances the only logical course of action was to proceed simultaneously with work upstairs and downstairs.

I began by gutting the entire upstairs save for the rooms that I had already redone. I had gained access to the upstairs through the closet of the downstairs master bedroom, which led to a hallway behind the house's front door and the stairway, but it soon became apparent that other arrangements would have to be made. The project raised a tremendous amount of plaster dust, which was quickly spreading throughout the house starting with the white carpet in the bedroom. As a result I stapled heavy plastic over the closet door to restrict the dust to the construction zone and used the front door of the residence exclusively to gain access to the upstairs. I also began to box my chemicals in the rear of the upstairs, the site of the polyacetylene project, so they could be moved to the basement for storage.

I had always been somewhat paranoid about burglars, but with much of the house under construction it was not going to be possible to secure every possible point of entry. The house was in a nice residential location with close neighbors, so rather than worry about security I simply raised my insurance coverage. With that taken care of I removed both sashes of an upstairs window which opened out onto the flat roof of the front porch and began to pile plaster and other debris on the roof. A friend borrowed a dump truck for me, and backed it across the front lawn up to the porch to be loaded as debris accumulated. The truck was no more than

50 feet from Clarendon Ave., and clearly visible from the street. In fact, the only obstructions between the Avenue and my house were two small trees midway up the lawn. The garage was also completely unobstructed, sitting at the end of my straight driveway. The dump truck stayed on the lawn for 2 or 3 weeks until it was heaped with plaster and wood, and then driven off leaving ruts in the grass.

Katrina and Lindsay moved to West Rutland in the middle of June, right after Lindsay completed the school year at Dana Elementary. We would have gone directly to the camp at Lake Bomoseen except that my brother, Tom, and his family had planned to stay there the week of July 4th. After Tom returned to New York we moved immediately to the lake so that I could start the downstairs renovations. After putting off the improvements to the house for more than 10 years, I was going to do whatever needed to be done, but the work on the bathroom, plumbing and Lindsay's bedroom had to be completed before Linds started school in the fall.

To get that much work done, I resigned myself to the fact that I was going to have to work on the house full time, and I reluctantly told my garage customers that I would be accepting no more work until my house was at least minimally fit to live in. Recognizing the magnitude of the task, I also hired a friend to work with me who was an expert roofer and experienced builder. Normally I would not have been able to afford his services, but his business was slow at the time and he needed something to carry him until he got another big job. From 8 or 9 in the morning until 5 at night, Monday through Friday, his BMW or truck and my Isuzu pickup could be clearly seen parked in my driveway. I spent nights and weekends with Katrina and Lindsay at Lake Bomoseen.

It turned out that even the floor of the bathroom had to be ripped out, and all the joists shimmed. A pile of construction waste, including the old toilet and drain plumbing, began to rapidly accumulate in the driveway and on the lawn next to the house, again readily visible from the street.

July 1990 was also the time of another fateful decision – my decision to be a candidate for the Vermont House of Representatives. I had often complained to my father during the time he was in the state Capitol that it was mostly morons that seemed to be running the government. In the spring of 1990 he informed me that my chance to change things had come as the Republicans were looking for a candidate from my district. After a thorough discussion with Katrina and Lindsay about the time that might be required to be a representative, I announced for the position. An article announcing my candidacy appeared in the *Rutland Herald* on July 6.

26

Although I was unaware of it at the time, others were very interested in what was happening in and around my house in July. According to a Vermont State Police Investigation Report[2] signed by Det. Sgt. James Baker[*] "Det. LaMoria continued to brief this officer [Baker] during the month of July 1990 concerning activity around accused Bloomer's residence." Since Det. LaMoria lived just down the street, he had to have known that the "activity" around the house was construction, and he also had to have known that no one had lived in the house since early July.

In June Sgt. Baker had "attempted to introduce an undercover operative to accused BLOOMER. This took place by sending Det. Douglas Robinson to accused BLOOMER's residence to inquire about a motorboat that accused BLOOMER had for sale." At one point Det. Robinson was outfitted with a hidden transmitter monitored by Dets. Baker and LaMoria. I never understood the purpose of Det. Robinson's visit, as surely there had been few instances where criminal suspects had blurted out confessions to complete strangers ostensibly trying to buy boats or cars. Sgt. Baker must have come to the same conclusion as, after a short time, "[t]his officer made the decision to discontinue the attempt to form a relationship with accused BLOOMER through this 'hap' meet format."[3]

The question was, why were the police so interested in what was obviously a construction site? The answer was not long in coming – Robert Spencer.

9

Unaware of the intense police surveillance of my house in West Rutland, I was enjoying Lake Bomoseen in my free time, and Lindsay in particular was very entertaining. The previous summer's lake activities had been abbreviated by Lindsay's summer camp and the Guatemala trip. For the same reasons, I had seen Robert Spencer only a few times during the summer of 1989, although he had been a frequent visitor in his boat the previous summer. In the intervening time, Spencer's relationship with the affable Debbie Mason had soured following numerous beatings and

---

[*] Sgt. Baker was the head of the Southern Vermont Drug Task Force, a loose association of federal, state and local drug enforcement officers.

denigrations. Even while Mason was still living with Spencer, he was carrying on openly with a married woman, Nicolette "Nicki" Samplatsky, and, following Mason's departure, Samplatsky and her two children moved in with Spencer. The relationship was stormy from the beginning, with frequent fights.

Part of the problem was that Samplatski was considerably younger than Spencer and Spencer was insanely jealous. Another part of the problem was that Samplatsky was much less tolerant of Spencer's beatings than his previous girlfriends. I would learn later that Samplatsky was working with the police to have Spencer jailed for abuse but, although she moved in to her own apartment on Pearl St. in Rutland, she continued to see Spencer. Probably unbeknownst to Spencer, he was not the only one with an interest in Samplatsky. A frequent nighttime visitor to Samplatsky's apartment was drug cop Raymond LaMoria, Jr. in his snakeskin boots and red Chevrolet Camaro provided by the drug task force.

Although I was unaware of the extent of Samplatsky's activities at the time, it was readily apparent that Spencer's boat had become a floating platform for further fights and arguments, and Spencer's self-control, always questionable, was ebbing. The previous summer, while he was in a good mood, he had had at least two near misses with other boats and had broken a passenger's arm in a wild maneuver that had ripped the boat's front seats out of the floor, but now he was constantly angry and was a serious menace on the water. He had cut a pair of water skis in half with his boat and nearly hit some swimmers, and Spencer simply became too unpleasant and dangerous to have around.

Although Spencer was no longer welcome to use my camp as a base of operations, he apparently thought it a good place to dump Nicki Samplatsky after a fight in early July of 1990. He then roared up to the dock from time to time to toss her a can of beer, "like you would toss an elephant a peanut" in the words of one onlooker. The situation was both intrusive and ridiculous, and I asked Katrina if she would take Samplatsky somewhere to get rid of her. Katrina returned about a half hour later after leaving Samplatsky at Woodard Marine.

About a week later on Saturday, July 23, 1990, I got a call from Spencer around 11:00 in the morning. He had been arrested and jailed for assaulting Samplatsky, and bail was $1000. Although the assault had allegedly taken place some time before, the police had apparently waited until Friday night to arrest Spencer, surely realizing that no judge would be available over the weekend to release him on his own recognizance. They

28

probably also thought that he would be unable to raise $1000 cash over the weekend and would therefore have to remain in jail until Monday.

Although I had seen little of Spencer socially due to the unpleasantness with Samplatsky, he remained a loyal motorcycle customer, as his expensive bike had suffered a series of breakdowns, largely on account of defective aftermarket speed parts. Spencer had finally decided to send the entire engine out to a racing shop in California and to hold it responsible for the outcome. The engine was removed from the motorcycle and crated at my shop and, since I was to reinstall it, he instructed that it be shipped to me. The transaction was to be C.O.D. cash, and Spencer had given me $1000 to pay for the engine when it arrived.

While I was not eager to leave the lake and drive to the jail in Rutland on a Saturday morning, I did have precisely the amount of cash required for bail, and it was sitting in an envelope labeled "Spencer Motorcycle" in my kitchen in West Rutland. Reluctantly, I drove to my house, picked up the envelope, and proceeded to the jail. The cash was counted several times by two guards, I was given a bail receipt, and Spencer was released. I took him to his mobile home on Curtis Ave., where he gave me a couple of hundred dollars in cash to restock the envelope, and then I returned to the lake.

When I arrived Katrina said, "Nicki Samplatsky called and she's really mad. She says Spencer is going to kill her, and you shouldn't have bailed him out of jail."

"I really didn't have any choice," I replied. "I had his money, and he knew it. What was I going to do? Refuse to bring him his money and leave him in jail for the weekend?"

I learned later that Samplatsky was much more specific with some of her friends. She believed that I was responsible for Spencer's release, and she intended to get even with me. Just three weeks later on August 11, 1990, Spencer's mobile home and my house in West Rutland were raided simultaneously by the Southern Vermont Drug Task Force, with much of the probable cause supplied to Det. LaMoria by Nicki Samplatsky.

10

"Drug Agents Raid House in Rutland" proclaimed the headline on the front page of Sunday's *Rutland Herald*, although my house was actually in West Rutland. There was an accompanying photo of someone with a baseball cap and white jumpsuit, carrying what appeared to be a white plastic gallon jug. At the time the police weren't saying much except that evidence was seized "supporting the presence of drug activity". Spencer was not named and no arrests were reported.

By Tuesday my case merited only the first page of the local section of the *Herald*, although it was to return to the front page occasionally. This time the police were more specific and the headline was that "State Police Suspected House Was A 'Speed' Lab". Again no arrests were reported although they were "expected in the future, according to one police officer." Again Robert Spencer was not identified, either by the police or the newspaper. Spencer had, however, called my brother, Rick, the day following the raid. Rick had represented him at one time on motor vehicle charges, and was representing him in connection with the assault on Samplatsky. Rick was not willing to represent Spencer on any drug charges, and Spencer did not ask him to do so. Indeed, according to Spencer, there were no charges. He described in some detail the events of August 11, from the entry of his mobile home by a SWAT team to the detailed search. According to Spencer, no drugs were found, although there was a considerable commotion for a short time when the police mistook hamster food for marijuana seeds. The police seized a few things from the trailer, but nothing of any great import.

Spencer's neighbor, Normand Gagne, was to tell me a much different story some seven years later. According to Gagne, following the search of Spencer's trailer he was led away in handcuffs. Although the search was conducted pursuant to a state warrant, Gagne was adamant that Spencer had been arrested by federal agents. Further, Gagne related that the day following the raid Spencer had told Gagne's girlfriend that the police had found cocaine. Over a year after the raid I finally obtained an inventory of the items seized by the police at Spencer's, and one of the items was a small bag of suspected cocaine. It had field-tested positive for cocaine at the scene, and the Vermont State Police Laboratory had subsequently confirmed this finding.

Although I didn't know it at the time, Spencer also wasted little time giving the police a series of confessions. The first was on August 20. A second was given on August 31 because "there were certain things in the statement that [he] wanted to correct."*

---

* Det. LaMoria asked Spencer , "Why – why didn't you tell me the truth the first time?" Spencer replied, "You're asking me a question I can't even answer. No particular reason. They say there's no difference between stealing one horse and a whole herd. I realize that. I don't know why I didn't say it."

Even as he was giving the confessions, he publicly maintained his innocence. The *Rutland Herald* on August 29 quoted Spencer as saying "They [the police] said they were looking for drugs. I told them they got the wrong place." This game was finally over on September 25 when the newspaper reported that Spencer had pled guilty to possession of cocaine.

I did not fully appreciate at the time that standard police procedure was to approach someone against whom they held a great deal of evidence. That person was then given two choices: face the full wrath of the law or cooperate and receive what usually was a dramatic reduction of the prison sentence. Cooperation often meant, besides providing information about criminal activity, that the cooperating individual serve as an agent provocateur to ensnare others.

In retrospect, it seems obvious that Normand Gagne had told the truth. The police had withheld news of Spencer's arrest, hoping to use him to gather whatever information he could. (A high school classmate told me in 2002 that Spencer and another cooperating individual had paid him a visit shortly after the raid, trying to engage him in a conversation about crimes that had allegedly been committed many years before.) In any event, my brother received another call from Spencer. This time his tune had changed. The police had mentioned the names of two women, Sharon Stickney and Monica Williams, and Spencer was very worried about what they might say about him. My brother, wary of Spencer, listened but did very little talking.

Spencer subsequently called me at the lake, saying that he was in "deep shit". Since I was sure that either the phone was tapped or that Spencer was calling from the police station, I told him that I didn't think my lawyer would want me to be talking to him, wished him well, and ended the conversation quickly. He never called back.

Meanwhile my father had been calling lawyers, trying to get the lay of the land and find me some representation should it be needed. Although my father was himself a lawyer, he did exclusively civil work and had virtually no knowledge of the criminal law. Likewise all three of my brothers were lawyers, but again did no criminal work except perhaps a DWI case or other relatively minor matter. None of the mainstream lawyers my father talked with wanted to be involved with the case except in an advisory capacity, and some advice was certainly needed. The search warrant was defective on its face, and, according to the newspaper, an inquest was planned.

On Tuesday morning, three days after the raid, police officer Raymond LaMoria, Jr. appeared at the my father's office with the missing piece of the search warrant, although the law required that a copy of the warrant along with an inventory of items seized be left with the owner of the property. In this instance a key part of the warrant had been omitted – the page detailing what items the court had authorized to be seized. The sheet that LaMoria left bore his signature beneath a less-than-convincing handwritten explanation that "THIS WRITER INADVERTENTLY FAILED TO LEAVE A COPY OF THE ATTACHMENT FOR OBJECTS, PROPERTY PERSONS TO BE SEARCHED FOR".

LaMoria's delayed delivery of the objects subject to the warrant was but one of many anomalies. First, it was difficult to believe that senior police officers and an assistant attorney general at the search scene would inadvertently leave a defective warrant. Second, it appeared to both my father and me that the list had been prepared after the search. "Computer " and "computer discs" were listed, although at the time the internet had yet to take off and home computers were a rarity. Third, there were some strange items like "surveillance equipment" and "booby traps" that I never possessed. Finally, even the suspicious list did not provide for the seizure of any property belonging to my live-in girlfriend, Katrina Carris, although items that were obviously her personal property had been seized.

Of the attorneys I was aware of that were willing to handle my case, I decided on Will Hunter, and Dad accompanied me for a consultation with Will in Ludlow on Wednesday, the 15th. Will was tall and handsome, with chiseled features and light hair, and not only did he look like a preppie, he had actually attended Exeter Academy in New Hampshire, and had studied at Oxford as a Rhodes Scholar. Will was the youngest person ever to be elected to the Vermont Senate, and seemed to have a bright future. He was noted for defending the downtrodden, and did not shy away from controversial cases.

Will thought I had serious problems, as it was obvious to him that the raid on my house had been botched. According to Will, a raid was just the icing on the cake during a criminal investigation, as the police could rarely predict what they might find on a given day. Even a big drug dealer might not have anything at a particular time. Consequently there would normally be no raid until sufficient evidence of criminal activity had been established through other means, typically a drug sale monitored by the police or an incriminating telephone conversation. If additional evidence turned up during the raid, so much the better, but there would already be enough for an arrest. In my case there had been no sale, no incriminating conversation and no seizure of drug. Law enforcement careers were at stake.

Further, both my father and Will thought that the raid was timed to influence the election. If they were correct, forces were at work beyond the police and prosecutors identified in the newspaper. One suspect that immediately came to mind was Ralph Wright, a Democrat and Speaker of the Vermont House of Representatives, the archenemy of my uncle John, a Republican, and President of the Vermont Senate. I had heard that Wright believed, "One Bloomer is enough in Montpelier [the state capital]." Wright, originally from Massachusetts, had changed the formerly genial atmosphere of the House into a take-no-prisoners, Massachusetts-style operation, and indeed an occasional Wright visitor was William Bulger, president of the Massachusetts Senate.*

Since Wright lived in Bennington, some 50 miles from West Rutland, I was a little surprised when he pulled into my driveway while campaigning on behalf of my local opponent, Democratic candidate Michael Chuse. I introduced myself, and Wright thanked me profusely for shifting the press's attention from him to me.

While the general public might have thought the investigation was just business as usual, those with a knowledge of how things were supposed to work were aghast. Clearly, if there had been any compelling evidence of criminality on my part, I would have been arrested within a day or two of the raid, but instead I was going to be left twisting in the wind until those in control of the situation decided what to do to save themselves. Not long after the raid I received a condolence call from a retired gentleman from Hubbardton who was a political junkie and frequent contributor of letters to the editor of the *Rutland Herald*. Well aware of my family's political ties, he said with great concern, "If they can do this to you, they can do it to anybody." `

11

I was anxious to know the basis for the search warrant and, according to Will Hunter, it was usually just a matter of going to the issuing court after the warrant had been executed. My case was different. The materials were sealed by order of the court "Only to be opened at time

---

* More recently Bulger came under suspicion of having knowledge of his brother's activities and perhaps having contact with him during the time he was a fugitive. James "Whitey" Bulger had been on the run since 1994, wanted by the FBI for racketeering, murder (18 counts), and extortion. He was finally arrested in California in 2011.

of arraignment or at request of [Assistant Attorney General] Gary Shattuck."

Will wasted little time filing motions to unseal the warrant documents and for the return of my property, and Katrina's attorney, Leonard Wing, also filed a motion for the return of Katrina's medical records on August 16th. Her gynecologist, Dr. Donald Wolins, had left town and had consequently given Katrina her original records. While they were in our West Rutland residence prior to the police raid, they were nowhere to be found afterward. Katrina was unable to understand the relevance of her gynecology records to a drug investigation into my activities, and was outraged that the police would take such private material.

It appeared at first as though the police weren't going to press the issue of the medical records. The *Rutland Herald* reported on August 21 "[Police officer Det. Raymond] LaMoria said Monday police would have no problem returning those records." Prior to the hearing on August 23 LaMoria had told Attorney Wing the same thing. The following exchange took place at the hearing between Leonard Wing and Gary Shattuck:

> MR. WING: Excuse me, Your Honor, the day after I mailed the petition for return of the goods, Detective Sergeant Lamouria [sic] called me and said that he had no intention of retaining Miss Carris' records, and that all she had to was come and pick them up and he gave me his phone number and his page number, and I passed that information on to my client. Apparently, there was a delay because Mr. Bloomer's attorney told her that, Why don't you wait and get everything at once because I'm going to get Bloomer's stuff on Wednesday. In reading the papers this morning, I see that he didn't get them yesterday so I'll just contact my client again and tell her if she wants her stuff, to go get it and, as I understand it, there's no objection from the State or from the officer.
>
> THE COURT: Is that true?
> MR. SHATTUCK: Correct, Judge. Without addressing the particular motion, just that we've had conversations and we've indicated to Mr. Wing that those materials belong to Miss Carris. The medical records we don't have any problem returning. And they've already – they've been separated from the file and all they're doing

is waiting to be picked up, making connection between the officer and Miss Carris.

Det. LaMoria surely knew that Katrina was living with me in West Rutland, as he had referred to her as my "cohabitating girlfriend" during the search warrant hearing before Judge Hudson.[4] Nevertheless, he called Katrina's mother advising that Katrina could pick up her belongings at the State Police Barracks in Rutland. I thought it best if she went with someone, but didn't want to go myself, so her sister, Anne Carris Reilly, agreed to go.

Although the gynecology records had supposedly been "set aside" and Katrina had called ahead, Det. LaMoria appeared disorganized when Katrina and her sister arrived at the State Police barracks in Rutland. An officer wheeled in my two filing cabinets with a hand truck and invited Katrina to search them for the records. She found no medical records, but did start to remove some of Lindsay's school papers. After a short time about a dozen State Police officers entered the room and began to giggle. They were followed by Det. LaMoria. He handed Katrina a paper, and said she'd have to sign for Lindsay's schoolwork.

"I'm not going to sign for anything," Katrina said.

"It doesn't make any difference. You're served," retorted LaMoria with a smile. The State Police officers present were also quite pleased with themselves. Katrina looked at the paper and it was some kind of subpoena. Katrina asked to call her attorney, but was denied by LaMoria.

"I don't want this," she said. "Where are my medical records?"

"That's all you're going to get today, honey," Det. LaMoria advised. "All you've got to do is tell the truth at the inquest and you'll be OK."

Katrina turned to her sister and said, "Let's get out of here." On the way out they slammed the door to the police barracks, and a State Police officer pursued them, threatening them with arrest for "destruction of police property". This incident was to be only the first in a series of attempts by the police to intimidate Katrina.

Lindsay, fortunately, had been spared the anguish of the raid itself. At the time she had been on her annual summer visit to her uncle in San Francisco, but had returned a few days later. News of the criminal probe had been on television, was in the newspaper frequently, and was the talk of the town. There was no way Linds could be shielded. Although Katrina and I did the best we could to explain the situation to her and assure her that everything would be all right, we had some doubts ourselves.

Our choice of the West Rutland school system turned out to be a good one, especially under the circumstances. The school was very small, with only about 20 students in Lindsay's 7th grade class. She was immediately drafted for the soccer team, and quickly adjusted to her new surroundings.

Katrina and I had planned to be married, but had not set a date. After the service of the inquest subpoena, Will Hunter suggested that it might be a good idea to have the wedding soon as in theory there was a spousal immunity. Katrina was not eager to testify at the inquest because the police had apparently stolen some of her jewelry and Lindsay's allowance money, and she saw no reason to trust the authorities. She had even less reason to trust law enforcement following the medical records imbroglio, and the inquest process lent itself to abuse.

Although the procedure outwardly resembled a grand jury proceeding, it had important differences. A judge convened an inquest on behalf of a prosecutor, and the function of the judge was primarily to threaten reluctant witnesses with imprisonment. As with a grand jury, witnesses' attorneys were barred from the proceeding. Will Hunter called the inquest "monstrous" and defense attorney Theodore Robare referred to it as an "archaic procedure" that was in limited use in only a few states. Others thought the inquest unique to Vermont. According to Robare, "It allows the prosecutor to have the opportunity to question anyone he wants about absolutely anything. He can even ask the oft-joked-about question, 'Do you still beat your wife?'"[5]

Katrina and I were married on August 27 at the Mountain Top Inn in Chittenden, with the civil ceremony performed by my brother, Bill, a justice of the peace. The guests consisted entirely of family with the exception of Frank Gorham, who Katrina had seen on the street shortly before the wedding.

Although we were married, inquest Judge John Morrissey disallowed Katrina's spousal immunity, and she was forced to testify on August 29. She was asked questions about my drug dealing, but had no knowledge. Also testifying were my neighbor, Rick Prenevost, and my ex-wife, Mary Ann. Apparently Mary Ann had thought that her presence would be a secret, as she was not happy when my brother, Rick, spotted her in the courthouse. Another subpoenaed witness, former Spencer girlfriend Debbie Mason, was fighting the subpoena and refused to testify.

A few days after the inquest Katrina and I, accompanied by Will Hunter, granted a lengthy interview to *Rutland Herald* reporter Julie

Hoogland. The article appeared on September 6, and we denied any criminal activity. In the same issue an editorial appeared on the legality of inquests. The editor opined that, "Now that the inquest procedure is being questioned in two different instances simultaneously and even Judge Mahady seems dubious about the law, its days may be numbered after nearly 100 years on the books." Despite the editorial optimism, more than 25 years later the inquest procedure remains on the books.

<h2 style="text-align:center">12</h2>

My motions to unseal the search warrant affidavits and compel the return of my property had been pending before Judge McCaffrey for about two weeks, but the decision came down on September 10, the day before the primary election, guaranteeing that it would be in the newspaper on election day. The judge had accepted Gary Shattuck's rationale that unsealing the search documents "might jeopardize the investigation". He further thought it premature to return my property, which Shattuck had represented was necessary for the investigation.

Under the circumstances, it came as no surprise to me when I was badly beaten in a three-way primary race for two seats in my district. Incumbent Ted Pendleton from Proctor received 480 votes, former Clarendon selectman Alphonse Bourassa received 371, and I got only 175. Michael Chuse of Proctor, a professor at Castleton State College, was to be the unsuccessful Democratic challenger in the general election.[*]

In response to Judge McCaffrey's ruling Will Hunter filed a motion for extraordinary relief in the Supreme Court, but eventually the Court ruled that Hunter had not shown that there was not an adequate remedy in the lower court. And so we went, around and around, getting nowhere. Although it was unknown to me at the time, as I was seeking the return of my property, and as the state was claiming all of it was necessary for the investigation, Pollution Solutions of Vermont was systematically destroying my chemicals. Ironically, the police had represented to the newspaper that one reason for the delay in bringing any charges was the necessity of analyzing "many" of my chemicals, but documents I obtained more than a year later showed that out of the 100 or so chemicals only 4

---

[*] The election was star-crossed. Within three years I would be in prison, Chuse would be shot dead by his wife as he slept, and Bourassa would be disgraced by charges he sexually molested a young girl. In July of 1995 Bourassa would plead guilty to sexual assault on a minor.

had been analyzed. (There was little reason for any analysis of three of the four, as they were in the original factory containers with factory labels.) It is worth noting here that chemicals were seized and destroyed (such as road salt, baking soda and powdered iron) that were neither hazardous nor indicative of drug manufacturing.

Since our first wedding had been a hasty affair, Katrina and I decided that we should do it again the way it should have been done, and on September 15th we renewed our vows and held a reception for about 250 people at Katrina's parent's house in Rutland. A band was hired, and a big tent pitched on the side lawn. Lindsay participated in the ceremony, and it was a beautiful day in every sense.

As Will Hunter was fruitlessly pursuing remedies in court, Gary Shattuck held another inquest on September 19. This time the witnesses were friends Tom and Debra House, and Robert Firpo. The final witness was Sharon Stickney, an alleged associate of Robert Spencer whom I knew only slightly. Proving the accuracy of attorney Robare's contention that a prosecutor conducting an inquest could question "anyone he wants about absolutely anything", Gary Shattuck had asked Debra House, "Did you ever see Robert Bloomer light a firecracker?" Firpo later characterized the inquest as "garbage" for the newspaper. In spite of the gag order imposed by Judge Morrissey, Firpo related to me that Gary Shattuck had inquired about napalm, which no one ever linked to drug manufacture. And none of the witnesses, with the possible exception of my first wife, had linked me with any illegal drugs whatsoever.

Two days after the inquest Det. Raymond LaMoria called my father's law office, subsequently delivering my computer, computer disks, computer manuals and answering machine although the police continued to hold a great deal of my property that could have had no connection to a drug investigation. The police apparently weren't too familiar with computers as they had ripped out the cables for the peripherals without first slackening the retaining screws. Thus I was greatly surprised when, after reconnecting everything, it worked.

Apparently Robert Spencer's usefulness to the government dwindled, or perhaps the state decided that it needed some positive publicity to justify the retention of my property. In any event, the front-page headline of the September 25th *Rutland Herald* read "Drug Plea Implicates Bloomer". Spencer had entered a guilty plea to a misdemeanor charge of possession of one-quarter gram of cocaine and had received a sentence of 6 to 12 months probation. The government had agreed not to bring any felony charges against Spencer "as long as Spencer provided a complete statement about his drug activity and alleged involvement with

38

Bloomer…" The plea agreement provided that "The defendant [Spencer] will provide a full, complete, truthful and sworn statement detailing his own actions and his involvement with Robert Asa Bloomer Jr. in all drug-related activities."

The state had failed to reveal that Spencer's truthfulness could reasonably have been questioned in light of his contradictory confessions. Significantly, in the second "correction" confession both the quantity of drugs and my alleged involvement with them increased. An affidavit filed with the court in connection with Spencer's plea stated that "police received 'reliable' information from two informants stating that the two main people involved in the [drug trafficking] network were Spencer and Bloomer." Of course, the informants were not named and Spencer's confessions were kept secret for more than a year after the plea. Under the circumstances I was unable to offer much of a defense except a blanket denial. The next day Will Hunter told the newspaper that, "It now seems like somebody's trying to do him [Bloomer] in. Somebody whose identity I don't know. Now we've got statements made public about 'reliable' evidence, and we're still not being allowed to see what anybody's basing this on."

Spencer had retained William Sessions III, widely regarded as one of the best criminal lawyers in the state, and clearly Spencer thought he had solved his own legal problems by transferring them to me. However, both Sessions and Spencer were soon to learn that they had seriously underestimated the treacherous nature of their new friends in the government, especially Gary Shattuck.

Immediately following Spencer's plea, Will Hunter again tried to get the search warrant documents, but they remained sealed. He then filed a motion to unseal, and the *Rutland Herald* filed a similar motion of its own on the basis that there was a public right to see court documents. A hearing was held before Judge Theodore Mandeville on October 17. At the same time Katrina's attorney, (State Senator) Vincent Illuzzi, also asked for the return of her property remaining in the hands of the police, including her gynecology records. Although Atty. Wing's motion had specifically requested the gynecology records of Dr. Donald Wolins, and both the police and Gary Shattuck had said that such records had been set aside to await pickup by Katrina, they now were claiming that they never had them.

Had I known at the time that Judge Mandeville was not impartial, I would have seen the proceedings for the farce they were. As I was to learn later, Judge Mandeville had also presided at Spencer's plea hearing on the cocaine possession charge, and the question of the $1000 bail had come up. When Spencer had been arraigned previously on the assault charge, the court clerk had given him a check in the amount of $1000 made out to Robert Bloomer, as I was the one who actually gave the money to the jail guards. It was Spencer's intention at the time to have me cash the check and return the money to the motorcycle fund, but before he could give it to me, the police had raided his mobile home and seized the check.

During the cocaine plea hearing Gary Shattuck represented that the state wanted the check for "evidence", and Spencer wanted the money. Shattuck also falsely represented that Spencer "had asked another person who is potentially a co-defendant in this case to actually get the money from the defendant's account and then put up as bail money…" Judge Mandeville obliged both Shattuck and Spencer, although he at first opined "it sounds like a civil case to me". He also noted "the State doesn't want to find itself as a defendant." Nevertheless, the Docket and Disposition report of Spencer's cocaine charge shows "9/24/90 – By order of Judge Mandeville – void check issued to R. Bloomer and issue check to R. Spencer". While the source of the bail money was, in fact, Spencer's motorcycle fund the only hard evidence before the court was that I had put up the money. I was never consulted about the bail money prior to Mandeville's ruling, nor notified about it afterward.*

On November 27 Judge Mandeville finally ruled that the search warrant materials would remain sealed. The notation sealing the documents had stated "Only to be opened at time of arraignment or at request of [Assistant Attorney General] Gary Shattuck." My claim, as restated by Judge Mandeville, was "that the information supporting the search warrants issued on August 10 are no longer required to remain sealed inasmuch as an arraignment has taken place in the case of Mr. Spencer." The government's problem was that the same affidavit was used to obtain both Spencer's and my warrants, and it wanted to keep me in the dark.

The Vermont Supreme Court had been explicit in the *Tallman* case that "papers relating to causes in the district court…together with the records of the court, shall be subject to inspection and examination…"

---

* In 1995 I was still attempting to recover property seized in 1990. I sent an inquiry about he bail check to the District Court Clerk dated November 5, 1995. It was finally answered on May 24, 1996. My father subsequently went to the district court with his secretary and had her transcribe the taped hearing before Judge Mandeville.

Since Spencer had been arraigned the records of his case should have been public. However Judge Mandeville inexplicably ruled that there was "no cause or action now pending in the district court" and therefore there was no right to see the documents. Apparently if Spencer had entered a plea of not guilty and had been awaiting trial the documents would have been available, but since he pled guilty, the papers would remain a secret.

It was not until nearly a year later when the file was finally unsealed that I knew the extent of Mandeville's perfidy. Judge Hudson had made detailed statements on the record about his reasons for sealing the file and the conditions for its unsealing:

> I had a request on the phone last night by Mr. Shattuck that these two warrants [Spencer and Bloomer] be sealed until they are executed and until a person or persons are charged, and because of the ongoing investigation in the case, because of what I have heard with regard to the utilization of weapons and particularly as to the express intent of Mr. Spencer to use force, as well as for mainly considerations of public safety at what we believe to be the clandestine laboratory at Mr. Bloomer's residence, I am going to approve that both of these be sealed and kept under seal until the first person is either charged or the Assistant Attorney General [Gary Shattuck] indicates to the Court that there will be no charges.

There was no requirement that both Bloomer and Spencer be charged, just the "first person". Outraged, my father went to the court clerk's office and demanded to see the file. The clerk was not initially disposed to produce the file, but after an angry confrontation she threw the entire file on the counter, including Judge Mandeville's personal notes. Although Judge Mandeville had ruled, "For the foregoing reasons this court denies both motions to unseal the documents at issue", his own notes indicated that the "affidavit...in [the] Spencer case has already been disclosed."

The file itself bore a notation that it had been unsealed by Judge Mandeville on October 4, 1990 nearly two months before he issued his opinion, and clearly the only reason to break the seal was to read the file. Thus while publicly ruling that I had no right to the search warrant documents, Mandeville had concealed Judge Hudson's explicit order and had apparently given those very documents to Spencer.

41

It is worth noting here that Judge Hudson himself and Gary Shattuck, as well as Judge Mandeville, knew exactly what Judge Hudson had ordered. In addition, Spencer's attorney, William Sessions III, had to have known that Judge Mandeville was talking out of both sides of his mouth. Attorneys and judges are all officers of the court, and all have a duty to the truth. Not one of these men ever came forward in this matter.

13

I was not only on the defensive, but seemingly blocked at every turn. Aside from the serious problems Katrina and I faced, there was also annoyance of Det. LaMoria. He would run into Katrina from time to time at the local Grand Union (later renamed Price Chopper) supermarket, and would acknowledge her with a wolf whistle or comment like "Hey, baby!" He was not deterred by Lindsay's presence, and she could do a pretty good imitation minus, of course, LaMoria's bushy moustache and snakeskin boots. Lindsay also instantly recognized LaMoria during his frequent drives by our house, slowing down as he passed. LaMoria was hardly undercover in his red Chrysler K-car with its white convertible top and license RAYME, so we often speculated about exactly what it was that LaMoria hoped to observe.

While I saw LaMoria more as a boorish clown than a serious threat, Lindsay's eleven-year-old eyes may have seen things differently. Katrina and I did our best to hide our stress at the enormity of our situation, but surely Lindsay could sense it. My father was convinced that our telephone was tapped, and urged that we not discuss anything regarding our legal situation by phone. Further, the police frequently followed me, and sometimes Katrina. Although some no doubt escaped my detection, others were so obvious as to be laughable, and after a while, I began to carry a camera to take pictures of the most incompetent of the surveillance bumblers.

There was no escaping, however, the fact that either LaMoria or one of the other officers at the search had taken Lindsay's allowance money, and whatever the direct cause, Lindsay began to suffer from nightmares. One fear she was able to articulate was that people were outside the house at night. I went out numerous times at Lindsay's request with our dog, but never saw anyone. Another of her fears was that the police would come back. While I thought this farfetched at the time, I later learned that Asst. U.S. Attorney David Kirby actually considered obtaining another search warrant to look for a typewriter.

42

We were getting nowhere fast and under the circumstances it seemed reasonable to attack the problem from a different direction. On November 27, 1990 I filed a civil lawsuit against Det. LaMoria alleging damages from the loss of my property, damage to my reputation and emotional distress. In response Asst. Attorney General Gary Shattuck prophetically commented to the *Rutland Herald* that, "We will let the facts speak for themselves ... when they become known."

Shortly after I filed the suit against Det. LaMoria, Katrina filed a suit of her own against both LaMoria and the State of Vermont demanding the return of her medical records generated by Dr. Wolins. Despite Gary Shattuck's statement to the court, the records still had not been returned, and the State's subsequent position was that the police never had them.

Discovery was proceeding in both Katrina's and my civil cases, and we were about ready to take depositions of Ray LaMoria, Gary Shattuck and others. Shattuck, in particular, could be shown to have made false statements, and clearly the state had a problem. Despite two inquests and Spencer's cooperation I had not been charged, and the courts weren't going to allow the police to keep my personal property forever. The criminal investigation was unraveling, and both Shattuck and LaMoria were at risk.

Katrina, Lindsay and I were vacationing in Florida during January of 1991 when we received the news. Lindsay's father called to tell us that, according to the newspaper, there was now a federal grand jury investigation, and that Gary Shattuck had become a special assistant United States Attorney.

On the surface, at least, Shattuck seemed completely unqualified for his new position. He had been a State Police officer who had embarked on a career change by going to law school. However, he had little practical experience as a prosecutor, having been in private practice for only two years and an Assistant Attorney General for only one. Further, he had bungled his first big case. The decision to promote Shattuck into the federal arena was, therefore, entirely for the purpose of protecting him from the consequences of his own mistakes. Because of the intense publicity surrounding my case, the decision to transfer jurisdiction to the federal arena had to have been made at the highest level – Attorney General Jeffrey Amestoy* Amestoy was certainly aware of the proceedings, as he always looked away during his occasional encounters

---

* Amestoy was later appointed as Chief Justice of the Vermont Supreme Court.

with my uncle in the halls of the State House, refusing to make eye contact.

Shattuck's mentor and savior was David V. Kirby, chief of the criminal division of the U.S. Attorney's Office for Vermont. Superficially, the two men couldn't have been more different. Shattuck was perhaps six feet five inches and quite thin with a head that seemed too small for his body. His pale complexion highlighted his short red hair worn in the military style. Kirby, on the other hand, was a slight man of about five feet five with red blotches on this face from psoriasis or eczema. His thick black hair and full beard were mottled with gray. While Shattuck's competence was certainly questionable, Kirby had been a law clerk to Supreme Court Justice John Paul Stevens, and had had extensive prosecutorial experience. While one lawyer referred to Kirby as "The Kirbibbler" he was more universally and aptly known as "The Prince of Darkness".

I was unconcerned at the time about the federal investigation. I thought that a complete lack of evidence was a complete lack of evidence, regardless of the forum, but I was to learn soon enough the hard lesson that the federal government had nearly limitless power, and that power could be wielded by men with few ethical constraints.

14

It came as no surprise that the both the state and federal governments were trying to halt discovery in Katrina's and my lawsuits. Both governments' claims in my case were that allowing discovery to proceed would jeopardize their investigations, which on the surface seemed persuasive, and especially so since Judge Mandeville had concealed the search documents. It would later turn out that Det. LaMoria's affidavit in support of the warrant contained numerous errors and outright lies, but I did not have the affidavit and could make no such showing to the court.

Will Hunter questioned the timing of the federal investigation in an interview with the *Rutland Herald* on February 8, 1991:

> I wonder whether this is really a bona fide investigation or whether this is something that has been arranged in order to give somebody a reason not to answer the discovery request…The federal involvement seems to have arisen around the time we were to have taken depositions. The raid took place Aug. 11. Six months later, we are told

now that there is a federal investigation that's beginning.
I wonder what happened to the state investigation. It just
doesn't make any sense."

Vermont Judge Silvio Valente subsequently ordered on February
21 that "all discovery in this proceeding is stayed pending the conclusion
of the related criminal proceedings", but he also ordered that the "State
and the United States shall, however, return to plaintiff any materials
seized on August 11, 1990 from 96 Clarendon Avenue, West Rutland,
Vermont which are not necessary or material to the criminal
investigation."

The government finally got around to complying on April 3,
returning such incriminating items as photos of my cats, equipment
catalogs, a Sears catalog, my high school diploma and maintenance
manuals for the West Rutland water system. Neither the state nor the
federal government ever explained its justification for seizing these
materials in the first place, much less refusing to return them for nearly
eight months.

The government conceded that Katrina was not a suspect, and that
her medical records were not necessary for any investigation, so discovery
was allowed to proceed in her case, although the questions allowed by the
court were very narrow. Depositions were taken from Det. Raymond
LaMoria, Jr., Gary Shattuck, and Lt. John Krupp who was in charge of the
Rutland and Castleton State Police barracks. And there were certainly
some questions that needed answering.

. Two days after the fiasco at the State Police barracks regarding
Katrina's gynecology records, Det. LaMoria had left some of Katrina's
property at the offices of her attorney, Leonard Wing. The receipt showed:

1.   MISC PAPERS FROM SILVER THREE DRAWER FILE
      CABINET GIVEN TO KATRINA CARRIS 08-24-90
2.   #9   FILE WITH MISC MEDICAL PAPERS ETC.
3.   #15 MISC PAPERS & CHECKBOOK STATEMENT

Numbers #9 and #15 apparently referred to the inventory left with
the search warrant. Number 15 on the inventory stated "MISC
PAPERWK CHECKBOOK M BDRM INC. NOTEPAD", which seemed
to correspond to LaMoria's list. However, #9 stated "Folder w/ ph. Bills
ect.". There was no mention anywhere in the inventory of "medical
papers" or anything of a medical nature.

Among Katrina's papers returned by LaMoria to Leonard Wing was a certificate from Beech Hill Hospital indicating only that Katrina had completed a seminar there in 1988, and both Ray LaMoria and Gary Shattuck were now claiming that this certificate was the "medical record" to which they had referred.

Shattuck even went so far as to claim that he and Katrina's attorney, Leonard Wing, had had a conversation before the court hearing on Wing's motion for the return of the records to the extent that the Beech Hill certificate was the only "medical record" that they were talking about. Shattuck's contentions were contradicted by Mr. Wing, who subsequently gave an affidavit:

> I specifically deny that statement. The medical records
> that were discussed were those which were the subject of
> the motion, namely Dr. Donald Wolins' medical records
> pertaining to Katrina Carris. Those were the only medical
> records which were the subject of that motion and I had no
> conversation with Mr. Shattuck prior to the hearing before
> the Court relative to the medical certificate to which he
> referred...

Clearly, things were spiraling out of control, but fortunately for Shattuck and LaMoria, the courts stepped in. By Order dated November 26, 1991 Judge Arthur O'Dea stayed any further proceedings in the case until the final resolution of the government's criminal case against me – a process that was likely to take years. Although Katrina had represented that Dr. Wolins' missing records were pertinent to her present medical care, the "court [saw] no good purpose to be served by allowing further discovery and engagements in this civil proceeding." The Supreme Court refused to hear an interim appeal.[6] When Katrina's case was finally reopened years later, the medical records were largely irrelevant, and by then she had lost her will to fight and never pursued the matter. Her gynecology records were never found.

(It turned out that Judge O'Dea was unpopular with others beside Katrina and myself. Following allegations of improper courtroom behavior in Family Court, the judge was thrown off the bench in 1993 by a vote of the General Assembly.)

15

As Katrina was trying to compel the depositions of Gary Shattuck and Ray LaMoria, the government tried a trick of its own. In early February of 1991 Sgt. James Baker, the head of the Southern Vermont Drug Task Force, showed up at my house in West Rutland to serve me with a subpoena for a federal grand jury in Burlington. The subpoena also demanded that I provide handwriting samples, fingerprints and photographs, and was signed by David V. Kirby, Chief of the Criminal Division of the U.S. Attorney's office.

The government had already tipped off the newspaper that I might be served, so the subpoena itself was not a complete surprise, but the service was bizarre for several reasons. First, Sgt. Baker was a Vermont state policeman, and not an officer of the federal government. Second, it must have been rare for someone of Baker's rank to be serving subpoenas. Third, Baker was stationed at the Shaftsbury barracks, some 45 miles south of West Rutland. And finally, no one could have seriously believed that I intended to say anything to a grand jury investigating my own activities.

While lawyers are not permitted to attend grand jury proceedings, witnesses can leave the room to consult with their attorneys during questioning, and under the circumstances it seemed prudent to have my attorney present. On the day specified on the subpoena, Will Hunter and I drove the 70 miles from Rutland to Burlington, only to discover that there was no grand jury meeting that day. Neither was anyone available to take handwriting samples. Although I did have the pleasure of meeting the Prince of Darkness himself, David Kirby, overall the trip was a complete waste of both my time and the money I had to pay Will.

I was eventually photographed and fingerprinted by U.S. Marshals in Rutland, but had to drive to Burlington twice to give handwriting samples. I never did get another grand jury subpoena, although others were not so lucky. My friend Frank Gorham, a farmer from down the road, gleefully recounted his encounter with Ray LaMoria. Officer LaMoria had come to Gorham's farm, and had served the subpoena while Frank was fixing his tractor. Frank then shook LaMoria's hand, thereby transferring a liberal amount of grease, grime and diesel fuel to the policeman.

I cautioned Frank that the grand jury was no laughing matter. "They've got a drug case with no drugs," I said. "Careers are at stake. They're going to hang somebody from the yardarm. Maybe it will be you." I advised him to discuss his situation immediately with a criminal attorney.

In West Rutland, Frank Gorham kept pretty much to himself, working on his farm. He was initially in the dairy business, but his cows had died off and his operation shifted to sheep farming, firewood and vegetables with maple sugaring and trapping providing extra income. But Gorham had not always been a farmer. His father was an executive with Union Carbide, and the family had lived in Berkeley Heights, New Jersey, an affluent suburb 15 miles west of Newark. Frank, according to his own account, preferred to pass his time in Newark collecting debts for organized crime and consorting with thugs. He claimed to know the details of unsolved murders in the area.

Something caused him to change course, and he attended the State University of New York at Delhi, majoring in agriculture. After graduating he took over the farm in West Rutland, which had been in the family since the Civil War. I met him while selling a pickup truck cap, and we began a working arrangement that turned to friendship. He needed constant mechanical help to maintain his farm equipment, and I frequently needed a hand moving heavy things around in my house and garage, both of which were in a state of more or less permanent renovation. We became occasional drinking buddies until I stopped drinking for good in 1987. I often shot guns at the Gorham farm, and stored my two snowmobiles in the barn. Frank owned about 250 acres, but an electric power transmission corridor ran through his property, allowing connection to miles of fields and trails.

Frank had frequent visitors from New Jersey that would spend the weekend at this farm, most of whom I didn't meet. Two I did meet were a girl and her boyfriend, who was pursuing an advanced degree in chemistry at Dartmouth. Another was Frank's best friend from his days on the streets of Newark, a slight character with shifty eyes. The friend had brought a co-worker with him, a blubbery young man with a thick southern drawl. The southerner delightedly related his favorite hobby – shooting razor-edged hunting arrows into the air in the largely black ghetto of Newark without any notion of where they might fall. "I shot an arrow into the air…" he'd say with a big grin. Noticing the carcass of a dog the pair had shot that morning with an old military rifle, I decided that I didn't want to know them any better and left the Gorham farm. I never saw those two again, and had no desire to do so.

According to Frank money was tight, and he wanted me to explain to his wife why he needed to see a lawyer, although perhaps the real reason was to focus on my problems and shift attention away from his past

48

in Newark. I had no way of telling if the Newark stories were true, but Frank certainly wasn't in jail nor had he ever been to the best of my knowledge, leaving open the possibility that he had been a police informant. Considering his position as husband and father to two young children, and his own statements, I had thought that Frank had broken whatever connections he might have had to the city of Newark, but that supposition had been disproved by the visit of the former best friend and his arrow-shooting compadre.

Apparently Frank's wife consented to the legal consultation, as afterwards an ashen Frank Gorham showed up at my house and handed Katrina a check for $200, which he owed me for a gasoline engine. On the advice of counsel, he told Katrina, he could never see me again. While I had no idea at the time what Frank Gorham would ultimately say about me, there was little doubt in my mind that it would be precisely what the U.S. Attorney's office wanted to hear.

Another of the subpoena recipients was Nicolette Samplatsky, Robert Spencer's sometimes girlfriend. A *Rutland Herald* article stated that Spencer had learned that he might be the target of a federal indictment, and was worried about what Samplatsky might say. The worry apparently metamorphosed into something more violent, with Spencer banging Samplatsky's head against a table and grabbing her by the throat according to a police affidavit.

Although she had had little to say at Gary Shattuck's inquest, Debbie House received a grand jury subpoena from Det. LaMoria. A short time later she showed up at my house, very upset. According to Debbie, LaMoria had told her that if she didn't change the testimony she gave at the inquest, she would be charged with perjury, although LaMoria later denied making such a specific threat. However, if the intent was to terrorize, it certainly worked.

Debbie had worked for years at the Rutland General Electric plant performing highly skilled final finishing on jet engine blades. She became bored with the routine, went back to school and received a paralegal degree. She had only been at her new job a short time when Det. LaMoria came calling. In all he called several times, always with the message that Debbie should tell the "truth" at her upcoming grand jury appearance.

At some point, Debbie was also advised that the government had two witnesses that she had been selling drugs at General Electric. "I never sold any drugs at GE, " Debbie said plaintively. "Who could these witnesses be?"

"It really doesn't make any difference," I replied. "If they're lying, it could be anybody."

(The government eventually revealed to Debbie the identity of the witnesses. Neither had ever worked at General Electric, and neither could have had any first hand knowledge of anything that had gone on there.)

Perhaps Debbie's real concern was the huge marijuana plant growing in her living room. Marijuana cultivation was of course a federal crime, and could have resulted in the forfeiture of her house to the government. Everyone who had ever been to Debbie's house in Middletown Springs had seen the plant, and apparently one or more of the visitors were police informants.

She discussed at least a part of her dilemma with her new employer, but was not happy with the response. According to Debbie, the employer wanted nothing whatsoever to do with the situation. Innocent or not, if Debbie were to be charged with perjury, she would be fired. As the grand jury date approached, Debbie became more and more agitated. "What am I going to do?" she whined to me. "My husband's business isn't doing well. We've got the payments on the vehicles. We've got the house payments. And we've got the girls. I can't lose my job."

I thought to myself, "I know what you're going to do. You just haven't rationalized it to yourself yet."

Debbie wanted me to find her a lawyer for her grand jury appearance, but I had no intention of doing so. First, virtually all the local criminal attorneys were already representing either principals or witness in the case. Second, and more importantly, I was in a very awkward position. I was sure she was eventually going to testify against me, and I did not want to expose myself to charges of obstruction of justice or witness tampering. She eventually found her own attorney in Burlington on the morning of her grand jury date.

A day or two after her performance, Debbie tearfully recounted what had happened. First, she and her attorney had gone to the U.S. Attorney's office in Burlington to meet with Gary Shattuck and David Kirby. The basic question she had was, "What do I have to do so that you'll leave me and my family alone?" She volunteered that she had bought a small quantity of drugs from me, but that was rejected as insufficient. When the quantity was increased, that was deemed adequate and she was then brought before the grand jury to deliver the performance rehearsed in the U.S. Attorney's office.

While Debbie wanted to remain friends, and wanted Lindsay to continue to associate with her daughters, I saw myself in a very dangerous position. Debbie was denying to herself what she'd done and the likely consequences. While I didn't want to antagonize her, I thought it imperative to have as little to do with her as possible.

50

The account of one of my motorcycle customers, Chuck, closely mirrored Debbie's experience. Chuck was a local roofer who had been an inmate at the Rutland Regional Correctional Center during the time that Det. LaMoria had been a guard there and, apparently unafraid of heights, LaMoria had visited Chuck several times on his roofing jobs to make threats.

For reasons neither of us understood, Chuck was subpoenaed to the federal grand jury. As he later told the story, Chuck took the grand jury seriously, and wore clean jeans and his best pair of sneakers on the day of his appearance. I would have liked to see his outfit, as he habitually wore a black leather motorcycle jacket covered with a grungy, sleeveless denim vest, as well as the other traditional accoutrements of the "one-percenter" Harley Davidson riders. However, Chuck never made it in front of the grand jury. Once again, he was first interviewed in the U.S. Attorney's office by Shattuck, Kirby and Det. LaMoria. Chuck denied any knowledge of drug activity on my part and explained that, "I wouldn't even call us friends. We're just good acquaintances. He works on my motorcycle."

Chuck was then told his appearance would not be needed, and he could go. However Det. LaMoria, apparently unconvinced that Chuck was telling the truth, followed him out into the hallway of the federal building, yelling a horribly tangled mixed metaphor, "Piss rolls downhill, and you're going to get all wet if you don't tell us about Bloomer."

My scientific friend, Mark Malmros, also told of a similar meeting with Kirby, Shattuck and LaMoria where he was threatened out of sight of the Grand Jury. Unlike Chuck, however, Mark was asked to testify about chemicals and our polyacetylene project.

Even if they were squeaky clean, the witnesses were in great danger. However those with a skeleton or two in the closet, like perhaps Debbie House or Frank Gorham, were under tremendous pressure to please the U.S. Attorneys. The situation was even more precarious because of the government's power to compel testimony.

The way it usually worked was that the prospective witnesses were given subpoenas. Those with no lawyers and little knowledge of the system, like Chuck, had no idea of what their rights were, and were vulnerable to the predations of highly experienced U.S. Attorneys like David Kirby. Those with attorneys generally asserted their Fifth Amendment rights against self-incrimination as a matter of course. The government then granted them immunity and demanded that they testify. If the witness refused, he or she could be sentenced to up to 18 months in prison. Another grand jury could be convened, the same witness subpoenaed, and another refusal to testify could result in another 18 months. The law allowed the government to do this up to three times for a total of 4 1/2 years in prison.

The truly dangerous part was that the government rarely granted total immunity or, as it was called, transactional immunity. Instead, usually it granted only use immunity, which meant that whatever testimony a person gave couldn't be used against that person in a subsequent prosecution. In theory, the government couldn't follow any thread provided by the witness's testimony, but in practice the government could simply claim that it received the information from another source and use the very information the immunized witness provided against him or her.

I had heard that this is precisely what the government was doing with my former motorcycle customer turned government witness, Robert Spencer. Apparently the government had subpoenaed people that Spencer had named as drug associates. The U.S. Attorneys were then saying, in so many words, "Spencer told on you. That's why you're here. What can you tell us about him?" As word of the grand jury subpoenas spread, my motorcycle repair business dwindled to almost nothing, and I was sure many of my customers were reluctant to answer questions of the type, "Did you ever know anybody who used illegal drugs?" I hoped that something would happen soon regarding the investigation, regardless of what it might be.

16

As the grand jury investigation inched forward, there was little the government could tell the newspaper. Apparently they thought something was better than nothing, and on June 8, 1991 an article appeared in the *Rutland Herald* entitled "Narc's Life Is Never Boring". The occasion of the article was an award given the previous month to Detective LaMoria by the New England Narcotics Enforcement Officers Association. There was a fairly extensive biography and details of a couple of LaMoria's undercover operations unrelated to my case, and an interesting quote:

If you're dealing drugs in Rutland County, someday, sometime, somewhere, you'll hear, "Hi, we're with the Southern Vermont Drug Task Force. You're under arrest." We will meet in person someday.

Twenty-five years after his bold statement law enforcement has utterly failed to control drugs in Central Vermont. Rutland has been in the grips of an unprecedented decade-and-a-half-long heroin addiction epidemic with no end in sight.

A day following the anniversary of the August 11th raid on my house, the *Rutland Herald* ran an article entitled "One Year Later, Bloomer Still Not Charged" with a detailed recap of events and a timeline. Two days later the front-page headline was "Bloomer Indicted for Making Drug". The first notice I had received of the indictment was a call from a reporter the previous day.

In addition to the indictment, the government filed papers for the forfeiture of my house, but I had anticipated the move and had made Katrina co-owner a couple of days before. No matter what happened to me, she would be eligible to retain her half, or at least its value.

The forfeiture statutes had been sold to the public as a mechanism for depriving criminals of their ill-gotten gains, but the process had been abused from the beginning and often amounted to little more than legalized theft by the government. Moreover, title in real estate passed immediately to the Attorney General upon the issue of the warrant, depriving a criminal defendant of what was likely his major asset just at the time he needed money to pay a defense attorney. While the forfeiture could be contested later, in the meantime the property was unavailable.

No proof was required that the assets were purchased with tainted money, but only that they were the "instrumentalities" of a crime, i.e. a car used to transport drugs could be forfeited even if it could be shown that it had been bought with funds from an untainted source. Consequently, agents or informers working for the government often tried to structure illegal transactions such that the government could go after the maximum number of assets, and there seemed to be no end to the greed. In Vermont it was not uncommon for a defendant to plead guilty to a state drug charge, only to have the feds show up a month or so later to confiscate his property. Although I could readily show the sources of all monies for major expenditures on my house, it was irrelevant to the proceedings.

While neither the forfeiture nor the indictment came as a surprise, it was surprising that Robert Spencer was also indicted on 15 counts relating to conspiracy to manufacture and distribute methamphetamine with me. These were precisely the charges he thought he had resolved in his plea and cooperation agreement with Gary Shattuck more than a year before.

I was never arrested in connection with the indictment, but appeared in court on August 19, 1990 with Will Hunter and was arraigned, or formally charged, with the six counts of the indictment. Robert Spencer was also arraigned on 15 counts. I entered a plea of not guilty to all, as did Spencer. Judge Franklin S. Billings III gave me personal recognizance bail pending trial, meaning that I didn't have to put up any cash or security, but there were various conditions of release including that I not leave the state and that I "avoid all contact" with numerous people believed to be potential or actual government trial witnesses. Among those on the list were obvious prosecution witnesses like Robert Spencer, obvious defense witnesses like Mark Malmros, and people I didn't know at all. The government even went so far as to ask that Spencer avoid all contact with his then-fiancé, Nicolette Samplatsky, but in that instance Judge Billings agreed with defense counsel that such a requirement would be unworkable.

Apparently no one thought it unworkable that I was prohibited from contacting potential defense witnesses. It would turn out that the government was deliberately preventing me from talking with Mark, and had no intention whatsoever of calling him as a government witness as Mark had given grand jury testimony that could and should have formed the basis of my defense. Specifically, he had testified that virtually all the chemicals that the government sought to link to my alleged methamphetamine manufacturing had a relevance to our polyacetylene project. Although the government had a specific legal duty to advise me of this - and any other - exculpatory evidence, it concealed the material until well after trial.

The day following the arraignment Will Hunter went to the Vermont District Court in Rutland to get the long-denied search warrant documents, only to discover they weren't there. Judge Mandeville had supposedly removed them for "review". Will was then forced to attend – at my expense - a hearing two days later (August 22, 1991) in Bennington, nearly 50 miles south of Rutland, where Mandeville finally turned over the documents.

It was immediately clear that there had been no reason whatsoever for any hearing, and that the search warrant affidavit and transcript should have been available to anyone who wanted them following Spencer's arraignment on the cocaine charge. Judge Mandeville had unsealed the file months before in connection with Will's previous motion, read Judge Hudson's explicit instructions, ignored them and concealed them.

The only reason that occurred to me, then or now, for Judge Mandeville to remove the file from the court was to change something himself or allow the government to do so. In the transcript I was provided of the search warrant hearing, Judge Hudson had referred to a possible

54

"induced ignition ...of the natural resources that go into the methamphetamine", but nothing whatsoever was on the record to suggest anything of the sort, suggesting that part of the transcript had been deleted. In addition the transcript contained the following statement of Judge Hudson:

> We're going to approve entry after 10 p.m. without knocking at the Bloomer residence as well because at the Bloomer home there also appears to be some weapons present, and although he has been less express in any kind of an offer to use force, that nevertheless in a panic situation where a candidate for public office finds himself confronted with a warrant of this magnitude, he might be provoked to do something that would be extremely out of character and endangering the police, endanger himself and the residents of his home.

One resident of my home, Lindsay, age 11, was never mentioned. Neither was there any mention on the record of any "offer to use force" on my part, or any factual basis for the judge's conclusion that there were "some weapons present". However, the next day the officers executing the warrant were briefed to expect an armed confrontation and to be on the lookout for booby traps.[7] It
thus seemed that Judge Hudson was relying on information he received outside the record. Perhaps he received it during the telephone call he referred to during the hearing – the call from Gary Shattuck to the judge's home the night before - or perhaps information that was inflammatory and demonstrably false was simply erased from the record during the time Judge Mandeville removed the file from the court. If the warrant application had been changed after the fact as I suspected (and as I suspected had been done with the search warrant return), it was going to be very difficult to challenge the warrant's validity.

I later filed complaints against both Judge Mandeville and Judge Hudson with the Professional Conduct Board for their roles in concealing and failing to follow Judge Hudson's original sealing order. The complaints were quickly dismissed.

17

The indictment laid out the government's case in considerable detail. The six counts pertaining to me alleged that I had conspired with

Robert Spencer, manufactured methamphetamine, maintained a place for the manufacture of methamphetamine, and sold the drug to three individuals – Robert Spencer, Franklin Gorham III, and Gary Makovec. Makovec was the former brother-in-law of reluctant witness Debra House. While the indictment used only the witnesses' initials, it wasn't very difficult to figure out who they were.

In addition to the counts themselves, the indictment described the alleged conspiracy and listed a number of overt acts such as ordering chemicals and having Frank Gorham store chemical notebooks "in an effort to avoid detection". (The government was never able to produce the alleged notebooks, as Gorham claimed that he had destroyed them. Although he could give only a vague description of the notebooks, Gorham was nonetheless certain that they contained formulas for the production of methamphetamine.)

Before he had even received the search warrant materials Will Hunter filed a sweeping discovery request, demanding various evidence from the government, and while we were waiting for the result he asked me to review the search warrant documents and list any inaccuracies I found. I was glad to finally be able to do something. The previous year had been one of intense frustration, with the police withholding much of my personal property and the courts refusing to make them disclose the basis for it. The image I had of myself was as an insect pinned to a corkboard – alive and squirming, but going nowhere.

A quick look at Det. LaMoria's affidavit revealed numerous inaccuracies and innuendos. Nowhere was it mentioned that I had a motorcycle repair business with Spencer as a customer, which left the impression that any visit Spencer made to my house was for drug dealing. Much was made of the alleged secrecy of my laboratory, although it wasn't a secret at all. My company, Soron Engineering, was described as a "front to order chemicals" although it was registered with Secretary of State's office and I was listed as the owner.

LaMoria also insinuated that I had abused my position with the Fire District by using it to launder orders from chemical companies. LaMoria claimed to have obtained delivery slips from United Parcel Service and, after reviewing them, he "found that any orders for the Town of West Rutland Fire District had been documented as having been delivered to the Town of West Rutland at the Town Office." The exception was orders from Wallace & Tiernan, "a company which distributes chemicals and chemical equipment". Those orders had been delivered to my house. LaMoria then concluded that this "information is consistent with that of Robert Bloomer attempting to avoid detection by

56

law enforcement personnel, as to his ordering chemicals and laboratory hardware or glassware."

Both LaMoria's statements of fact and conclusions were demonstrably false. First, Fire District orders for anything were never delivered to the town hall. The Fire District maintained no offices, so the longstanding practice was for the persons needing parts or supplies to have them sent to their homes. I did many of the repairs on the pump house and chlorinator, so those parts were sent to me. Joe Skaza did other repairs, and parts for those were sent to him. Interestingly R.J. Elrick, a West Rutland volunteer fireman and police officer with Det. LaMoria in Rutland, had repair parts for the fire department radios sent directly to his house. The parts from W & T that LaMoria found so suspicious were all repair and maintenance parts for the West Rutland municipal chlorination system manufactured by W & T, a fact that could have been readily verified with a call to the company.

Much was also made of a previous DEA investigation beginning in 1984. Apparently some of the chemicals Mark Malmros and I had ordered in connection with the polyacetylene experiments had piqued the interest of the Drug Enforcement Administration (DEA). A thorough investigation had been conducted which included the accumulation of the chemical and equipment orders I had placed in connection with the polyacetylene project from 1982-1984, surveillance of my house, grand jury testimony, and the attempted intimidation of at least one witness, Beverly Hobson. The investigation was dropped due to a lack of evidence and a lack of leads.

While the DEA investigation apparently commenced with my chemical orders, at some point it turned up my association with Mark on the medical testing machine according to the Reports of Investigation I eventually obtained. (Many of the reports are still secret to this day, although some were provided.) LaMoria specifically stated in his affidavit that he obtained the reports of the previous investigation, so he had to be aware of the polyacetylene experiments, but no mention was made of polyacetylene or my research in the affidavit. Instead, LaMoria relied on the opinion given by a DEA chemist in 1984 (inaccurately reported by LaMoria as 1986) that "the chemicals that Bloomer was ordering were conducive and indicative to the manufacturing of controlled substances, specifically, methamphetamine." According to the DEA report itself the chemist had said, specifically, "phenylacetone", not methamphetamine. Furthermore, the list of chemicals submitted by LaMoria as purchased by me – the same list presumably relied upon by the DEA chemist - was not complete. Conspicuous by its absence was Titanium (IV) Butoxide, an essential component of the catalyst system to synthesize polyacetylene, but with no application to methamphetamine. It was never determined whether the chemist was aware of the polyacetylene experiments at the time he gave his opinion, or precisely what information he had relied on.

A key part of the search warrant affidavit was statements attributed to Confidential Informant #RL-90-007 who was obviously Robert Spencer's girlfriend, Nicolette Samplatsky. This was the same Nicolette Samplatsky who had allegedly made threats against me, who had played various games to have Spencer jailed, and who had entertained Det. LaMoria at her Pearl St. apartment. My own opinion of Samplatsky was that she was an alcoholic, cocaine addict and pathological liar, and I wouldn't have mentioned a speeding ticket in her presence. Perhaps Det. LaMoria thought it too farfetched to have Samplatsky claiming direct knowledge of any drug activity on my part. In any event, Samplatsky only claimed that Spencer had "informed" her of various things, including that I was making methamphetamine.

Samplatsky's credibility could have been challenged on yet another ground, of which I was not aware until later. Samplatsky had Diane LaMoria, the wife of Det. LaMoria, as her social worker as did several other women who were government witnesses, and there was no question that Diane had served as a go-between for Samplatsky and her husband. However, there might have been more to the relationship. Sharon Stickney, another witness and Diane LaMoria client, gave a sworn affidavit that she had had financial problems and was given welfare benefits to which she was not entitled. She was subsequently approached by Ray LaMoria, who somehow knew she had financial problems. When Ms. Stickney refused to cooperate with Ray LaMoria, Diane LaMoria was removed from Stickney's case and her welfare benefits "went down".[8]

While there were numerous other problems with LaMoria's affidavit, one more deserves mention here. Supposedly between October 23 and October 28, 1989 Confidential Informant #RL-009-89 (later identified as Michael Galarneau) went to Spencer's trailer wearing a wire but, although LaMoria could hear the conversation, he claimed he did not record it. This left him free to recall numerous statements by Spencer regarding our supposed drug dealing. Later, when Spencer was under oath and anxious to please the government at trial, he contradicted LaMoria by saying that my name didn't come up at all at that time, but rather in a subsequent conversation with Galarneau in December that was recorded.[9]

Even if the first conversation had occurred as reported by Det. LaMoria, it's questionable if he actually believed what Spencer was saying. I had long thought that many of Spencer's tales were gross

58

exaggerations, and later learned that some of the more dramatic ones had actually happened to someone else. Although LaMoria reported that Spencer "was going to be receiving some type of trip wires and dummy grenades...through the National Guard" and that "if his ex-girlfriend did say something, and he found out, he (Spencer) would kill her", Spencer does not appear to have been taken seriously – except regarding methamphetamine.

LaMoria tried again with CI Galarneau on December 8, 1989. This time the conversation was recorded, or at least part of it. With both the tape I was given and the transcript, the beginning of the conversation was missing, as well as a portion of unknown length in the middle at a crucial juncture. At that point in the conversation Spencer uses the word "unlimited", but he doesn't say to what he is referring. Nowhere does he utter the phrase "unlimited supply" although it is quoted in both LaMoria's affidavit and the indictment. The indictment states Spencer "expected an 'unlimited supply' of methamphetamine from ROBERT A. BLOOMER", and LaMoria's affidavit infers that, but that's not what even the government's transcript showed. The transcript was also missing the verbal comments "Bloomer – talk Bloomer" from someone, presumably a police officer, on the recording.

According to LaMoria's affidavit, Spencer expected to have something by Christmas, only two weeks after the recorded Spencer/Galarneau conversation. However, the very next day a three-man team from the Town of West Rutland went through my house from top to bottom in connection with a tax appeal. They were shown the laboratory area, and saw nothing suspicious. Nothing was set up, and nothing was operating. Despite Spencer's posturing and promises, Galarneau never obtained any methamphetamine from him in the more than six months between the initial wired conversation and the execution of the warrant on my house. And no methamphetamine was ever found, either at my house or at Spencer's - only alleged residues.

The transcript of the warrant hearing before Judge Hudson convinced me beyond any doubt that LaMoria, or someone working on his behalf, had entered my house and closely inspected what remained of my laboratory and chemicals before applying for the search warrant. In his testimony LaMoria stated:

> ...through my investigation I believe that the chemicals
> have been stockpiled, and when they are stockpiled they
> start to -- the containers start to rust and corrode and they
> become very unstable. Some chemicals that are used in

the process will explode on contact of any liquid or water
that would go into them, so if we would move a chemical
and there happens to be moisture on it and the chemical
which is contained in the container happens to come in contact
with the water, then it could explode.[10]

The fact was that I had a small amount of water-reactive sodium metal left over from the polyacetylene experiments stored in an unlabeled paint can under kerosene. While it was safe enough where it was, the container did have some surface rust. This meant that not only did someone observe the container, but they also opened it to at least observe, if not sample, the contents.

Questions about the affidavit and the subsequent search nag to this day. In an after action report of the raid Trooper R. W. Penka wrote[11]:

After receiving our assignments we were briefed on the
possibility of a clandestine lab being at the residnce [sic].
We were alerted to the potential dangers of the chemicals
involved. As well we were warned about the liklyhood
[sic] of weapons being involved. It was determined at this
time that the Tactical Operations Team (TOT) would be
used at both residences. Again the possibility of
'boobytraps' was discussed.

Det. Sgt. James Baker, the head of the Southern Vermont Drug Task Force and Det. LaMoria's boss, authored a report indicating that LaMoria had my house under surveillance for the month of July 1990, and he briefed Sgt. Baker "concerning the activity around BLOOMER'S residence."[12] In addition, LaMoria lived just down the road and probably passed my house a minimum of twice daily. How, then, was it possible no one knew that I hadn't lived at the house for more than a month? And why was no mention made of Lindsay? Arrangements had been made for fire trucks, an ambulance, a crime lab team complete with a specialized van, a DEA chemist from New York, a hazardous waste outfit (Pollution Solutions), and a Tactical Operations Team. Why had no one simply staked out the residence for one day before sending in the heavily armed Tactical Team expecting "weapons being involved" and "boobytraps"? An accidental weapons discharge by police in my residential neighborhood could have had disastrous consequences, and for nothing.

60

18

The numerous problems with the search warrant application gave me a brief moment of false hope. If the evidence from the search could be suppressed, the prosecution would be left with only the statements of a handful of witnesses, all of whom had admitted criminal activity and all of whom had made deals with the government. My hopes were diminished somewhat by the government's massive evidence production on September 6, 1991. While I had expected to see copies of my chemical orders and most of the government's other evidence, I was taken completely by surprise by the reports of the Vermont State Police Laboratory indicating that residues of methamphetamine had been found in some of my laboratory equipment. I knew at that point that someone was willing to falsify evidence, and that I had some very serious problems.

The reports indicated that methamphetamine had been found on a metal drip tray on bottom of my fume hood, and that simply was not possible. In the spring of 1990, only a few months before the raid, I had spilled some picric acid on the drip tray. Since picric acid was both a poison and a potent staining agent I had cleaned the tray very thoroughly, first with detergent and water, then with solvents. Consequently, there was no possibility whatsoever that there was anything on that tray from any activity of mine except dust from the construction project going on at my house.

The only question in my mind was whether the methamphetamine had been planted during the raid at my house or later in the police laboratory. The laboratory seemed more likely, since it made no sense for the police to plant residues instead of a bag of methamphetamine. Had a bag been found the day of the raid, I would have been arrested and that would have been that.

The reports indicated that methamphetamine had been found, but did not disclose the methods used to arrive at that conclusion, making it impossible to determine if proper scientific procedures had been followed. Federal law required only the production of the reports themselves, and prohibited the deposition of the chemist – or any of the other witnesses. Congress had also passed a specific law, 18 U.S.C. 3500, the Jencks Act, that required the production of witness's statements only after the witness had testified at trial. This was certainly intended to handicap a criminal defense, and left the government in sole control of evidence that could well have been exculpatory. Will Hunter's discovery request for witness statements was therefore either wildly optimistic or made in ignorance of federal law.

Will also seemed to have problems staying focused on the case. Part of the explanation was that he had "a lot of balls in the air" as he put it, and part of the explanation was adult attention deficit disorder (AADD) which was not to be properly diagnosed until a couple of years later. Under the circumstances I thought I needed to bring someone on board that was familiar with the federal criminal law.

The best-known criminal attorney in the area, William Sessions, was already representing my codefendant, and many other lawyers represented prospective witnesses in the case. After considering the possibilities, none completely satisfactory, I settled on David Gibson of Brattleboro. He had served with my father in the Vermont Senate, and Gibson's father had been a friend of my grandfather. More importantly, Gibson had been an assistant U.S. attorney and should have had an intimate knowledge of both the federal law and the way the system worked. Gibson formally entered his appearance on September 26, 1991. This was to be the beginning of the end, but I had no way of knowing it at the time.

My father, uncle, cousin and all three of my brothers were lawyers, but none did any criminal work with the exception of perhaps a traffic or DUI case; my father disliked all the rules in federal court and hadn't even tried a civil case there in two decades. Federal criminal law was different from Vermont state law and highly specialized, which left me with a family of lawyers unable to give me much help with my problems. David Gibson, however, got off to a fast start by filing with Will Hunter a motion to suppress evidence less than two weeks after entering his appearance. At last the counterattack had begun, I thought. It turned out that the motion was completely incompetent.

The 4th Amendment to the United States Constitution prohibited unreasonable searches and seizures, and required that "…no Warrant shall issue, but upon probable cause, supported by Oath or affirmation…" The Constitution, however, was silent on how one was to proceed if the oath or affirmation were false. The U.S. Supreme Court answered the question, with the controlling case at the time of Gibson's motion entitled *Franks v. Delaware*. The Franks case was mentioned nowhere in the motion to suppress, nor did Gibson comply with the requirements set down by the Supreme Court.

Will Hunter could be forgiven as he never claimed to be an expert on the federal law, but David Gibson, on the other hand, was hired specifically for that expertise and specifically charged me for legal research on the motion. While the law might be intimidating to a layperson, handbooks and practice guides are available to lawyers, leading

62

them through every step of a criminal defense just as service manuals guide auto mechanics. Mr. Gibson would later claim that he was aware of the *Franks* case, and was unable to comply with its provisions, but that's not what he told me at the time. I was led to believe that we had a good chance of invalidating the warrant, and that would have effectively ended the prosecution.

David Gibson was going to handle the suppression hearing himself, with Will Hunter only observing. At the very least we were going to expose all the lies and half-truths Det. LaMoria had included in his search warrant application. It was thus with high hopes that I attended the hearing on the suppression motion held on January 27, 1992 before the Hon. Franklin Billings, Jr., but the high hopes didn't last long as the hearing quickly degenerated into a fiasco. From the beginning Assistant U.S. Attorney David Kirby claimed that Mr. Gibson had not met the requirements of *Franks* and no hearing was required. There wasn't much doubt about what should have been done. As the Supreme Court wrote in *Franks*:

> To mandate an evidentiary hearing, the challenger's attack must be more than conclusory and must be supported by more than a mere desire to cross-examine. There must be allegations of deliberate falsehood or of reckless disregard for the truth, and those allegations must be accompanied by an offer of proof. They should point out specifically the portion of the warrant affidavit that is claimed to be false; and they should be accompanied by a statement of supporting reasons. Affidavits or sworn or otherwise reliable statements of witnesses should be furnished, or their absence satisfactorily explained. Allegations of negligence or innocent mistake are insufficient.

Gibson hadn't begun to comply with the requirements, and no affidavits or otherwise reliable statements had been provided. He tried to offer proof to the court himself unsuccessfully, and then he tried to have the hearing postponed so that he could comply with *Franks* – again unsuccessfully. Finally Gibson stated that *Franks* was wrong. Judge Billings answered, "May be wrong, but you got to get it reversed, seems to me."[13]

Gibson was allowed to call Det. Raymond LaMoria, Jr. to the witness stand over the objection of David Kirby, and I wondered how he was going to respond to questions about who had been in my house, inspecting my chemicals, before the court-authorized search. LaMoria was clearly terrified, as his hand shook badly enough to spill water from his cup on the witness stand, but he needn't have worried. David Kirby objected to nearly every question on the grounds that David Gibson had not complied with *Franks*, and the objections were upheld. We were never able to show anything. While I had much to fault Judge Billings for later, his decisions in this matter were correct. The rules were there for all to see, and David Gibson had either failed to read them or had chosen not to follow them.

There was no easy explanation for David Gibson's performance. I had given him two typewritten analyses of the search documents detailing even the smallest inconsistency. We could have easily obtained affidavits from, as but one example, the West Rutland Town Clerk regarding UPS deliveries to the Town Hall. The sole purpose of the hearing was to demonstrate knowing falsity or reckless disregard of the truth on the part of Ray LaMoria, but Gibson brought no proof. We had neither witnesses nor documents meaning that, unless LaMoria confessed to lying on the witness stand, the hearing was guaranteed to fail. Gibson didn't even bring the search documents he intended to challenge, and some had to be borrowed from Judge Billings, others from David Kirby.

In retrospect it is inescapable that David Gibson was either completely incompetent or he deliberately betrayed me. At the time, however, things were less clear, as in 1992 I didn't have the detailed knowledge of federal criminal law and courtroom procedure that I later acquired. Will Hunter hadn't worked out, and I was already on my second lawyer. I had neither the time nor the inclination to begin an in depth study of the law with barely months before my criminal trial, and it is doubtful that I could have learned enough in that time to have done myself much good.

Under the circumstances, I wanted to believe in David Gibson, and I had few options. His father and my grandfather had been good friends, and I thought that at least Gibson would be loyal. That belief was to be the worst mistake of my life.

19

It had been a very difficult year, and much of my attention was focused on keeping things together at home with Katrina and Lindsay. Besides the uncertainty of our situation, the police harassment continued. Supposedly the State Police were shorthanded, but they somehow found the manpower (along with sheriff's deputies) to escort Katrina from Rutland to Manchester and back (a distance of 60 miles), while she did her Christmas shopping. A month later, confirming Lindsay's fears, a contingent of a half-dozen U.S. marshals and State Police showed up at my house. Luckily Lindsay was at school.

I was working in my garage, and watched them knock on the door of the house and then enter. Katrina had met them at the door in her housecoat, and asked for whatever papers they had. Instead of showing any papers, they put their hands on their guns and pushed past her. I rushed into the house as Katrina retreated to the bedroom to get dressed. As she closed the door, the police began to wail, "Are there any weapons in there?"

"There are weapons all over the house," I replied.

"She can't be in there alone. Someone's going to have to go in there with her."

Fortunately for Katrina a female State Trooper, Helen Moritz, was present and went in to watch her dress. Had Moritz not been available the duty might have fallen to the ringleader, Deputy Marshal Jeffrey Paine. There was another female present, a small, mousy woman in civilian clothes, but she shrank into a corner near my woodstove and refused to give her name. I advised Katrina in front of everyone to, "Keep an eye on your jewelry. You know what happened with the last bunch."

It turned out that the purpose of the unannounced intrusion was to document the condition of my house and property. Under the federal asset forfeiture statutes, title to my property had already passed to the United States Attorney General, Janet Reno, upon no more than an allegation. No hearing was required, although I could request one to try to get my property back. In the meantime the government owned it, and wanted to document its condition. In order to stay in our own home Katrina and I had to execute a tenancy agreement with the marshals.

The police suspected that their high-handed tactics might provoke a response, and brought along Trooper Gary Boutin as a self-described "negotiator". At least some of the police were very nervous, first about Katrina alone in the bedroom and then about me as I followed Deputy Marshal Paul Whelton while he videotaped the premises. Walking directly behind me, in lockstep, was Trooper Cacciatore with his hand on his pistol. Finally Paul Whelton said with a slight smile, "I've worked with Mr. Bloomer before. You don't have to do that."

Probably Katrina didn't help matters when she told one of the cops, "Don't go upstairs in the garage. That's where Bob keeps his bombs." No one did.

20

As Mr. Gibson was working on the suppression matter, we were attacking the case from another direction, an investigation into the government's witnesses, and for that purpose I executed a contract with the Continental Detective Agency owned by Edward Lucas. Lucas had been a police officer in New Jersey, a Vermont State Trooper and had later founded Continental.

My initial contact with Mr. Lucas had not been satisfactory. Within a few days of the raid on my house Lucas had appeared at my father's office professing to have knowledge of two women that could discredit Ray LaMoria. For a few dollars an investigation could be conducted, he said. As far as I know the women were never located, and the investigation was terminated. I checked myself at the address Lucas had given, and no one had heard of them.

David Gibson thought we should have the witnesses investigated, and while Ed Lucas had a personal animosity of unknown basis toward Will Hunter, both Lucas and Gibson indicated that they had a good working relationship with each other. Notwithstanding the earlier result, Gibson recommended that I hire Lucas. Although I had executed the contract with Continental, David Gibson directed the investigation from the beginning. All the reports were addressed to David Gibson, and all the bills were sent to him. He then forwarded the bills for payment and, I thought, the reports. I later learned that he did not forward all the reports to me.

Ed Lucas told me specifically that the information he was developing in his investigation was to impeach the credibility of the government's witnesses. In that regard he made two trips to New Jersey to investigate Frank Gorham's tale of killing a black pimp. Lucas also related that an old acquaintance in New Jersey, Anthony Imperiale, was willing to testify regarding Gorham's activities there, but the Imperiale testimony never materialized. Worse, the investigation quickly turned to people with no connection at all to my case.

There can be no doubt that David Gibson was well aware of what was going on as the reports were addressed to him, and Gibson was billing me for conversations he had with Ed Lucas throughout the multi-month investigation. From the first report dated October 14, 1991, it could be readily seen the direction that the investigation was taking, and that was to "discredit Robert Spencer and other witnesses" by interviewing people with no connection to my case. The report also made clear that Lucas was seeking "information concerning [prosecutor] Gary Shattuck".

The one person I thought should be interviewed without delay was Mark Malmros, my former partner in the polyacetylene/medical testing project. All the chemical orders the government had disclosed as evidence were between 1982 and 1984, which was at the height of my association with Mark. Only two people knew what those chemicals were used for, Mark and me, but Mark was listed as a government witness, and I had been ordered by the court to "avoid all contact" with him. If he were going to testify that he knew the chemicals were used to make methamphetamine, then no defense to the charges would have been possible, and it would have been senseless to go to trial. If, on the other hand, he were to testify that the chemicals had been used in the polyacetylene experiments, then the methamphetamine manufacture charges would have been on very shaky ground. Either way, it was crucial to know what Mark was going to say.

Since the polyacetylene project had ended in a dispute and a lawsuit, I could not be absolutely sure that Mark would not be vindictive. If he refused to submit to an interview, it could be inferred that his testimony would be damaging. The government, of course, knew that Mark's testimony would be crucial to my defense because he had testified before the grand jury, but that information was being concealed.

Mark's testimony was all the more crucial because my lab notebooks from the polyacetylene experiments had been seized by the police as well as numerous other chemical procedures copied from the chemical literature showing legitimate uses for my chemicals. These were not inventoried except as "File Cab & Contents". The procedures and notebooks were never produced by the government as evidence and disappeared in police custody, so not only could I not use these documents for my defense, I could not prove they ever existed.

David Gibson told me that the "avoid all contact" order was to be taken literally, and Ed Lucas warned me against contacting any of the witnesses myself. On the other end, Mark had been threatened by the U.S. Attorneys not to say anything about his grand jury testimony. He told me later that he was extremely wary and would not have said much on the telephone, but he would have revealed his grand jury testimony to my investigators - if they had shown up.

Ed Lucas and his associate, Guy Paradee, had taken two costly trips to New Jersey at my expense, but never crossed the Delaware into Pennsylvania to interview Mark, who lived just opposite Trenton. Years later David Gibson was to explain this oversight by referring to some undated personal notes. According to Mr. Gibson my relationship with Mark effectively ended in 1985 with the lawsuit and therefore he could have had nothing to say about subsequent events. However, all the government's evidence of chemical orders to make methamphetamine covered the period of 1982-1984, when Mark and I were actively involved together on our project. Mr. Gibson's "explanation" explained nothing, but did bolster my belief that the failure to interview Mark was deliberate.

It turned out that almost all of the $42,000 investigation was a waste of money. The criminal records of the witnesses had been given to us by the government in its September 6, 1991 evidence production - before David Gibson had even entered his appearance - and there was no need for an investigator in that regard. Ed Lucas did dig up some dirt on a few of the witnesses, but it was all going to be inadmissible at trial. Federal Rule of Evidence 608(b) provided that "Specific instances of the conduct of a witness, for the purpose of attacking or supporting the witness' credibility, other than conviction of a crime...may not be proved by extrinsic evidence." In plain language this meant that, even if Ed Lucas had developed overwhelming evidence that Frank Gorham had killed a black pimp, as Gorham had once claimed, it would not have been admissible to discredit his testimony in my drug case. The same rule would apply to the other witnesses.

A great deal of effort was expended investigating the alleged misdeeds of Detective Raymond LaMoria, but the best use of the information, had it been deemed admissible, would have been at the suppression hearing. However, David Gibson never complied with the requirements laid down by the Supreme Court to challenge a search warrant, and as a result we never got to the obvious lies in LaMoria's affidavit, much less misconduct in completely unrelated cases. Consequently, the information was really of no value to me at all.

Interestingly, in a report dated February 4, 1992 Ed Lucas related that he had been "focused on the Raymond LaMoria/Shattuck aspect of this investigation", and Gary Shattuck had been mentioned in Lucas's very first report to David Gibson. While Shattuck was clearly a target of the investigation, Gibson never told me what he intended to do with whatever information was developed. Shattuck and David Kirby were co-prosecuting the criminal case, so it was certain that Shattuck was not going to be a government witness.

In a report dated April 20, 1992 Lucas wrote, "Reliable confidential sources have indicated that Gary Shattuck was somehow involved in illegally accepting money in one instance and in another falsified information to get a conviction", but nothing more specific was

68

ever offered. More than ten years later during a conversation with Guy Paradee, I learned that he had specific information, and the source of that information, John Gray, had been a confidential informant developed while Paradee was with the City of Rutland police. According to Paradee he had submitted a complete report to Ed Lucas, and the subject matter of the report had come up during a meeting of Paradee, Ed Lucas, David Gibson, FBI agent John Hersh and State Policemen Kerry Sleeper and Nicholas Ruggiero.

Although I was paying for the investigation, I was never given a copy of the report, nor was I ever told of it at the time. I had had no direct contact with Paradee during the investigation, dealing only with David Gibson and Ed Lucas, and Paradee was astounded to learn that I had never been told of his findings. I wanted to follow up on John Gray's allegations, only to find that he was dead.

A few months after his revelations to Guy Paradee, John Gray was jailed after pleading guilty to federal marijuana charges. He was incarcerated at the Federal Medical Center at Carville, Louisiana due to a serious heart condition, and it was there that another inmate stabbed him in the abdomen. Gray was subsequently taken to an outside hospital for treatment, where he died of a "myocardial infarction" on January 10, 1994 at age 59. The death certificate didn't mention the stabbing, and neither did the letters from Carville's warden to Judge Billings and Gray's widow informing them of his death.

I filed two Freedom of Information Act inquiries to the Federal Bureau of Prisons with appeals beginning in 2005 to discover that the BOP could locate no internal investigation of the stabbing, no criminal referrals, and not even an Incident Report, although one was required by the BOP's operating procedures[14] based on the Code of Federal Regulations. The Bureau refused to divulge the name of John Gray's assailant.

However, a later FOIA request to the FBI revealed that there had indeed been an investigation and successful prosecution of Gray's assailant. A letter to Harley Lappin, Director of the Bureau of Prisons, asking for an explanation got no response.

In the end, the very expensive Continental investigation turned out to be almost completely worthless. The one potential political bombshell unearthed by the investigation never saw the light of day because I was unaware of it, and therefore unable to follow up on it. Moreover David Gibson, hired specifically for his expertise in the federal arena, was either unaware of the rules of evidence that would govern my upcoming trial or he deliberately ignored them. The investigators, under the direction of Mr. Gibson, avoided the one person who could have given me a credible defense, Mark Malmros, while they pursued various wild goose chases. Ed Lucas, meanwhile, was assuring me that the various witnesses' "credibility was shot" due to his investigation. The effect of the investigation, whether intended or not, was to give me false hope of victory at trial. The reality was that David Gibson was never going to mount a defense with even the slightest chance of success.

21

While Ed Lucas was assuring me that we were going to impeach the credibility of the government's witnesses, there remained the problem of the residues of methamphetamine, not only at my house, but also at Spencer's. The pieces fit perfectly. I was only alleged to have been involved with methamphetamine, and that's all that was found at my house. Spencer was alleged to be my partner in the meth conspiracy, and had also pled guilty to cocaine possession. Residues of both had been found at his mobile home as well as a small bag of coke.

Putting myself in the position of a juror, I was unable to come up with any plausible explanation of why, if I were innocent, my laboratory equipment would be tainted in numerous places with methamphetamine, even assuming that I had had a legal prescription for it. Of course, the real explanation was that there actually had been no methamphetamine, and that it had either been planted or that the tests had been faked in the police laboratory. But it was certainly going to be an uphill fight to prove irregularities in the police lab, especially since we didn't even know how the alleged meth had been detected.

The only idea anyone had at the time was to have our own chemist perform testing on my equipment to see if there was, in fact, any methamphetamine and, if there was, whether anything was suspicious in the distribution of it. This course of action was not without risk. If the methamphetamine plant had been expertly done, our chemist would confirm the police lab's result. However, barring a well-founded challenge, the lab's result was going to stand anyway. At the time I had no way of knowing that the police chemist performing my tests, Dr. Brendan McMahon, was severely addicted to cocaine, was stealing the drug from the police laboratory itself, and was using it on the job.

Besides the independent testing, there was another instance where our defense evidence could have best been presented through a chemist: the police inventory of the chemicals seized from my house. Piecing together eyewitness accounts and the documents we had, it appeared as though the police had initially inventoried the chemicals upstairs in my

70

house near the laboratory area. The chemicals had then been carried outside to my driveway, sorted into compatible groups by Pollution Solutions of Vermont personnel, and reinventoried for transport as hazardous waste. The police inventory had been prepared in the presence of two chemists, Jack Fasanello of the DEA and Dr. Brendan McMahon of the Vermont State Police Laboratory. This was the official inventory left with the search warrant return, and it was supposed to be correct under the law. Likewise Pollution Solutions was legally obligated to accurately describe what it was transporting as hazardous waste.

The police inventory indicated that 7 of my chemicals had been seized as evidence with the rest, approximately 100, going to Pollution Solutions. The inventories, therefore, should have been identical except for the 7 taken as evidence. Instead there were numerous discrepancies, which were not minor. More than a dozen chemicals seized by the police didn't show up on the Pollution Solutions inventory. Even more interesting, Pollution Solutions listed more than a dozen items never seized by the police. The number of containers for the same chemical did not agree, and neither did the quantities. In the case of Sodium Bicarbonate (baking soda), for example, the police listed the quantity as "1 1B" while Pollution Solutions listed it as "1/4 lb x ///". In the case of Hydrochloric Acid the police listed "1 Gal" while Pollution Solutions listed "1 Gal x 3, Pt x 2".

With only a couple of exceptions all my chemicals were in the original factory containers with the factory labels, a fact confirmed by Dr. McMahon at trial, and it was therefore astounding that the police, under the supervision of two chemists, recorded chemicals that didn't exist. Among the interesting entries on the police inventory were chalchal, sodium carbonite agent, 3D&H alcohol and ethyl acete. While one might have guessed what was meant, there was no certainty that a guess would have been correct. For example, I was unable to find any entry in any chemical reference work that began "ethyl acete". The seized chemical could possibly have been ethyl acetate, or it could have been ethyl acetone, or it could have been ethyl acetylene, or literally hundreds of other compounds. It appeared that both chemists were incompetent and, despite signatures and initials, no one had verified the inventory by comparing it to the chemical labels. I looked forward to having some real fun with these bozos at trial, but it was not to be.

Of course I had a very good idea of what chemicals were present in my laboratory, and I knew that neither inventory was correct, but I was never able to show what, in fact, existed at my house the day of the raid. As Will Hunter was filing motion after motion in the courts for the return

71

of my property, and as the governments, both state and federal, were claiming my property was necessary to their investigation, the chemicals were being systematically destroyed by Pollution Solutions over a period of months. By the time I realized what was going on, all but the half-dozen at the police lab were gone.

David Gibson had never asked me to find my own chemist, and said he would take care of it. We agreed to wait until after the suppression hearing as, had we won, the case might have been over without the need for further expense. On February 19, 1992, after the hearing but before the court's decision, Mr. Gibson wrote his friend, (former Governor) Thomas Salmon, President of the University of Vermont "to secure the services of an expert chemist in connection with the pending criminal prosecution of Robert A. Bloomer, Jr." Gibson also "hope[d] that I may have an early response to this request, as the Federal Courts are fairly prompt in scheduling trials."[15]

An analytical chemist, Dr. Karen Sentell, made herself available on or about March 1, 1992, and awaited a call from David Gibson. The court called Gibson on March 18 to advise him that trial would begin on April 1, but inexplicably Gibson waited until March 24 at the earliest to contact Prof. Sentell. Gibson then composed a Motion to Continue dated the 24th, but not filed with the court until the 25th asking that the trial be postponed. Gibson represented to the court that "Following the denial of defendant's motion to suppress evidence, defendant has sought to engage the services of qualified experts in chemistry…Defendant only recently has been able to obtain assurances from persons qualified …to perform such an analysis and review…In connection with the preparation of the defense to the pending criminal charges in this case it is essential that the chemical analysis and review of materials be performed prior to trial."[16] Judge Billings, noting that the defense had had months to perform the testing, immediately denied the motion.

Notwithstanding the date of David Gibson's motion, both Dr. Sentell's report and billing statement indicate that her first contact with Gibson was March 27th. Regardless of which date was correct, Dr. Sentell was unable to perform the independent testing on such short notice due to a previous commitment, so the testing that even David Gibson had described as "essential" was never done, leaving us with nothing to discredit Dr. McMahon at trial.

I had been raised in a legal family where the proper course was to give your lawyer the facts and let him handle the problem, and David Gibson played into this predisposition, asking questions but giving few answers. He blamed the lack of independent testing on Judge Billings, and

72

at the time I didn't have the documents to see otherwise. Gibson never told me his trial strategy, although I assumed he had one. Whatever it may have been, it was certain to fail, but I didn't know that until it was too late.

<h1 style="text-align:center">22</h1>

It came as no surprise when Spencer quickly pled guilty again, this time in federal court, and again agreed to testify against me. He had no bargaining power left, and part of his agreement was that he could be sentenced to up to five years in federal prison. Spencer, of course, hoped that he would be able to please the government to the extent that he would go free, and the quantity of methamphetamine with which I was supposedly involved increased again.

Robert Spencer's indictment on federal methamphetamine-related charges brought out a little known quirk of the American system: a person can be prosecuted twice for the same crime - once in federal court and again in state court, or vice versa. In spite of Gary Shattuck's misleading or false assurances to Spencer while Shattuck was an Assistant Vermont Attorney General, the fact was that Spencer could be prosecuted again by the federal government. Since Spencer had already confessed, a defense was impossible. Possibly the confessions could not be used directly against him, but they could be used to prove perjury if Spencer denied any of the charges to which he had confessed.

Two weeks before trial the government, citing adverse publicity, filed a curious motion to have the entire trial moved to Burlington or, alternatively, a jury selected in Burlington and brought to Rutland. It failed to mention the adverse publicity in Burlington concerning drug dealing. A crazed black drug dealer from New York City had accidentally gunned down an innocent 15-year-old white girl during an attempt to kill her boyfriend, with the dealer erroneously believing that the boyfriend was responsible for the arrest of the dealer's brother.

Judge Billings denied the government's motion stating that: "…we feel that an impartial jury can be selected in Rutland and thus, that a fair trial can take place here. We therefore think that the Government's concerns are meritless."[17] Apparently Judge Billings' clerk, Austin Burbank, disagreed because everyone one from the immediate Rutland area was secretly and systematically excluded from the jury pool, and perhaps anyone else that the U.S. Attorney's office didn't want on my jury, although I was unaware of it at the time.

Another factor influencing the fundamental fairness of my upcoming trial was the question of Judge Billings's impartiality. Although David Gibson was a personal friend of the Judge, he had had a longtime hatred of my father. Judge Billings had formerly been Speaker of the Vermont House and Chief Justice of the Vermont Supreme Court and he had wanted to be governor also, apparently to satisfy a megalomanical desire to be the head of all three branches of government. My father had had at least some part in thwarting the plan. More importantly, while Judge Billings was in private practice, a client became dissatisfied with his representation, sought other counsel, and wound up with my father. Judge Billings never forgave him.

As the odds were stacking up against me, David Gibson added a little grease to the skids himself. Two weeks before trial[18] he had written me asking that I stipulate that the handwriting samples I had given to FBI Agent McGinnis were, in fact, mine. Gibson continued:

> Similarly, the U.S. Attorney's office is requesting us to stipulate to the fact that certain records of companies from whom chemicals or other supplies were ordered are accurate. Again, we would not be agreeing to the admissibility of these records. Rather, we are asked to agree, if otherwise admissible, that the records are accurately reproduced. The purpose of seeking this type of stipulation is to avoid the necessity of having persons testify in person at a trial with respect to somewhat routine types of questions and answers concerning custody of those documents. It is not unusual to enter into this type of stipulation. Please look over the enclosed proposed stipulations and the documents referred to in the stipulation and then give me a call so that we can discuss it further.

The matter was not so routine as Gibson had suggested. First, many of the copies that he had sent me were very faint and mostly unreadable. Consequently I was not in a position to know what they said, much less to determine if they had been "accurately reproduced". Second, I was being asked to stipulate the accuracy of an order to Alfa Products (a chemical company) that had been allegedly placed by Vermont Solar Engineering, a company owned not by me but by Allan and Beverly Hobson. Third, I had no specific recollection of any of the orders placed so many years before and, fourth, the police had seized any papers from my house that I might have used to verify the orders.

I was from a legal family, and the standing advice had always been to never sign anything without a full understanding of what was being signed. Furthermore, I could see no benefit to cooperating with the government in any way considering its shabby treatment of not only me but my wife as well, and I told Mr. Gibson that I was not interested in the stipulations.

The day before trial, as I was waiting a block away in my father's office, David Gibson was in the U.S. Attorney's office signing the stipulations behind my back, but the ones he signed were not the ones he had submitted to me for my approval. In particular, the orders for chemicals that he had stipulated were not complete. While the offending Vermont Solar Engineering entry was gone, orders that could have been clearly identified with my polyacetylene project with Mark Malmros were gone as well, leaving only the orders the government wanted to use for the prosecution. Mr. Gibson knew I wouldn't be pleased, as he made no mention of the stipulations a few minutes later in my father's office. I was never able to get copies from David Gibson, and the copies I did get long after trial came from prosecutor Gary Shattuck. It would later turn out that some of the documents Mr. Gibson stipulated to were obvious phonies.

23

Trial began on April 1, 1992 with the jury draw. David Kirby and Gary Shattuck were co-prosecutors and both sat at the prosecution table. David Gibson and I sat at the defense table. Will Hunter was present, but sat in the audience and did not participate. My wife, Katrina, was there, as were her parents and my father. Kirby and Shattuck had an odd guest at the prosecution table, who would remain there throughout the trial: Detective Raymond LaMoria, Jr. LaMoria was not an attorney, was never called as a prosecution witness, and seemingly did nothing except sit there. Apparently the purpose of his presence was to have him bask in the glow of legitimacy from Shattuck and Kirby, as both knew of our investigation into LaMoria's activities.

Because of the extensive pretrial publicity, both the current jury panel and the previous panel were summoned to court to provide a larger pool from which to select unbiased jurors. During a recess, my father observed to David Gibson that no one from the immediate Rutland area was available in court for jury duty, but there were people from 50 miles away. Since Rutland was easily the biggest population center in Southern

Vermont, it was indeed an interesting fact, and especially so in light of the government's motion to move the trial. Gibson replied that he didn't think the jury composition would "rise to the level" that would interest the court, and said nothing at the time. This would later turn out to be a serious error.

The presentation to the jury began with the government's opening statement given by David Kirby. He related that the government had six witnesses who would testify that they had received methamphetamine from me, that formulas for methamphetamine had been found at my house, that I had ordered or otherwise possessed the necessary chemicals, and that residues of the drug had been identified in some of my equipment. Mr. Kirby admitted at the outset that all the non-expert or law enforcement witnesses were either drug dealers or drug users, and all had made agreements with the government. None of this was any surprise, and most of the government's evidence had been disclosed in some detail months before trial.

Since David Gibson had never revealed his proposed defense to me, I followed his opening remarks with great interest. The defense was to be that any crime had to be proved beyond a reasonable doubt, and that the government's witnesses weren't credible. The police inventory of materials taken from my house was mentioned as being vague, and Mr. Gibson argued that the materials, or at least some of them, had not been properly secured. He never mentioned that the inventory was wrong, and he gave no inkling of how he was going to overcome the finding of methamphetamine residues.

The first witness was my old pal, New Jerseyite turned Vermont farmer, Frank Gorham. While I was certainly not surprised to hear him say that I had sold him methamphetamine, I was surprised at the depth of detail he was prepared to offer. According to Gorham I had given him notebooks with formulas to make methamphetamine, explained the process in detail, and allowed him to watch the procedure. Furthermore, he claimed to have stored a machinegun for me as well as jars of methamphetamine in his cow barn.

There was, of course, no evidence of any of it. No machineguns were ever found or methamphetamine, and Gorham claimed to have burned the notebooks with nothing remaining. He was also unable to recall anything specific regarding the meth manufacturing procedures that might have given him a problem on cross examination, and he described the process itself only as "there was beaker with some fluid in it and something was spinning around inside it. And then there was some gas bubbling into it."[19] No one else was alleged to have been present during our supposed conversations about meth manufacturing, and certainly there were no conversations or incriminating phone calls monitored by the government, or they would have been produced like the Spencer-Galarneau conversation. I was hoping that the jury would wonder, as I did, why Gorham would confess to a crime for which there was absolutely no evidence. Part of the answer was surely revealed in Gorham's description of his deal with the government: "In exchange for my testimony they wouldn't try to take my father's farm and they wouldn't try to prosecute me for anything."[20]

As David Gibson's cross examination of Frank Gorham proceeded, it soon became obvious that Ed Lucas's very expensive investigation was not going to be used to impeach Gorham's credibility. Gorham admitted telling some stories about crime in New Jersey, but he denied telling others, and when something was denied, that was the end of it. As far as he went, David Gibson did a good enough job making the point that Gorham had told numerous stories of criminal activity, and that they all were inventions except, according to Gorham, the stories involving methamphetamine. What Gibson never did was to give the jury an alternative theory of the evidence. Gorham's frequent visitors from New Jersey or his chemist friend from Dartmouth could have been the source of both Gorham's and Spencer's methamphetamine, and this possibility became especially important as trial progressed.

The government's version of events had me as Robert Spencer's sole source of methamphetamine, but I had not made any during the year 1988 because of my pending divorce from Mary Ann, and my supposed fear that she would say something about it. David Kirby argued this specifically in his opening statement, and this nicely tied together the testimony from Gorham, Spencer and Mary Ann. However, there was a large hole in this theory. According to Spencer whatever meth he had obtained from me in the fall of 1987 was gone by the first of the year[21], and didn't receive any more until the spring of 1990. Meanwhile Det. LaMoria's search warrant affidavit[22] described an interview in March 1988, with a "reliable informant, #GJB-88-02", stating that Spencer "was selling between one to two ounces of speed (methamphetamine) a week." Also, the government's indictment of Spencer[23] listed 10 separate counts for methamphetamine sales during a period that included 1988,[24] with the year 1988 stated explicitly in 7 of the counts.[25] The government admitted the methamphetamine didn't come from me, so it was an open question just where it did come from. Mr. Gibson never pursued the matter, nor did he pursue the relationships between the government's witnesses independent of any relationship that they had with me.

While the jury might have had some doubt about the credibility of some of the witnesses, the chemical experts were unshakable. Both had had extensive courtroom experience, and their testimony was devastating. Brendan McMahon of the Vermont State Police Laboratory had a doctorate in chemistry, and explained in detail how he tested equipment removed from my house and discovered methamphetamine. DEA chemist Jack Fasanello explained how my chemicals could have been used for three separate synthetic routes to methamphetamine, how certain pieces of my equipment could have been used only for the manufacture of methamphetamine, and that his opinion was that methamphetamine had been manufactured in my lab.

The federal rules of criminal procedure required that the results of any scientific testing be produced before trial. However, despite that requirement Dr. McMahon went beyond what he had written in his reports to testify that he had found another chemical in my equipment, n-formylmethamphetamine, which he characterized as "a commonly found byproduct in methamphetamine specimens that were manufactured using a particular syntheses…". He also called it an "intermediate" in methamphetamine manufacture.[26] Mr. Gibson did not object.[27]

It turned out that DEA expert Jack Fasanello had also done some testing, and had generated a report, which had never been produced to us at all. David Kirby claimed that he had never received the report, even though some seven copies had been sent to various people. David Gibson raised quite a commotion regarding the government's failure to produce the DEA report and unsuccessfully asked for a mistrial but, interestingly, what he did not do was demand the contents of Mr. Fasanello's laboratory file on his testing. David Kirby had already indicated that the government provided those materials as statements of the chemist in connection with his testimony, and had done so with Dr. McMahon. This followed the requirements of the Jencks Act (18 U.S.C. 3500), and under the Act Gibson was entitled to demand the DEA file. In the event the government refused to provide it, the Act specified that "…the court shall strike from the record the testimony of the witness, and the trial shall proceed unless the court in its discretion shall determine that the interests of justice require that a mistrial be declared…".

Had Mr. Gibson obtained chemist Fasanello's DEA laboratory file, he would have immediately seen that Fasanello had lied, and that either crucial test results were missing or that the chemist had simply made up the results. However, Mr. Gibson never asked and I did not obtain the file until several years later through the Freedom of Information Act.

24

Day after day, the Rutland Herald covered the case in headlines: "Man Testifies Bloomer Sold Him Illegal Drugs", "New Witnesses Describe Bloomer Drug Deals", "Spencer Says Bloomer Supplied Him With Drug", "Prosecutor Tries to Link Bloomer with Chemicals". As the trial progressed, I thought myself like a boxer pinned on the ropes, absorbing blow after blow, waiting for a chance to counterattack that never came.

Our defense to the government's case consisted of calling three of my neighbors to testify that I was a good guy and they hadn't seen me with any illegal drugs. Also Daniel Pratt was called to testify that he had inspected my house in connection with a tax appeal at the time Spencer was promising police informant Michael Galarneau an imminent delivery of methamphetamine. Pratt had seen the entire house, including the lab, and had not seen anything he could identify with illegal drug manufacture. Pamela Linton, President of Pollution Solutions, was called as that was the only way Mr. Gibson could introduce the Pollution Solutions chemical inventory into evidence. Shortly after the inventory was introduced, Mr. Gibson rested the defense case without ever getting into the discrepancies between the police inventory and that from Pollution Solutions.

Certainly the most bizarre aspect of our case was the testimony of Det. Raymond LaMoria as a defense witness, as no part of the government's case depended on LaMoria, and the government had not called him. Part of David Gibson's strategy was to get LaMoria to deny using drugs, and then later have criminals that LaMoria had busted testify that he had used drugs and skimmed them. Judge Billings properly refused to allow that testimony, but even if he had allowed it, it was pointless. Assuming LaMoria could have been shown to be corrupt, that would not have refuted any part of the government's case.

David Gibson also questioned LaMoria about a number of items of concern to Katrina and me: her missing gynecology records, Lindsay's stolen allowance money, and the storage of much of my seized property in the police garage where dozens of people had access to it. Again, this was completely pointless. Only one of the government's trial exhibits had been stored in the garage, and it was not essential to the government's case. As to the missing items, LaMoria denied any knowledge, and that was the end of it. In order to make the point that things had been lost or stolen, either Katrina or I would have had to testify to what was in our house prior to the police raid, and David Gibson never planned to have us testify.

The jury got the case on Tuesday, April 14, 1992, but had not finished deliberating by the end of the day, and Katrina and I went home exhausted. I didn't see how I could possibly win, but still hoped for some kind of miracle. Katrina couldn't have had much hope, either, and we didn't talk about it. The next day the jury announced that it had reached a verdict, and everyone took his or her place in the courtroom. Two U.S. marshals stationed themselves at the exits, and I was soon to understand why. The jury then gave its verdict – guilty on all counts. At Mr. Gibson's request the jury was polled individually, but that could hardly have changed the outcome. David Kirby then rose to address the court, asking that I be immediately detained, that is, immediately taken to jail. This came as a shock as I had assumed that, even if I were found guilty, I would remain out on bail pending appeal. I hadn't much time to consider the matter when Judge Billings ruled that he was not going to order me detained. A frustrated and angry David Kirby tried to argue with the court, but to no avail. Dazed, I left the court with Katrina and went home to await further developments.

25

Years after trial David Gibson would excuse his inadequate representation by pointing to the supposed overwhelming evidence of my guilt. According to Jerome O'Neill, a lawyer (and former U.S. Attorney) hired by Mr. Gibson to defend his performance, I was virtually certain to be convicted and Mr. Gibson did a great job under the circumstances. At the time of my trial, however, Mr. Gibson didn't tell me that I was certain to be convicted but, on the contrary, led me to believe that the government had a weak case because no methamphetamine had been seized, and that I had a good chance of winning at trial.

I later learned that when a case is considered unwinnable, the usual course is to pursue plea negotiations with the government. It really made no difference if a defendant were innocent or guilty. The only consideration was whether the government's case could be contested sufficiently to create at least a reasonable doubt and, if not, it made no sense to go to trial.

Even if a conviction was virtually certain, the government was still very interested making a deal for a guilty plea because pleas removed any uncertainty, as well as saving the government considerable time and expense for both the trial and the inevitable appeals. The United States

Sentencing Guidelines, in effect at the time of my sentencing, made an explicit provision for a sentence reduction in exchange for a guilty plea under the rubric of "acceptance of responsibility", but the advantages of a plea often went beyond the reduction for acceptance, as drug sentences were determined largely by the quantity of drugs involved. A judge would almost never dispute a drug amount provided by a prosecutor in connection with a plea agreement, and thus the prosecutor had considerable latitude to reduce a sentence even further than the actual facts of a case might warrant. Finally, the U.S. Attorney's office had at least some influence on where a prisoner would do his time, and federal prison camps were definitely more desirable than the higher security institutions.

The only time David Gibson and I ever discussed a plea agreement was on January 22, 1992, while we were at the State Police barracks in Rutland examining the government's evidence. Cash seized from my house was kept in a locker there, and some of my chemistry books and papers were made available in a small room. As I was conducting a fruitless search for my laboratory notes on the polyacetylene experiments, Gibson left to confer with Asst. U.S. Attorney Gary Shattuck in another room. When Gibson returned, he related that the government was offering a ten-year sentence in exchange for a guilty plea. When I asked what sentence I would receive if I were found guilty, Gibson replied, "Ten years." I asked what, then, I had to lose by going to trial, and Gibson replied, "Nothing." At the time, I knew nothing of the Sentencing Guidelines, and certainly had no notion that I was risking life in prison.

David Gibson's later explanation for his failure to pursue plea negotiations was that I hadn't instructed him to do so, but this ignored the fact that I had no idea what to do and was relying on Gibson's advice. Had he told me at the time that we were not going to mount a serious defense, that I was virtually certain to lose at trial, and that my risk exposure was life in prison, it wouldn't have taken me long to figure out what to do. I was later to learn in prison that the government was particularly eager to enter into plea agreements where the defendants also agreed to the forfeiture of assets.

While the government may not have had much problem seizing my half of the property at 96 Clarendon Ave., Katrina owned the other half, and this was certain to complicate matters. Katrina had sold her house in Rutland, and she and Lindsay had made the West Rutland house their home. A forced eviction and sale of the property would certainly have generated a great deal of adverse publicity for the government, and especially so since a similar case involving children in Northfield, Vermont, had already made numerous headlines. In that case, the government had come across as overwhelmed by greed at the expense of the hapless children whose parents were both going to jail following a setup by an agent provocateur working with law enforcement. At the time, I was unaware of the possibility of a global agreement encompassing both the civil and criminal matters, and David Gibson never mentioned it, either then or later.

Since Gibson had made up my mind for me to fight instead of negotiate, he should have put on the strongest defense possible. Instead, we didn't even use what we had. First, no real defense was possible without either Mark Malmros or myself testifying about the laboratory, its chemicals and equipment. Since there was no testimony as to the actual uses of my chemicals, DEA chemist Jack Fasanello was free to engage in rank speculation as to what the chemicals might have been used for. The fact that he proposed three separate synthetic routes for methamphetamine using my chemicals indicated that there was no proof for any of the routes, and Fasanello could have had no knowledge whatsoever of what might have been used in the polyacetylene experiments, as they were cutting edge research.

Second, the failure to do independent chemical testing on my laboratory equipment left us with nothing to challenge the government's expert, Dr. Brendan McMahon. Moreover, I had no idea of how Dr. McMahon had identified the alleged residues of methamphetamine. I did know that David Gibson had engaged Dr. Karen Sentell of the University of Vermont Chemistry department as an expert for the defense, but he had waited to do so until just days before trial and she was unable to do any testing on such short notice. What I did not know until a couple of years later was that Dr. Sentell had immediately contacted a colleague who had formerly worked for Rhode Island's State Forensic Lab to ascertain testing methods used by forensic chemists. It turned out that the methods were identical to those used by Dr. McMahon and, had I been aware of Dr. Sentell's information at trial, I would have realized that Dr. McMahon did not testify accurately.

The only methamphetamine ever found in my case was the residue supposedly discovered by Dr. McMahon, and even Mr. Gibson later argued that his testimony was of crucial importance, but Dr. Sentell was inexplicably not in court to hear either of the government's experts. David Gibson was, as he later admitted, no chemistry expert, but I was left out of any conversations he had with Dr. Sentell. After Dr. McMahon testified, Mr. Gibson faxed her the instrumental printouts, or at least some of them, and visited with her on the phone, making it highly unlikely that Dr. Sentell had an accurate picture of McMahon's testing.

Even more interesting, DEA chemist Fasanello was unintentionally critical of one of Dr. McMahon's testing procedures, a fact that David Gibson failed to emphasize at trial. Dr. Sentell had already written her report before Fasanello testified, so she could not have been aware of this disagreement between the government's own experts, and Mr. Gibson never told her. Dr. Sentell's report indicated that she could find nothing wrong with McMahon's testing, and that apparently ended the matter for Gibson. It didn't end it for me, and I later developed solid evidence that Dr. McMahon had rigged his tests, but that development was long after trial.

Curiously, Mr. Gibson failed to pursue defects in the government's evidence that he was well aware of. He knew months before trial that the tape (and transcript) of the conversation between Robert Spencer and informant Michael Galarneau had mysterious gaps in it, but when the government wanted to play only the excerpts it thought incriminating to me, Gibson made no inquiry regarding the tape's deficiencies or objection on that basis.[28]

Neither did Mr. Gibson object to David Kirby's improper vouching for the informant. Before playing the Spencer/Galarneau tape, Kirby explained to the jury that Galarneau agreed to wear the wire because a friend of his was dying from drug use and he wanted to get drug dealers. The information I had, which I did not verify, was that Galarneau agreed to wear the wire after police found him growing marijuana. Galarneau himself never testified. At the time I asked David Gibson, "If David Kirby is going to testify, can we cross examine him?" Gibson never responded, and Kirby's speech to the jury never appeared in the official trial transcript.

Prior to trial I had thought that we could have the police tied in knots trying to explain how chemicals that didn't exist could have been seized and why the inventories of the police and Pollution Solutions, both signed by police officers, could have so many discrepancies. Our position was even better than I thought as Pollution Solutions documents bore the signature of Det. Sgt. James Baker, the head of the Southern Vermont Drug Task Force, on separate forms for metallic mercury and sodium azide. Neither of these was listed on the police inventory as having been seized.

The U.S. Attorneys were certainly aware of our investigation into the activities of Det. LaMoria, and introduced the police inventory into evidence during the testimony of Dr. Brendan McMahon, although it was LaMoria's signature, not McMahon's, on the document. McMahon described the process as:[29]

Officer Ray LaMoria positioned himself right here. There
were a couple tables out here, but there was one work
table that was set up right here. And he sat at one end it
and began to write. And we systematically started
carrying bottles and various containers out to him. And he
would write down what the bottle said or what we told
him. And we would carry it down to Pollution Solutions
to be gotten rid of.

McMahon also testified that the inventory was prepared in his presence
and it was accurate.[30] Of course it wasn't accurate, and this should have
been the opening we needed. In addition, a quick look at the inventory
itself revealed that Dr. McMahon's account simply could not have been
true.

The government's inventory exhibit (trial exhibit 44) consisted of
six pages of the police inventory, which were numbered, in the upper right
corner as pages 3 through 8. The first page of the exhibit, numbered page
3, listed seven chemicals that were collected by "JF", presumed to be DEA
man Jack Fasanello, and recorded by "LaMoria". However, on pages 4, 5,
6, 7 and part of page 8 the recorder was "R.P." with "Ray" listed as having
recorded the final five items page 8. Unless Raymond LaMoria was going
by the initials R.P. as well as LaMoria and Ray, Dr. McMahon's account
could not have been true.

Before the court ruled on the admissibility of the exhibit, David
Gibson was allowed to question Dr. McMahon about it in what is called a
voir dire. Gibson was able to determine that none of the initials, signatures
or notations on the inventory reflected Dr. McMahon's handling of the
items, and that Dr. McMahon was in and out of the room as the list was
being prepared.[31] The only signatures appearing on the document were
those of Raymond LaMoria as the EVIDENCE OFFICER and as the
misspelled INESTIGATOR on every sheet and Jack Fasanello "for DEA"
on the last sheet. Gibson made no attempt to determine if the signatures
meant that these two had verified the inventory, and made no attempt to
even discover the identity of "R.P." who had recorded – and misrecorded –
most of the chemicals.

Since Mr. Gibson had earlier shown a great interest in getting his
hands on Det. LaMoria, this seemed to be the perfect opportunity. Instead
Gibson made no objection to the exhibit and it was admitted. He never
inquired of anyone how chemicals that didn't exist could have been seized,
and never exposed the numerous discrepancies between the two

84

inventories, both signed by police officers. This failure, along with the stipulations that Gibson had secretly signed regarding chemical orders, would come back to haunt me at sentencing.

Considering that I had spent more than $40,000 on an investigation with the purpose of impeaching the credibility of witnesses, it was surprising at the time that our star witness, Sharon Stickney, didn't testify. She was the only defense witness that could have directly challenged any of the government's case and, based upon the affidavit she had given detective Ed Lucas prior to trial, her account would have contradicted part of the testimony of Robert Spencer, his girlfriend Nicolette Samplatsky, and longtime Spencer drug associate Frank Elnicki, Jr. Furthermore, Stickney's welfare caseworker was Diane LaMoria, wife of Det. Raymond LaMoria, and Sharon believed that Diane LaMoria had manipulated her benefits depending on whether Sharon had cooperated with her caseworker's husband. Several of the women who were government witnesses were also clients of Diane LaMoria.

All I knew at the time was that Sharon was willing to testify for the defense, but could not testify without immunity as she was an unindicted co-conspirator and her testimony would include confessing to her own criminal involvement with Spencer. A meeting was held in Judge Billings' chambers to consider the matter, and afterward the prosecution team put on an odd, clownish performance in the hallway outside the courtroom. The 5 foot 4 David Kirby was in the lead, followed by the 6 foot 6 Gary Shattuck with Ray LaMoria as the caboose in a ridiculous parody of a choo-choo train. Each man was pressed tightly against the man in front of him, walking in lockstep and pumping his arms in unison, all grinning broadly. I assumed that they were pleased with Judge Billings's ruling that Sharon Stickney did not have immunity and therefore would not be testifying.

It wasn't until two years later, when I received a complete copy of the trial transcript, that I realized what had actually happened. Although Sharon Stickney had been given immunity for her inquest testimony and was listed as a government witness, the government not only refused to grant her immunity for any trial testimony, but also threatened her with prosecution. Judge Billings asked David Gibson for any legal authority for the court to grant Sharon immunity over the objection of the prosecution, and Gibson answered: "I have not been – have not researched the issue. [Stickney attorney] Mr. Griffith thinks that a case in the Third Circuit has so held, but I'm frank to say I don't know."[32]   Relying on law cited by David Kirby, Judge Billings found he had no authority to order immunity. Researching the question myself several years after trial, I found that not only did Judge Billings have the authority, but also that there was a well-defined test specified by the Second Circuit Court of Appeals for the circumstances under which court-ordered immunity was appropriate. Sharon met all the criteria.

There were other oddities in the Sharon Stickney matter. Judge Billings had asked Gibson, "What I wondered what your proffer was whether you've demonstrated that the testimony [of Sharon Stickney] would be materially exculpatory or not cumulative."

Gibson replied: "Of course, it's a little difficult, your Honor, to know exactly what Ms. Stickney would testify to in terms of her reticence in giving information…" [33] All the while Gibson was aware of Sharon's affidavit that was given months before trial, and that Ed Lucas had described her as "extremely cooperative". More than two years after trial Sharon was interviewed by private detective Guy Paradee on October 19, 1994.[34] According to Sharon, she was never told why she hadn't testified, but speculated that it was because her testimony would have been helpful to the defense.

I wasn't the only one puzzled about the defense. The government called as witnesses old friends Allan and Beverly Hobson to support the theory that I had tricked them into ordering chemicals for me and had then had stolen those chemicals to make methamphetamine. Beverly had been subpoenaed twice to the Grand Jury and related that she had been threatened by two police officers that if she didn't cooperate fully she could be charged with obstruction of justice.[35] Later at trial Det. LaMoria admitted that he did "remind" Mrs. Hobson about obstruction.[36] Under the circumstances they had their own attorney in court during their testimony. Later Beverly related that the lawyer was amazed by Gibson's performance and had observed, "This guy's making a lot of mistakes. Hasn't he ever tried a criminal case before?"

26

Katrina, Lindsay and I tried to carry on with our lives, but the threat of imminent incarceration weighed heavily. David Kirby was very anxious to have me jailed, and was surely pursuing that goal vigorously. I didn't really understand the technical legal arguments, and left those matters in the hands of David Gibson, but I did know that one of the considerations was the likelihood of the success of the motion Gibson had filed for a new trial. One of the grounds was the court's failure to immunize defense witness Sharon Stickney, which sounded good at the time. I didn't know then that Mr. Gibson had failed to do any legal research on the question, failed to give the court any legal authority for immunity, and failed to be truthful with Judge Billings by indicating he didn't know what Sharon would say.

Another of the grounds for a new trial was Gibson's contention that the court had erroneously admitted into evidence the chemical orders, even though Gibson himself had stipulated to them and had made no objection at trial. I didn't understand that one, but I did understand much of what the government's chemists had said at trial, and thought I could do myself the most good by seeing if I could poke any holes in their testimony.

I knew for sure that Dr. McMahon of the police laboratory had lied at trial, and concluded that he was the one who had either planted the methamphetamine in my equipment or falsified the tests. McMahon had testified that he had found methamphetamine crystals "embedded into a gummy residue" in the drip tray of my fume hood.[37] Since the crystals were embedded, Dr. McMahon concluded they were manufactured there. The problem was that there were no "green, oily residues" as he otherwise described them.[38] I had thoroughly cleaned the drip tray following the picric acid spill in the spring of 1990, and the only residue was plaster dust from the construction project at my house.

Dr. McMahon had described one of his techniques as swabbing a test reagent, which he called a Marquis reagent, onto a potential target area. If the reagent turned the appropriate color, methamphetamine was presumptively present. A sample was then scraped from the area that tested positive, and this sample was analyzed by instrument called a gas chromatograph – mass spectrometer or gc-ms. If the output values of both the gas chromatograph and the mass spectrometer closely matched values produced by a sample of pure methamphetamine previously run through the machine, then Dr. McMahon declared the unknown to be methamphetamine. This was the accepted procedure in the scientific community.

The police laboratory had a large collection of very high purity samples of various drugs and drug-related chemicals which had been already run through the instrument to create reference values in the machine's computerized reference library. If an unknown compound was injected into the machine, the test results were automatically compared to the reference library and the closest matches printed out.

Dr. McMahon's other analytical instrument was an FTIR microscope. He claimed to have zeroed in on a single methamphetamine crystal in the "green, oily residues" allegedly found in my fume hood. It was then irradiated by an infrared laser beam, with the result being a graph

87

of transmittance vs. frequency over a part of the infrared spectrum. This graph was superimposed on a graph resulting from pure methamphetamine to show that they were virtually identical. Since there were no "green, oily residues" Dr. McMahon had completely faked this part of his testing, probably using his pure methamphetamine reference standard to produce both the reference graph and the graph for the unknown supposedly taken from my equipment. However, with nothing but the graphs and Dr. McMahon's testimony, it wasn't going to be easy to show that there was anything wrong.

I had run an infrared spectrophotometer in college and had some knowledge of its operation, although McMahon's FTIR machine was far more elaborate than the one I had used. I had also run a gas chromato-graph, but never a mass spectrometer, and didn't have much of a feel for it. If I were going to really analyze the test results, I would need to study all the instruments in depth. Another immediate problem was that I had no idea of how forensic testing of a suspected clandestine drug laboratory should have been conducted. Brendan McMahon and DEA chemist Fasanello had testified, but I wasn't going to take their word for it.

This was a few years before the explosion of the internet, and the closest place I thought adequate to begin my search was the library at Castleton State College 10 miles away. The library had recently computerized the index of its holdings, and listed as well the holdings of the other Vermont state colleges and the University of Vermont. I didn't know how to use the computer system at the time, and thought it would take considerable time to learn, so I struggled without success in the card catalog for about a day. Finally, in desperation, I tackled the computer system. Fifteen minutes later I was ready and typed in the search term "methamphetamine". There were only a couple of hits, but one was in the government documents section of the Castleton State library, where I would never have thought to look. The National Institute on Drug Abuse published a small monthly journal, and one was devoted entirely to methamphetamine. There were various articles, but the ones most interesting to me were those relating to testing for the byproducts of meth manufacture. One article by Irvine and Chin was heavily footnoted, and the bibliography contained the names of forensics journals – just the information I had wanted. It also turned out that the state of Oregon had had a big problem at one time with clandestine meth labs, and had published a handbook for law enforcement. I sent away for a copy immediately.

For whatever reason David Gibson had never given me copies of the reports, notes and printouts produced by the government's chemists at trial. I finally asked for them and Gibson sent the materials by letter of June 5, 1992 – nearly two months after trial - but by then time was running out for me. The Second Circuit Court of Appeals had agreed with David Kirby and had remanded the matter of my bail to Judge Billings to determine if there were exceptional circumstances or that there was a substantial likelihood that I would receive a new trial. A hearing had been held on May 8, and Judge Billings had subsequently ruled that I was to be detained, with the order stayed if I were to appeal. The Second Circuit wasted no time upholding the detention order, and on June 26 Judge Billings ordered that I surrender to U.S. Marshals by 2:00 p.m. on June 30. On June 29 I wrote a lengthy letter to David Gibson pointing out what I believed were serious problems with testimony of both of the government's chemists along with my recent discoveries regarding accepted forensic practices and procedures in drug manufacturing cases.

While Judge Billings had originally given me the option of surrendering to either the marshals or the institution in which I was to be incarcerated, in the second order I was to surrender to the marshals. Apparently David Gibson saw nothing significant about the difference between the orders, and I certainly did not at the time, but nonetheless there was. The United States Bureau of Prisons used a manual of over 200 pages to determine the security level of its inmates wherein numerical scores were given for various factors such as the severity of the offense and length of the sentence. The scores were then totaled to give the security level, which determined the type of institution and sometimes the programs for which the inmate was eligible. Self-surrendering directly to an institution was worth a whopping minus six security points, while surrendering to the marshals under otherwise identical circumstances might be worth nothing.

Had Gibson realized the importance of this subtlety, he might have arranged things differently. As it was, I showed up at the marshals' office on the second floor of the federal building in Rutland at 10:00 a.m. on June 30 accompanied by my father and Katrina. I was then taken into custody, a chain was passed around my waist and my hands cuffed together and to the chain belt. For what they said were security reasons, the marshals refused to divulge my destination, but I was allowed to take a bag of textbooks from home that I thought might be handy to alleviate any prison boredom. I was then loaded into a car by deputy marshals Paul Whelton and Donald Russell, and driven 2 hours to the Federal Correctional Institution at Ray Brook, New York. It turned out that the prison was the former Olympic village for the 1980 winter Olympics in Lake Placid.

The marshals informed me that people they transported usually wore leg irons, and they had done me a favor by not using them, which was true, but the whole exercise with the chains was a little silly. I had been out on bail for two and half months following my conviction and could have left either the state or the country with little difficulty. It made no sense that I would surrender to armed marshals and then try to escape on my way to prison.

27

The Bureau of Prisons classified inmates by security level using a complex scoring system, and there was a matching set of institutions. At the top was the supermaximum security facility built inside a mountain in Florence, Colorado that once housed John Gotti and Timothy McVeigh. A notch down were the high security penitentiaries like those in Lewisburg, Pennsylvania and Leavenworth, Kansas. Then came the medium and low security FCIs (Federal Correctional Institutions), and finally the fenceless prison camps such as the famous "Club Fed" Allenwood Camp in central Pennsylvania.

Ray Brook was a medium security facility, and was constructed in the same general pattern as numerous other FCIs. From above, each of the housing units looked like a dumbbell, that is, two more or less circular ends connected by a narrow corridor. Each of the rounded ends contained two-man cells arranged around the circumference in two tiers. The center was open and had a few tables, a couple of exercise bicycles, a pool table and a chin-up bar. At the end of each tier were two single-person showers, and there was a small office for guards on each side of the housing unit as well as two rooms devoted to televisions. The bar of the barbell contained the unit administrative offices, laundry rooms with washers and dryers and more television rooms. Outside was a small exercise yard with a basketball hoop, two or three picnic-style tables and an area to play handball against the wall of the unit.

Ray Brook had five individual housing units to contain its approximately 1,100 inmates and these were spaced about 75 yards apart along the fence at the eastern part of the compound. At the north end was a recreation area consisting of a softball field, walking track, outside weight pavilion and basketball court that doubled as a skating rink in the winter. Adjacent to the outdoor rec area was a nice gymnasium with a full basketball court and well-equipped exercise room with numerous machines and weightlifting stations. Arrayed along the westerly part of the compound were the disciplinary segregation unit, aka "The Hole",

90

medical facilities, administrative offices, R & D, the mess hall, educational classrooms and libraries, prison industries, psychological services and the chapel. The middle of the compound was open but crisscrossed with a web of sidewalks separated by well-manicured lawns.

The perimeter of the compound was enclosed with two fences, one inside the other, each festooned with coils of razor wire, and some areas had three fences. The wire was more than decorative. An inmate trying to escape from the state prison in Rutland, Vermont only made it over one fence of an arrangement similar to Ray Brook's, and was found unconscious due to loss of blood without having surmounted the second fence.

Outside Ray Brook's fences, two pickup trucks constantly patrolled a paved roadway around the perimeter of the compound. The drivers were prison guards, one to a truck. Each guard was armed with a 9mm pistol in a holster as well as both a 12-gauge pump shotgun and an M-16 assault rifle (in 3-shot burst fire configuration) carried in a hunting-type rack in the rear window of the pickup.

While the trucks probably gave the townspeople a sense of security, it was debatable exactly how alert the drivers were performing this boring duty, especially at night. One New Year's Eve the two trucks had collided head-on, with the drivers alleged by inmates to have been drunk, and it was not uncommon for the trucks to have dents from inadvertent collisions with the fence or whatever else happened to be in the way. After I had left Ray Brook, the trucks were successfully distracted by a staged melee on the compound, and two inmates escaped over the fence in broad daylight. They were, however, badly cut in the process as well as abandoned by their getaway driver, and were taken into custody a few days later in poor condition after wandering aimlessly in the woods.

28

When the marshals and I arrived at the gate of FCI Ray Brook, a guard emerged with a 12-gauge pump shotgun and stood about 30 feet from the car. The marshals then removed their sidearms, put them in a lockbox, and drove into the prison. I was extracted from the car, placed in a holding cell and unchained. Subsequently I was ordered to remove all my clothing and personal items, and everything but my sneakers and books was placed in a cardboard box to be sent home, even my old wind-up watch. I was then issued the bare minimum of prison clothing – one pair each of underpants and socks, one t-shirt, green pants with no belt, and a green shirt. In addition to the clothing I was also supplied with razors, soap, towels and bedding. A case manager interviewed me, moving his pen down a form item by item, asking about various things including communicable diseases and any medicines I was taking. He finally asked if there was any reason that I should not be placed in the general inmate population, a thinly disguised query as to whether I had snitched on any inmates at Ray Brook. Answering in the negative, I was ushered out the door of R & D (Receiving and Departures), and onto the empty prison compound with directions to report to the unit officer (guard) of Ausable Housing Unit, the most southerly of the five units at Ray Brook.

With more bewilderment than trepidation I walked up the short hill from R & D to Ausable, opened the outer door and entered a glassed-in mudroom. The inner door was locked, so I stood there and waited for a few minutes until a guard from inside the unit unlocked the door with a large key, perhaps six inches long. He led me to a 2-man cell on the upper of the two tiers, and left me there to make my bed, collect my thoughts, and visit with my cellmate. Although I had been issued a pillowcase, there was no pillow.

My cellmate was a black man, perhaps of Jamaican origin, about 30 years old. He wasted no time telling me about his faith in Jesus, and began to quote scripture. From what I could discern, he had been caught more or less red-handed dealing cocaine, or crack cocaine, but nonetheless thought God himself was going to intervene and set him free. I hoped that this was going to be our only conversation on the subject, as I would be trapped all night in the cell with this gentleman, and really didn't want to hear any more of his religious views. Unfortunately I was awakened at perhaps three in the morning on several occasions by loud praying, and more than once he came within a foot of my face spouting quotations from the Bible. My own prayers were answered a few weeks later when my cellmate was transferred to another prison.

The cells were all alike, about 8 by 12 feet, with two beds stacked one atop the other against a tall, narrow window. The only exceptions were the cramped 4-man cells at the end of each tier. Each 2-man cell had a small table with two plastic chairs, and a stainless steel combination sink/toilet with buttons for hot and cold water that could not be left on. The door was sheet steel with a 6 by 10 inch window about eye height, and the door was left unlocked except from 11 p.m. to 6 a.m. The original plumbing fixtures were porcelain, but had been destroyed by disgruntled Cuban inmates some years before and replaced with stainless. The rest of the prison had the porcelain fixtures with normal water faucets, but I was on the wing for so-called "holdovers" and condemned, at least temporarily, to the metal fixtures.

Holdover was the official name for inmates housed in Bureau of Prison facilities, but not in the custody of the Bureau of Prisons. They were either pretrial detainees ineligible for - or unable to - raise bail, or convicted criminals awaiting sentencing such as I was. Technically holdovers were in the custody of the United States Marshals Service, and were in a sort of limbo. The Bureau of Prisons couldn't force the holdovers to work, but then again it didn't have to allow them to leave the housing unit except to eat. Under the circumstances the arrangement was usually for holdovers to perform nominal cleaning duties in the housing unit in addition to the staff of inmates formally assigned that position; in return they were allowed to go to the libraries and recreational facilities. Of course, I wasn't aware of all that when I arrived, but there was a short learning curve owing to the willingness of other inmates to tell me the rules, written and unwritten.

It took three days on and off to complete the various intake procedures. On the second day I went to the hospital for a cursory physical exam, a tetanus shot and a tuberculosis test. Blood and urine samples were taken for unknown tests. Although prison personnel denied testing for HIV, it became certain after a time that they had, indeed, done such a test as some inmates had been told they were HIV positive. Fortunately I wasn't positive for any disease they were testing for.

On the third day I finally got a toothbrush and some shaving cream, as well as most of the prison issue clothing package – three pairs of socks and underwear, ankle boots, a coat and a hat. I had to wait three more days to get my second green uniform shirt and pants as well as my belt. The whole operation was inefficient, and everything took much longer than it would have under other circumstances. The same applied to the process allowing Katrina to visit.

She had wanted to visit the first day, but people couldn't just show up at a federal prison to visit someone. All visitors had to be on an approved visiting list, which of course took time to approve. Fortunately there was an exception of sorts for wives and immediate family, and Katrina was allowed to visit on the evening of my third day in prison. Both my parents and Katrina came to visit on Sunday, the sixth day.

Ray Brook had visiting hours three evenings a week and from 9:00 to 3:00 on weekends. Only people from the immediate area came on weeknights, but on the weekends busses brought friends and families up from the New York City area, and the visiting room could be crowded. The room was perhaps twenty by fifty feet, with floor to ceiling glass panels on one side looking out on the compound. There were blinds covering the glass making it difficult to look inside, as boorish inmates were prone to stare at visitors, particularly the women. Plastic chairs were arranged in rows, and several vending machines were against the wall opposite the glass dispensing everything from drinks to chips to microwave-ready meals. Visitors entered through the prison's main gate, and passed through a metal detector. Inmates were pat searched before a visit and strip searched afterward in an attempt to prevent contraband from entering the prison.

For both Katrina and me, it was important to see each other frequently to offer mutual support and ease the transition to a much different lifestyle. We did talk on the telephone, but a visit was better, especially at the beginning when the telephone system was nearly impossible to use. When I first arrived at Ray Brook, each side of Ausable Unit had only one telephone, and that was for collect calls only, a very expensive method. Inmates lined up to use the telephone for 15 minutes at a time and there was always a line.

About a week after I arrived, Ray Brook became part of a system-wide change. Instead of collect calls, inmates could direct dial up to twenty numbers on a pre-approved list. The BOP had negotiated a reasonable rate with a long distance company, which charged five cents a minute for most calls. Inmates created telephone accounts in which they could deposit money from prison jobs or sent in from friends or family on the outside, and this was automatically debited by the phone system. Every call was disconnected after 15 minutes, but now there were 8 phones per housing unit instead of 2. If no one were waiting in line, an inmate could call back for another 15 minutes.

The new phone system certainly made it easier for Katrina and me to stay in touch, and carried us through between visits. For the first few months she came to visit several times a week, but gradually less frequently as winter set in and the winding mountain roads became more treacherous.

29

The roads weren't the only things treacherous at Ray Brook. Having seen first hand the damage that people cooperating with the government could cause, I was extremely wary of my fellow inmates, and the situation was even worse than I had imagined. It seemed logical to suppose that once someone had been sentenced for his own crime, any opportunities to cooperate in exchange for a sentence reduction were foreclosed, but this was not the case. One could cooperate at any time, and, upon motion of a U.S. Attorney pursuant to Federal Rule of Criminal Procedure 35(b), a federal judge could reduce the sentence. The rule specifically exempted the court from any mandatory minimum sentencing laws. Other inmates recognized me as soon as I walked into Ausable Unit due to the extensive TV and newspaper coverage my case had received, and I wondered if I might be the target of someone desiring a sentence reduction.

Those who hadn't cooperated had great disdain for those who did, and I learned almost immediately that I was in the midst of various schemers looking for an easy way out. Many of the inmates from Vermont had cooperated in one way or another, and there was even a father-son snitch team from Burlington. Also, the reality of a long sentence was beginning to sink in for some of the new inmates, especially the younger ones, with the likely loss of wives and girlfriends. A few were crying at night, and surely it crossed their minds that a facile solution to their problems might be to inform on someone else, even if the story had to be invented out of whole cloth.

While some of the schemers might have been very clever, others were so inept as to be laughable. A self-professed motorcycle gang member showed an unusual interest in the several defendants of the Billy Greer hashish case, where 54 tons of the drug had been found floating in barrels on the St. Lawrence River near Quebec. The motorcycle gangster could often be seen lurking behind the massive 2 foot by 2 foot cement columns in the open area of the housing unit, straining to overhear any conversation involving a Greer defendant. This amateurish performance must have pleased someone as, despite what the inmate had described as years remaining on his sentence, he abruptly disappeared. A suspicious acquaintance called the biker's mother's house in Pennsylvania to be told that he had just stepped out, but would be back soon.

I was fighting my conviction, and became fearful that someone might claim I had confessed to something, which could have undermined the new trial I was seeking on appeal. This fear turned out to be very well founded, and was emphatically confirmed when I later met Premnath "Winston" Birbal and heard his story. However, I had been tipped off at the outset about the way things worked and my instinct for self preservation had already been well honed. Under the circumstances I thought it best to be courteous to other inmates, but not to tell them much that they might weave into a false story to give it the appearance of credibility.

Since my trip to Guatemala I had wished for an opportunity to continue my Spanish studies and prison seemed to be the ideal place. While the racial and ethnic compositions of different prisons varied somewhat, Ray Brook was about evenly divided between Hispanics, blacks and whites. Among the Hispanics there were numerous foreign nationals, with quite a few on the holdover wing with me. I began to hang out with a couple of the Colombians who spoke little English, practicing my Spanish. In addition, I was able to do some rudimentary translations for the Colombians with their legal papers, prison rules, etc. I also thought that I was relatively safe with them, believing it would be a tough sell to a Vermont jury that I was learning Spanish to confess to deportable aliens in their own language.

30

My first week in prison was consumed organizing and trying to adapt to my surroundings. Time not spent getting laundry and medical tests was spent with other inmates playing cards, walking, playing basketball and even tennis. (There were two outdoor tennis courts at Ray Brook.) I still had the mission to discredit the government's chemists, and finally went to the prison library on the seventh day. As I suspected there was nothing I could use, and the only research tool was Books in Print, meaning that I had to identify potentially useful books only by their titles. To compound my difficulties the prison librarian, Inger Curth, was initially not very cooperative.

My work took on a new urgency when I received the draft of my Presentence Investigation Report (PSI or PSR) that recommended a prison sentence of 30 years to life, a great shock considering David Gibson's assurance of 10 years. The PSI was prepared by United States Probation, which was employed by the court and was theoretically impartial. However, since no one from U.S. Probation attended my trial, and the transcript had not yet been prepared, the likely source of information regarding trial testimony was the U.S. Attorney's Office.

The PSI appeared intended to inflict the maximum amount of emotional distress. The sentence was based mostly upon the quantity of methamphetamine I might have produced, with the PSI stating: "At trial, an expert chemist affiliated with the Drug Enforcement Agency [sic] testified that three kilograms was a conservative estimate of the amount of methamphetamine that could have been manufactured with all the chemicals ordered and received by Bloomer." Clearly the preparer, Teri J. Ames, never verified the three kilogram figure (6.6 pounds) as the expert had guessed only 3 to 4 pounds at trial. There was also an enhancement for possession of "automatic firearms" that, even if correct, would not have applied in that nobody had linked any such weapons to the crimes of conviction. (As it turned out, Ms. Ames's meanness would catch up with her a few years later.)

It was now obvious that my sentencing was going to be a battle of experts guessing how much methamphetamine might have been made by methods unknown, each trying to convince Judge Billings of the accuracy of his conjecture, and I was going to have to redouble my research efforts to aid myself in any way possible.

After a few conversations, Mrs. Curth warmed up to me a bit. She was in her mid-30's and very Scandinavian in appearance – fair skinned, blue eyed and blonde. She was attending night classes at SUNY in Albany to earn an advanced degree in library science, and had taken the job at the prison to help support her family in the meantime. Unlike the guards and most of the employees at Ray Brook, Mrs. Curth was a contract worker who did not plan to make a career with the Bureau of Prisons. She had actually put together a pretty good library, considering the limitations, and it was part of the New York State library system. This meant that Ray Brook could obtain copies of articles from periodicals and books throughout the system via interlibrary loans. The printout of periodicals available was over an inch thick.

I identified a few books on drug analysis and gc-ms theory and practice from Books in Print and tried to order them through interlibrary loan. Most were unavailable, and the rest were going to take a while to work their way to Ray Brook. I had better luck with my initial periodical requests. I submitted a list of articles that I had obtained from the NIDA methamphetamine book I had found at the Castleton State College library, and some of them had come in. Just as I was making a little progress, the court (on October 7) set sentencing for November 3, 1992. It took a few days for the news to reach me, but when it did I wrote to David Gibson in somewhat of a panic on October 14, explaining the difficulties I'd had obtaining materials, and stating that "…I don't believe I can possibly be ready for a hearing on the 3rd of November, especially without the [DEA chemist] Fasanello trial transcript." Considering that my sentence was apparently going to be based on Fasanello's opinions I further told Mr. Gibson that "It's important that you realize that Fasanello has been mistaken or is lying about virtually everything."

Despite the knowledge that I was having difficulties finding appropriate materials, Gibson didn't inform me of, or provide me with, Dr. Sentell's report of April 15, 1992. According to her report, she

97

"performed extensive literature research to confirm the current protocol for the identification and analysis of methamphetamine, particularly in terms of forensic samples. She also consulted about the latter protocol (March 29) with Mr. Michael E. Swartz in the Applied Technology Group at Waters Chromatography Division of Millipore, who has in the recent past been employed at the state of Rhode Island's State Forensic Lab." Thus Dr. Sentell already had what I was looking for, and I had already paid for it, but David Gibson didn't tell me.

Even without Gibson's help I continued to make steady progress. After going around and around with the prison authorities, I finally got permission to have chemistry books sent in from outside the prison and, between my mother and my wife, Katrina, I received more than two hundred dollars worth. Mrs. Curth continued to order periodical articles as fast as I gave her the requests, and they would usually arrive within a couple of weeks.

As I read the scientific materials an interesting picture developed, creating even more doubt about the competence and integrity of both the government's chemists. DEA chemist Fasanello had testified about references in the chemistry literature allegedly found at my house and their relevance to methamphetamine. When I obtained the articles themselves, it turned out that Fasanello was, in many instances, wrong, and some of the references had nothing whatsoever to do with methamphetamine. Even when the articles might have had some application, Fasanello had not described them correctly. Since this was supposed to be Fasanello's field of expertise, I thought this was significant, and it convinced me that Fasanello was at least sloppy if not incompetent.

As for Dr. McMahon, his testimony seemed riddled with inconsistencies. He had testified that he had expected to find residue of manufacturing in my fume hood, and that's why pieces of it were taken back to his laboratory.[39] He had also testified he had performed a screening test for methamphetamine with his Marquis reagent, and "[i]f you don't get the positive screen reaction, it's not there."[40] (Tr. II-178) However, he and Fasanello had performed dozens of these tests at my house the day of the raid, leaving the test kits behind, but they hadn't discovered any methamphetamine. I had brought the abandoned used test kits to trial for several days, and had requested that David Gibson ask McMahon how it was that he could find no methamphetamine the day of the raid but, once he was back at the lab, found it over and over using the same methods in the same places he had already looked. Gibson never asked.

98

A closer examination of Dr. McMahon's printouts from his gc-ms revealed another part of the story. He had performed the first test on August 13, 1990 at 2:58 p.m. on the drip tray from my fume hood, and had found no methamphetamine. The next test was at 5:44 p.m., when presumably everyone else had gone home, and this time there was methamphetamine. All the tests that followed of the drip tray showed methamphetamine.

There was another interesting aspect to the gc-ms printouts: by the time Dr. McMahon finished testing the fume hood parts on August 14, his scrapings were almost pure methamphetamine. This was odd, since in a manufacturing environment by-products and intermediates of manufacture would be expected to be present. These chemicals were well known, and had been described in numerous articles in the forensic literature written by DEA and other forensic chemists. Dr. McMahon's own opinion that methamphetamine was manufactured in my equipment was based on a crystal embedded in some green goo. The green goo, therefore, should have contained by-products and intermediates – except it didn't (with the exception of n-formylmethamphetamine).

The n-formylmethamphetamine was even more interesting. According to DEA chemists, it was only associated with one method of meth manufacture – the Leucart synthesis. The problem was that I could not be shown to have the chemicals necessary for this method, and again there were other characteristic by-products of that process that simply weren't there. Just before going to prison I had written to David Gibson (on June 29) that I believed that Dr. McMahon had created the n-formylmethamphetamine himself.

After researching the matter more thoroughly in prison, I prepared a six-page monograph heavily footnoted with references to the chemistry and forensics literature justifying my earlier conclusion that the n-formyl-methamphetamine was a reaction product of the Marquis reagent and methamphetamine. The source of this damning substance was thus Dr. McMahon himself using an improper test procedure, a procedure that created something that wasn't there originally. Later DEA chemist Fasanello would agree with me, although his motive may have had more to do with politics than chemistry: the Leucart synthesis was not very efficient, and would have resulted in a lesser amount of methamphetamine and thus a shorter prison term.

While I had a lot of circumstantial evidence, what I really needed was a smoking gun. I then organized the data from the gc-ms printouts in a table and the result leapt off the page: the reference values for methamphetamine were changing from test to test! This invalidated the basis of the test and was contrary to McMahon's testimony at trial that the reference values did not change.

Even more interesting was the reference value for lignocaine (lidocaine). Lidocaine was a common cutting agent for cocaine, and had been found in materials seized from Robert Spencer's residence. It's value, too, had changed, and in an astounding manner. According to the reference values printed out by the gc-ms in one case lidocaine would have exited the machine before PCP and in another case afterward, which was physically impossible. The essence of the testing was that the machine was operated in exactly the same way for each test, and consequently the exit order could never change. If the reference values for the gc-ms were changing, the test results were worthless.

There were only two possibilities: the machine was malfunctioning or Dr. McMahon was deliberately tampering with it. Because of the way digital data is stored, there was only one real possibility – tampering. Since there was no other methamphetamine in my case except for what Dr. McMahon had claimed to find, I thought a new trial was a certainty, but I was to be bitterly disappointed.

31

I was in Ray Brook for just a month when the reality hit home that there were more dangers in the prison than inmate cooperators. As my parents were about to leave the visiting room on August 2, all entries and departures were suddenly suspended. After a short time guards, accompanied by a priest, wheeled a gurney past the windows of the visiting room and toward the main gate of the prison. The patient, an inmate with the upper portion of his head heavily bandaged, lay face up on the gurney. His hands were clenched into fists, which rested upon his face with the thumbs poking his closed eyes. There were no medical personnel, and the guards were in no hurry. A short time after the procession had passed, normal visiting resumed, and my parents left. Soon afterward there was a prison-wide lockdown with all inmates locked in their cells.

Normal procedure for lunch and dinner was for each of the five housing units to be released sequentially in approximately twenty-minute intervals following an order that changed from week to week. The prison compound itself was left open for a time afterward so that inmates from other units were free to mingle. Because of institution's fear of additional violence following the killing, each unit was released individually. The inmates were given about one-half hour to eat and return to their units to be again locked in before the next unit was released.

By the following morning the prison authorities apparently thought they had the situation under control, as the compound was opened for breakfast by unlocking all the doors of the housing units. Breakfast was not well attended, and any inmates wishing to eat or just wander about on the compound were allowed to do so from 6:30 until the 7:30 work call.

I was glad to be out of my cell and went to breakfast with another inmate who was my basketball-playing partner. Just as we were about to sit down with our food, a wild melee broke out at the opposite end of the mess hall with guards and inmates alike running to join the fray. While my companion was inclined to sit and watch, I immediately put down my tray and walked quickly to the exit. He reluctantly followed me back to Ausable. As we looked back down the hill, another altercation broke out on the prison compound in front of the mess hall. Shortly thereafter an announcement came from the prison's ubiquitous loudspeakers - all inmates were to return immediately to their housing units. Again everyone was locked in his cell for the day, with units going individually to lunch and dinner.

The next morning, the feeding procedure began with breakfast. Before we were locked back in our cells, a number of us were leaning over the railing of the upper tier. A black inmate about my age turned to me and said, "These people don't have a clue what's going on. It's D.C. boys versus Dominicans." He was referring to black inmates from Washington, D.C. and inmates from the Dominican Republic.

Clueless or not, the prison authorities put on a show of force, and by mid-morning the goon squad had been activated. This was nothing more than volunteer guards in black outfits with helmets and clubs, but twenty of them marching out on the compound were an intimidating sight. My cell was situated such that I could see much of the compound from my window, and I could clearly observe the procedure. Three-man goon squad details would enter a housing unit. Shortly thereafter they would emerge with a chained inmate between two of them, with the third following, and the inmate would be escorted to R & D. The procedure was repeated for about two-dozen men.

After three days of lockdown, we were released from our cells and normal activities resumed. In all, about two hundred inmates had been shipped out over the violence, and busses had been running all night, dispersing inmates throughout the system. It was an effective strategy, as whatever alliances had been formed at Ray Brook were scattered as leaves in the wind. Fake disciplinary transfers were also an unobtrusive means for the Bureau of Prisons to move the most treacherous of its inmate informers from institution to institution without raising any suspicions.

Actually, a transfer for alleged participation in a disturbance gave the informers an instant credibility with their new victims. Unfortunately it was virtually certain that inmates who had had no connection whatsoever to either violence or informing had been inadvertently caught in the net and had been sent far from friends and family.

With inmates mingling once again, it wasn't difficult to find out what had happened. There had been a simmering feud between Dominican inmates and black inmates from Washington, D.C., and the week before a Dominican working in the kitchen had had his face smashed into a cooler by blacks. His friends spotted the perpetrators in the exercise yard, grabbed two aluminum bats from a softball game in progress, chased the men down and clubbed them. The dead man on the gurney was presumably the one that had been taken off his feet with a tremendous blow to the head, hitting the ground in convulsions. The ringing of the bat could be heard throughout the area, as its metal crushed the victim's skull.

The prison authorities had no credibility with inmates, and it was easy to see why in the aftermath of the killing. The official story was that the dead inmate was in an outside hospital, and was going to be all right. Within a few days prisoners were repeating this version in a campaign apparently orchestrated by the prison's psychology department. A few men actually claimed to have seen their dead comrade walking about the prison. Since the authorities themselves were promoting this nonsense, they should not have been surprised to learn that inmates never believed them, even when they were telling the truth.

32

The killing of the black inmate brought out more sad facts of prison life than the administration's compulsion to lie. Any prison's management wanted to institutionalize its inmates as soon as possible, that is, adapt them to prison life. The flip side of this coin, however, was that many of the inmates became fully invested in their situation inside the prison and, in the process, lost their perspective. Those with life sentences were, of course, going nowhere, but the vast majority would be released sooner or later. Given that reality, the successful inmates were those that survived to go home.

Some quickly lost sight of that objective and became involved in activities virtually guaranteed to put them in harm's way like drug use and gambling. Others engaged in unprotected homosexual activity with other inmates, whose rate of HIV infection was much higher than the population at large. Some, perhaps, had little choice. Gang members on the street were expected to remain members in prison, and that may have been the situation in the Dominican/D.C. Boys altercation. Regardless of gang affiliations, disagreements between inmates often became group confrontations along ethnic lines, a very dangerous situation.

For me the strategy was crystal clear: avoid any controversial activities, treat everyone with the greatest respect, and avoid most of my fellow inmates whenever possible. It was also desirable to be unobtrusive, so that if the guards were looking for suspects one's name would not readily leap to mind. Still, it was more than possible to be in the wrong place at the wrong time.

Although I needed some time to work on legal matters, I spent an inordinate amount of time in the Ausable housing unit and thought I would be better off elsewhere. Another holdover had volunteered to work in the education department as a tutor, and I did likewise. August 24th was my first day on the job.

The federal prison system ran a GED program for those without high school diplomas, and college courses were also offered in conjunction with a local community college. While college was optional, the BOP made GED class attendance as close to mandatory a possible and, while some took advantage of the opportunity and made a serious effort, others were there physically but refused to participate.

At the beginning I was tutoring math and reading, but over time my students were all readers with severe learning disabilities. Although it was demanding to work with them, it was also rewarding as most made steady, if slow, progress.

33

Fortunately my sentencing hearing, originally scheduled for November 3, 1992, had been postponed until December 9, as I needed a little more time for my scientific investigations. Although my sentencing had been put off, the date for my codefendant, Robert Spencer, remained on November 9. I had heard that Spencer appeared to be very confident, and had purchased another car as well as having his motorcycle tuned up. Although his plea deal was for a prison sentence of zero to five years, Spencer clearly thought that zero was the most likely result. Fearing that Spencer would be sentenced only to probation, I asked Katrina to attend the hearing.

Prior to the formal start of the proceedings, but in the presence of the judge, there was some loud banter between Spencer's attorney, William Sessions, and the U.S. attorneys to the effect that "Bloomer was the one with the guns." Spencer was also frantically arguing with his attorney that part of his deal was that he was supposed to be sentenced after I was, and that the sentencing should be postponed. The reason was obvious at the time - Spencer wanted to curry more favor by testifying against me again - but that fact would be confirmed beyond any doubt shortly. When Judge Billings sentenced Spencer to five years, Katrina said he looked as if he were going to cry.

Although I didn't know it at the time, the delay in my own sentencing was especially fortunate since David Gibson had not lined up any expert chemist by the original sentencing date. In fact, according to Gibson's personal notes I obtained years later, his first calls to prospective chemists were on November 24, and he was unable to find one until a week after that.

Perhaps Mr. Gibson had no intention of hiring a chemist at all in spite of my impending 30-to-life sentence based on DEA chemist Fasanello's speculation, but events intervened. On November 20 an inmate from Burlington, Vermont gave me a copy of the *Burlington Free Press* with an article that Dr. Brendan McMahon of the Vermont State Police Laboratory had been relieved of duty for taking and using regulated drugs from the lab. Four days later, on the 24th, David Gibson and my father came to Ray Brook on a legal visit, and we were given a private room for that purpose just off the main visiting room. Although my father had nothing to do with the criminal case, he was representing me in some civil matters, and was allowed into the prison along with Mr. Gibson.

When I excitedly told David Gibson about Dr. McMahon, he went rigid and nearly collapsed. I thought it was a strange reaction at the time, but I was swept away by exuberance and gave it only fleeting consideration. McMahon had called his own credibility into question with his apparent criminality, and I had amassed a great deal of evidence that he was both incompetent and corrupt. I naively imagined myself home for Christmas.

I had kept David Gibson apprised of my progress regarding Dr. McMahon and made sure that he was aware that it was almost a certainty that the gc-ms testing was rigged. At the very least the testing was invalid. Gibson replied that a new trial was a "possibility, not a probability" although another criminal lawyer with more experience than David Gibson told me later that if the tests had been rigged a new trial would have been virtually automatic. Mr. Gibson and I discussed my evidence regarding Dr. McMahon, and he indicated that he was going to use it. Subsequently I simplified the data from the gc-ms as much as possible along with my conclusions and, on November 30, mailed to Gibson "proof McMahon

104

massaged GC data".[41]   Although Gibson was not as upbeat as I expected he would be, my father referred to lawyers as "paid pessimists", and I attached no particular significance to it at the time. I would have been much more pessimistic myself had I realized that Gibson was going to file a new trial motion based only upon newspaper articles, and that he intended to ignore all my evidence of incompetence and corruption.

However, the revelations about McMahon's illegal activities apparently lit a fire under Mr. Gibson, because he began to call chemists the same day as our meeting at Ray Brook. A week later he left a telephone message for our eventual chemist, Dr. Edward Brown of California. Finally, just six days before the sentencing hearing, Gibson sent Dr. Brown a package of materials including a transcript of DEA chemist Fasanello's trial testimony, the stipulated chemical orders, my calculations regarding possible methamphetamine amounts, chemistry articles I had culled from the scientific literature, and even my monograph on n-formylmethamphetamine.

Conspicuous by its absence was my evidence that McMahon's tests had been rigged, although Gibson certainly had that information in typewritten, simplified form at the time he wrote Dr. Brown. Gibson made no mention at all of the flawed chemical testing, stating only "As I indicated, I can [sic] primarily in need of being able to present an alternative opinion that the amount of methamphetamine that could have been made was less than what the DEA chemist stated."[42]

34

By late November, I had done everything I could to help myself. I had given David Gibson calculations regarding methamphetamine manufacture, articles from the scientific literature and evidence that Dr. McMahon's chemical testing was almost certainly rigged. Since Gibson had given me no specific information regarding his plans for sentencing, I assembled books and documents I thought might be useful, and awaited my trip from Ray Brook to the federal district court in Rutland, Vermont. I was sure that no one would be willing to take my word on the subject, and therefore had a box of chemistry textbooks and another box of documents to back up my opinions. On December 8, I reported to R & D to be transported to federal court in Rutland by U.S. Marshals Whelton and Russell along with a surprise passenger, fellow inmate Premnath "Winston" Birbal.

Birbal would eventually give me the tool I needed to free myself from prison, but in the meantime he had serious problems of his own. His life had spiraled completely out of control and he was frightened and bewildered. Perhaps he was seeking allies, or perhaps he just wanted some reassurance that everything would be all right, but in any event he gushed details of his case – "diarrhea of the mouth" as a friend put it.

According to Winston, he was an ethnic Asian Indian and a citizen of Trinidad. He had come to Rutland, Vermont on some sort of work visa and was initially employed at a local dairy farm. A musician of some talent, he began to frequent the local bars that featured live entertainment, and in the process, he made an exciting discovery: while the Indian girls in Trinidad saved themselves for marriage, many of the bar girls in Rutland were promiscuous. Winston also discovered that he could eke out a meager existence by playing occasional guitar gigs and selling small amounts of cocaine in the bars. He wanted nothing more out of life and things went well – for a while.

Unfortunately one of Winston's girlfriends from the bars had another lover who became jealous, and decided to eliminate the competition by informing the police that Winston was a drug dealer. One night Winston heard a strange noise outside his apartment and looked out the window. Observing some unusual activity, he immediately decided to flush whatever cocaine he had just as the police broke down the door, leaving several more or less empty plastic bags floating in the toilet. The police laboratory later scraped a total of 2.5 grams of cocaine from the bags, less than 1/10 of an ounce.

The investigation stalled at the beginning. The girlfriend claimed to have had no knowledge of any drug dealing by Winston, and said her lover had simply made up the story in a fit of jealousy. This left the basis of the search warrant in serious jeopardy. In addition, none of Winston's purported customers could be identified. Winston hired a lawyer, and a deal was made. As Winston understood the deal, he was to describe his cocaine operation, such as it was. In return, he was to be deported. Involved with Birbal's confession (also known as a proffer) were two people intimately involved in my own case, Detective Raymond LaMoria, Jr. and Asst. U.S. Attorney Gary Shattuck.

At the end of his confession, Birbal was then asked about his involvement in heroin dealing. When he denied any involvement with heroin, he was told the deal for deportation was off. The real agenda was now clear. Birbal was supposed to be the government's star witness against an acquaintance, John Wright, who had allegedly provided a friend with the heroin that resulted in a fatal overdose.

Winston always thought that his lawyer was colluding with the prosecution, but whether he was or not, the lawyer apparently made no
106

effort to have Winston's confession excluded or destroyed on the basis that it had been obtained by fraud and deceit. A defense to the cocaine charges was now going to be very difficult, but the prison sentence for possession of 2.5 grams of cocaine was a few months at most, followed by a deportation, which Winston had planned on anyway.

The government must have figured that Birbal could be pressured into testifying if the ante were raised, as he was abruptly transferred from the state prison in Rutland to the Addison County Jail in Middlebury, Vermont. On or about the same day Edward Gabaree of St. Albans, Vermont was transferred to the same facility. As the government later put it, they got lucky in that Gabaree, who was already cooperating with the government, was coincidentally present to hear Birbal confess to a tremendous drug dealing conspiracy involving 54 kilograms (119 pounds) of cocaine. Birbal vehemently denied to me that he had confessed any such thing, and I later talked to another inmate who had observed Gabaree's performance at Addison. Apparently Birbal couldn't go anywhere without Gabaree following closely, almost in lockstep. Cooperation with the government paid well as Gabaree, looking at a mandatory minimum 15-year sentence for being a career criminal, was instead released in 1994 because of his substantial assistance.

Despite the new possibility of a prison sentence in excess of ten years due to Gabaree's allegations, Birbal still hadn't agreed to cooperate. Since no proceeding had been scheduled in his criminal case, Winston was mystified as to why he was being removed from Ray Brook with me, and he was also very uneasy. The mystery was solved when the marshals entered R & D to shackle us for the trip to Rutland. One marshal broke into a broad grin and said, "Hey, Winston, you know that heroin overdose death? You've just been indicted."

35

Winston was visibly shaken when he received the news of his indictment, and I thought it would be a quiet trip to Rutland. However, he spent much of it arguing the merits of his case with the marshals, and it was now easy to see why he had been such an easy mark for a predator like Ed Gabaree. My own theory was to be courteous and compliant with guards and marshals, but certainly not to discuss my case with them. There was nothing to be gained and much to be lost, as I was sure that any worthwhile nuggets of information would be reported to the U.S. Attorney's office.

The state prison in Rutland housed federal inmates on a temporary basis, and Winston and I were taken there. The closest federal prison to the federal court in Rutland was Ray Brook, but the state lockup was only a few blocks away, making it very convenient for the marshals. What was not convenient for them was carrying my boxes of books and legal papers. I couldn't do it myself as my hands were cuffed together and shackled to a chain belt. With my permission Deputy Marshal Whelton took my books to the marshals' office just outside the federal courtroom, but I retained the box of legal documents at the state prison.

Winston and I were strip-searched and asked to fill out various forms including a personality inventory with questions like "How often do you think about your mother?" Ray Brook didn't have any similar forms, and it made me very uneasy wondering what mischief could be done with such a document. Consequently I refused to fill it out. Winston, angry and bitter in spite of his fear, refused also.

Perhaps we were the only inmates in the history of the institution to refuse to complete the form, because the guards didn't know what to do. A grossly overweight man, later identified as Chief of Security Wallett, threatened that if I didn't fill out the form I would be locked in my cell 23 hours per day. Since we were in the high security section of the prison with no privileges anyway, it made little difference, and we continued to refuse.

After the strip search and intake screen, Winston and I were issued the bare essentials for toiletries and bedding and ushered into a small common area in the high security section of the prison. The usual procedure was for federal prisoners to be isolated for a time, after which they were put into the general prison population and, since Winston had already been in general population in Rutland, we both thought it a little odd that he would be isolated. In theory inmates had individual cells in high security, but the facility was seriously overcrowded so Winston and I were put in a cell together.

While we were isolated from the general population, there were other inmates in the high security section, and everyone was allowed to come out of his cell into the common area for much of the day to watch TV on a cart that was wheeled in and out of the room at the whim of the guard. The other inmates were, for the most part, young punks who were put in high security for disciplinary reasons. Winston and I hadn't set them much of an example by our refusal to complete the forms, which turned out to be a suicide risk assessment.

That evening a younger, more friendly guard, Officer Fernandez, came in to talk with us. "Look, they left this up to me. Please – just put

108

something, anything, and sign it." I was afraid that I might be denied my legal papers as retribution and, facing 30-to-life, wanted to be in a position to help myself at sentencing. Winston and I looked at each other, and agreed we should put something on the paper. I circled most of the left hand responses, and then drew a line down connecting some of the circles. I also placed some circles between the choices. Winston did likewise and we both signed the forms thus completed. The guard left, satisfied. I was given my box of legal papers in our cell as well as a sweatshirt that Katrina had brought to the prison. Katrina had also brought dress clothes for my court appearance, which was standard procedure.

The following morning we were released individually to walk a few feet to the shower, and I asked for a razor at that time. Correctional Officer Dorothy Day informed me that I should have asked for a razor at 5:00 a.m., breakfast time. I explained that I had just arrived the night before, had no rulebook, and no one had informed me. Ms. Day was unmoved, and I didn't get the razor. A few minutes later, Ms. Day threw my suit bag on my bed and told me to get dressed as the marshals were on their way to pick me up. My tie and shoes were missing and, although the marshals waited, could not be found. The result was that the newspaper and a local TV station got some nice file footage of me shackled and unshaven, with an open collar under my suit jacket.

36

The sentencing hearing was, in most respects, a farce. While none of the trial witnesses had ever mentioned guns in connection with my alleged drug deals, the government now wanted the court to increase my sentence for that reason. The evidence was photos of a locked gun cabinet in my bedroom taken the day of the raid and a few empty gunstocks standing in the corner of my office/hobby room/bullet reloading room. Among the wooden gunstocks was one gun, a World War II M-1 carbine with a folding stock, to which Det. LaMoria tried to attach great significance as a military weapon. I then had to call my sister-in-law to testify that it wasn't even mine. I had purchased it at the request of my brother-in-law and had subsequently given it to him.

My other witnesses were called to advance the proposition that I was a good person. While this might have had a beneficial effect on Judge Billings, he was bound by the Sentencing Guidelines, and the Guidelines made no provision for a downward sentencing adjustment for being a good guy.

At the end of the hearing, I was returned to the state prison along with my box of legal documents. David Gibson had asked me to perform some drug quantity calculations for use the following day in court, but my papers, necessary to determine the yields of various synthetic routes, were denied to me despite repeated requests. According to C.O. Day, that was because they contained procedures to make "crystal meth". When I explained that this was exactly the topic for the court hearing, she then said that the papers, file folders tightly packed in a cardboard box, were a fire hazard. Despite a call from the U.S. Marshal ordering the institution to give me my legal papers, it was not done. Instead C.O. Jones produced a form and demanded that I sign it to the effect that my papers had been placed in "storage".

Fearing that I would once again run afoul of some obscure rule, I asked Ms. Day for a copy of the rulebook. She angrily complied, and demanded that I read the whole book and sign it. I did read everything, but didn't sign it. There was nothing in the book about the time to request razors, but it did state that inmates were expected to shower and shave daily. It also said that inmates in E-block, where I was, were specifically permitted to have legal papers.

Winston and I were locked in our cell about 9 p.m. About two hours later C.O.s Dewey and Jones came into our cell to conduct a shakedown. Mr. Dewey informed me that they had been waiting several months for me to come to Rutland, and that the search had been ordered by Tom Terenzini. The purpose of the search was strictly harassment. First, both Winston and I had been strip-searched, had only prison-issue property (my sweatshirt had been confiscated), and virtually no opportunity to encounter any contraband. Second, there were no lockers in E-block, and the only place to have hidden anything was in the bedding or under the gym mats we slept on. These weren't searched. Mr. Dewey's comment also left no doubt that the harassment was preplanned and had nothing to do with our refusal to fill out the suicide inventory. This was curious in that I had no enemies I knew of on the prison staff. A former guard had been a frequent drinking buddy during my years in the barrooms, and we had run into Tom Terenzini on numerous occasions without any indications of animosity.

The next morning I was again denied a razor with the incredible explanation by C.O. Potter that Deputy Marshal Whelton had ordered that I not be given one, and that federal policy prohibited inmates from shaving the day of their sentencing because they might commit suicide. I was finally allowed to shave, but was not given my legal papers until about 5 minutes before the marshals arrived to take me to court. My files had been ransacked and I was unable to even reorganize them before being taken to court. On the way I told Deputy Marshal Whelton of my treatment at the Rutland jail, allegedly on his orders. He snapped, "You know better than that."

"Yes, I do," I replied, "but that's what they said."

Unfortunately, my files were not the only things in disarray. Apparently Dr. Brown had arrived in the middle of the night, and Mr. Gibson had him performing calculations just prior to the hearing. The biggest farce of all was about to begin.

Judge Billings could have added up the quantity of methamphetamine the government's witnesses said they had received from me, and sentenced me on that basis. That method was not without problems in that the biggest customer, Robert Spencer, had given so many different accounts that the judge would have been faced with the impossible task of determining which time, if any, he was telling the truth. Instead, Judge Billings decided to determine how much methamphetamine could have been manufactured with chemicals allegedly available to me. But this method had problems of its own, since the synthetic route was unknown and the differing routes had widely varying yields of methamphetamine. In addition it had to be presumed that all the chemicals were used for methamphetamine manufacture even though some had been used for polyacetylene and others had not been used for anything, remaining on my shelves on the day of the police raid. The judge was ultimately going to have to consider some very technical and conflicting expert testimony to arrive at a quantity.

I remembered working for my father in his law office and how he had prepared witnesses for trial testimony. He had gone over their testimony in detail, and had asked likely cross-examination questions so that the witness had a ready answer and wouldn't fumble on the stand. Mr. Gibson, on the other hand, could not have spent more than a few minutes preparing Dr. Brown for his complex testimony. As a result Asst. U.S. Attorney David Kirby was able to confuse Dr. Brown, the court and everyone else by asking a series of hypothetical questions and having Dr. Brown calculate the results on the stand.

While the calculations were not particularly difficult they were involved and, done hurriedly, likely to result in errors. At one point Dr. Brown asked for a recess to double check a calculation he had made just before the hearing at Gibson's request, and on another occasion was forced to admit that he had made a mistake on the stand. At the end of the day his testimony was so confusing that the Second Circuit Court of Appeals, after reading the transcript of the hearing, couldn't determine if Dr. Brown's previous mistakes had affected his final determination. The government's expert, DEA chemist Jack Fasanello, avoided a similar dilemma by stating flatly that he didn't perform calculations on the stand. The whole exercise was absurd and, notwithstanding the severity of the consequences, laughable.

There was one surprising development. The government unsealed the grand jury testimony of Mark Malmros as proof of its proposition that I deserved a sentencing enhancement for abusing my special skill as a chemist. Since I had no degree in chemistry or anything else, Mark's testimony was to demonstrate my competence. I was amazed that, in their zeal to give me more jail time, the U.S. Attorneys had handed me a tool to reduce my sentence or even obtain a new trial. The government had a well-established duty to provide exculpatory evidence, and failure to do so could result in the reversal of a criminal conviction. However, the government didn't seem worried about that possibility, and it turned out there was no reason for worry.

While I didn't know it until years later, David Gibson had actually received Mark's grand jury testimony two days before the hearing, so he wasn't surprised at all.[43] In spite of this, he made no protest to the court about the government's withholding of exculpatory evidence, and filed no motion for a new trial. Neither did he use Mark's testimony to reduce the amount of chemicals available to make methamphetamine, as obviously whatever chemicals had been used for the polyacetylene project could not have been used for anything else.

(In April of 2007 I finally obtained material from my client file that Mr. Gibson had been withholding for years, and discovered a copy of the government's petition to Judge Billings to unseal Mark's testimony, and the Judge's order.[44] These documents were sealed by the court, and my attempts to get them from the court or even determine their subject matter from prison were unsuccessful, although Mr. Gibson had them all along.)

When we returned to the jail after the hearing Deputy Whelton specifically instructed the guard at the desk that I was to have both boxes of my legal materials in my cell with me. I asked repeatedly for my documents, but again the prison staff denied them. At around midnight, guards awakened Winston and me, and he was removed from my cell with one of them muttering something about state law prohibiting two men in that cell. Although my evidentiary hearing was over, Winston had a court appearance the next day, and being rousted in the middle of the night couldn't have helped his mental clarity. The following morning, Friday, December 11, I was transported back to Ray Brook by marshals in a van along with nine other shackled inmates.

112

37

I spent only until December 16th at Ray Brook when the marshals took me again to Rutland for sentencing. I was delivered again to the state prison at Rutland, and was treated better this time, but since there was to be no hearing I had no papers, and it really didn't make much difference. Marshals picked me up the morning of the 17th, and I spent the day in their holding cell in the federal building except for the time of my appearance in court to receive my sentence from Judge Billings - 121 months, a little more than 10 years, and 5 years of supervised release, a form of probation.

I was eventually removed from the federal building and transported, not back to Rutland, but to the Addison County Jail in Middlebury, Vermont, a town famous for its liberal arts college. The Addison Jail, an old brick building on Main St., turned out to be a much better facility than Rutland. County sheriffs ran the place, but the U.S. marshals had a contract for the temporary housing of federal prisoners.

The cellblock seemed to be a very old prefab design of steel plates riveted together and formed into about 20 cells in 2 tiers. Although the block itself was locked, the lower tier cell doors were always open, and the upper tier had no doors at all. Outside the cellblock, but still in a secure section, were a shelf of well-worn books and a couple of decrepit exercise machines.

Unlike Rutland and Ray Brook, where rigid adherence to procedure was the norm, the atmosphere at Addison was relaxed. Inmates had only a few cleaning duties, but otherwise were free to watch television or read. Street clothes were allowed, and inmates could receive packages from friends or family with food, books or clothing. Particularly noteworthy were the visiting procedures. While the hours were shorter than at Ray Brook, visitors to Addison weren't given the third degree, and inmates and visitors were seated at tables. In addition the jail's proximity to Rutland made it convenient to visit for Katrina, my parents, and friends I hadn't seen for a while like Bob Firpo.

Although the visiting was unquestionably better than Ray Brook, the telephone situation was considerably worse, with but a single telephone in the cellblock, set up for collect calls only. Besides being very expensive, the calls were for all intents and purposes public as the phone was simply hanging on the wall. Upon request inmates could have private conversations with their attorneys using one of the sheriff's phones outside the cellblock, but it was common knowledge that telephones in prisons were tapped, and conversations were recorded at the discretion of the authorities. Occasional articles in the newspapers about stupid prisoners picking up additional criminal charges by making threats through the prison phones only confirmed the obvious. In theory attorney calls weren't monitored, but one had only the word of the authorities for that and, considering their overall veracity, a prudent inmate said little of importance on any prison telephone.

The only real downside of the Addison County Jail was the cramped quarters and lack of any suitable exercise facilities. There was no outdoor recreation yard at all, and the only indoor equipment was a low-end universal machine and a barely functional stationary bicycle. As a result, inmates ran up and down the stairway connecting the tiers of the cellblock and did chin-ups on a steel pipe near the shower. Addison was never intended to be a long-term federal facility, and those that spent more than a few weeks there were in protective custody awaiting a possible court appearance to testify against codefendants.

I was told later by a fellow Ray Brook inmate that my own codefendant, Robert Spencer, had been at Addison during my evidentiary hearing. Spencer had represented to David Gibson (through his attorney, William Sessions) that he was remorseful about his role in my difficulties, and could be helpful at sentencing in keeping the drug amount in the conspiracy low, but his real agenda was otherwise. According to my inmate informant, while my evidentiary hearing was under way, Spencer was on the telephone crying to his attorney that five years was too long for him to serve, and that he had to testify again to reduce his sentence. The other inmates were not impressed, and some urinated on his bed.

I suffered no such problems, although another Addison resident, Jim Nutter, began to ask a lot of questions regarding drug chemistry. In his eagerness to engage me in conversation, Mr. Nutter did a lot of talking and soon convinced me that he had had the benefit of an extensive dossier on me that could only have come from the government. Keenly aware of the Gabaree-Birbal encounter at the same institution, I gave Mr. Nutter the same respect as I would have given any poisonous snake.

While I needed no confirmation that Nutter was trying to set me up, it came anyway a few weeks later in the newspaper. According to Mr. Nutter, his daughter was a drug addict and had stored drugs in Nutter's home against his specific instructions. When the daughter was busted, she had implicated her father, and the police had found her hidden drugs in a subsequent search. However, according to the newspaper, Nutter himself had made seven sales to undercover federal agents.[45]

After enjoying the hospitality of the Addison County Jail for Christmas and New Year's, and enduring the machinations of Jim Nutter, I was transported back to Ray Brook by marshals on January 6, 1993.

114

During my absence I had been permanently designated to the Delaware Housing Unit, a considerable improvement over Ausable. My cell even had porcelain fixtures.

38

I had barely settled into Ray Brook when the news came that Judge Billings had denied my motion for a new trial on January 7, 1993. The motion had failed to mention anything about any of the problems with Dr. McMahon's testing, and relied entirely on the proposition that McMahon's illegal drug activities at the police lab "would have constituted significant grounds for impeachment of the testimony of Brendan McMahon, resulting in a severe blow to his credibility. As a result, there is a significant possibility that this information could have induced a jury to have reasonable doubt so as to avoid the convictions of the defendant."[46] Judge Billings found this to be the wrong legal standard, stating that "…evidence that bears on the credibility of a government witness but not on the substance of the government's case, will seldom warrant a new trial…Moreover, there is no indication that Dr. McMahon's trial testimony was untrue."[47]

Three weeks later, Mr. Gibson sent me a letter (dated January 27) along with "two State Police Investigation Reports concerning the State Police laboratory problems and the activities of Brendan McMahon."[48] The report from Captain James Candon was dated January 13, 1993 and that of Capt. Kerry Sleeper January 14, a week after Judge Billings had denied the motion. Although they did not so state, the reports certainly could have indicated that Dr. McMahon was too strung out from drug abuse to do his job properly. Obviously, neither report was available to David Gibson as he crafted his motion for a new trial, and neither was before Judge Billings when he decided it.

Considering the basis of Judge Billings' ruling, the contents of the police reports probably would have had no effect on the outcome, although David Gibson could not have known that when he filed the motion. And there were a couple of interesting points that I would have liked to follow up on if I had had the opportunity. According to Capt. Sleeper's report, Dr. McMahon admitted having a "substance abuse problem with cocaine" and "in June and July of 1990 removed for his personal use, cocaine from the Destroyed Evidence Locker… he voluntarily entered a substance abuse treatment program in January 1991 to resolve his problem." A glaring omission from Sleeper's report was what McMahon was doing between

July, 1990, and January, 1991, the time he was involved in the raid on my house and the subsequent testing of evidence. An interesting tidbit from the Candon report was that among the items missing from the lab was the pure methamphetamine standard used to calibrate the test instruments, and it occurred to me immediately that the source of the methamphetamine that Dr. McMahon had allegedly found in my equipment was the lab's own missing standard.

The laboratory was clearly out of control. Of the five forensic scientists employed there, at least two, Brendan McMahon and Glenn Welker, were drug addicts helping themselves to the lab's drugs. Furthermore, the Sleeper report had Dr. McMahon indicating, "Welker had often displayed the symptoms of a narcotic user while at work, i.e., drowsiness, slurred speech, cotton mouth." Ostensibly all this had gone unnoticed by lab boss Dr. Eric Buel and laboratory director Vermont State Police Capt. James Candon.

At the time it was inconceivable to me that David Gibson would never put before the court the evidence that Dr. McMahon's testing was fatally flawed, although he never did. I had no real understanding of how the criminal justice system worked, and trusted that there was some strategic reason to withhold the evidence about Dr. McMahon at the time, and as a result I continued to refine my analysis of his testing on the misguided assumption that I would eventually get a chance to use it. Shortly after the court's denial of the new trial motion I wrote to Mr. Gibson on January 28, 1993, and "briefly summarized what I now know about [the problems with] McMahon's test procedures" listing eleven separate items.[49]

39

I have since come to the conclusion that David Gibson deliberately betrayed me, but at the time I had only a vague uneasiness. I didn't understand the system and was incapable of representing myself, but things were moving ahead anyway with the appeal. My father continued to have faith in Mr. Gibson that I did not entirely share, but I didn't know where to turn. I not only was out of money, I was in debt, with a financial affidavit filed with the court at the time of my sentencing showing a debt to Katrina of $50,000, her brother $13,000 and my parents $20,000.[50] I proceeded on appeal in forma pauperis, with Gibson appointed by the court to represent me.

Knowing that Burlington attorney Mark Kaplan was involved with the American Civil Liberties Union, I wrote him on February 4, 1993

116

seeking representation. Leslie Williams of the ACLU replied on March 18 to the effect that I already had counsel, and that I "should talk it over with [my] attorney and have the attorney contact us if he feels that there is a substantial civil liberties issue involved in your case, and if he feels that ACLU involvement would be beneficial." It hardly seemed wise to alert Gibson that I was trying to replace him, so I let the matter drop.

Katrina later wrote to Harvard University professor Allen Dershowitz, who was much in the news following the release of the Oscar-winning movie *Reversal of Fortune* chronicling his successful representation of Claus von Bulow. Desperate people from all over the country must have been writing to Dershowitz, because the response Katrina got was a form letter of rejection. I was unable to come up with another plan of action, and Gibson continued on the appeal.

With the appeal pending, there was little I could do on the legal front except continue to refine my work on Dr. McMahon's testing, which was not particularly time consuming, and I returned to work at the Ray Brook prison education department. My theory of prison was that if I made good use of my time in prison it would not be wasted, and I thought that perhaps I should be pursuing some education of my own. Inger Curth, the librarian, offered to help me enroll in the college program available through the prison so that I could get my degree, but I declined, perhaps unwisely, in favor of pursuing studies on my own.

Since the Guatemala trip I had wanted to improve my Spanish language skills, and Ray Brook seemed an ideal place with its large Hispanic population. Incredibly, the education department offered English as a second language (ESL), but not foreign languages. I had heard from a friend in Ausable Unit that a Colombian in Delaware Unit was running a private class for a few inmates, and I sought him out after being relocated to Delaware myself. Jaime was a bit disillusioned by the lack of commitment of his former students, but I finally struck a deal in which he was to teach me Spanish grammar in return for my help in English pronunciation. While the university-educated Jaime's command of English and its vocabulary was better than at least half of Ray Brook's American inmates, his pronunciation left much to be desired. Our first class was February 22, 1993, and we tried to keep to a schedule of five nights a week, an hour each night.

I had also wanted to make a serious study of electronics, but had had little luck on the street. I had forgotten much of my engineering math from my university days at Cornell, and my life with Katrina and Lindsay simply didn't leave enough extra time to first review math and then go on to electronics. In prison, the challenge wasn't finding time for projects, but rather filling idle time with something worthwhile.

I had brought a college calculus book with me when I entered Ray Brook, and Jaime's brother, an engineer, had a wonderful 900-page math review text. Without bringing myself anywhere near the proficiency I had at Cornell, I was nonetheless ready to begin electronics, and coincidentally, the education department decided to offer an electronics course taught by a regular member of the department, Richard Salemi.

The course was well received by inmates with about ten times as many people signing up as could be accommodated. Someone then struck on the idea to give a math test and award the course positions to the top scorers. The test was essentially eighth-grade algebra with a little trigonometry thrown in, and I would have been able to do it easily even without my extensive math review. Unfortunately, the same was not true for most of my fellow test takers, and it was immediately determined that the mathematical aspect of the course would have to be simplified as much as possible.

By all measures the course was a success, due in no small part to the effort made by Mr. Salemi, but ours was to be the only class due to a mission change at Ray Brook. The higher security institutions were full, and the only thing that could be done in the short term was to reduce inmates' security levels whenever possible and move them to lower security institutions. If people were to be crammed together, it was best to do it in a low or minimum-security facility with relatively non-violent offenders. Medium/high security facilities like Ray Brook were left to absorb the overflow from high-security penitentiaries like Lewisburg, and inevitable changes occurred. While the level of violence at the prison went up, the level of education went down. It turned out that too few of Ray Brook's new charges had the skills to justify the electronics course, and it would have to be dropped.

40

While the education department at Ray Brook functioned relatively well, given the limitations of its students, the medical system did not. Shortly after arriving at Ray Brook I had injured both knees playing basketball. I figured I had pulled or torn something and, being in considerable pain, went to the prison hospital to at least obtain a pair of crutches. I expected that the knees would heal on their own if I could stay off them for a while, but at Ray Brook one had to walk to work, walk to eat, and generally walk to do anything.

118

I soon learned that one didn't automatically see a doctor. The first line of defense was that an inmate had to report to sick call early in the morning and sign up for treatment. The second line of defense was the team of physician's assistants, and these were the people inmates generally saw. The third line of defense was to suggest that the inmate was lying, or any other excuse to postpone meaningful treatment, and this is what happened to me. The PA started, "Can you imagine 1000 men with crutches…", and then stopped himself. Crutches were not "medically indicated", he said.

"Look," I said, " I'm not trying to get out of work. I just want to take some weight off my knees for a few days."

The final diagnosis was that I didn't need any crutches, and that I should watch the callout (daily computer printout of appointments) for an x-ray, although the x-ray wouldn't show soft tissue damage. Since the prison didn't take its own x-rays, and since the outside technician was brought in only sporadically, I was going to be in for a long wait. I returned to the housing unit and wrapped myself up with Ace bandages for about a month, leading to the atrophy of both knees.

After threatening to sue the institution, I finally got to see an orthopedist brought in from time to time to examine inmates. His recommendation was to do exercises to strengthen my knees and, while the right knee eventually healed completely, the left one still isn't right and may never be.

Considering what had happened with my knees, it was with great dread that I went to the dental clinic about a severe infection around a right lower molar, as the dentists were arguably worse than the PAs. There were only two of them for over 1000 inmates, some of whom had had little dental care, and the dentists' task was probably hopeless. On the other hand, they didn't even try. Most of their fillings were temporary and fell out after a short time, and they had been observed by more than one inmate napping in their state-of-the-art chairs.

Waits for treatment were long, unless one wanted an extraction, and then an immediate appointment was made. Not surprisingly, extraction was the recommended treatment for my infection. In an attempt to convince me, the dentist, a Dr. Cohen, hailed an overweight female guard from the hallway outside the dental clinic. After examining my x-ray, the guard agreed - extraction was the only way. I then knew why most long-term inmates wore dentures.

I wasn't anxious to begin the process of removing all my teeth, and suggested that we try an antibiotic first but, although Dr. Cohen told me he would prescribe one, he had lied. Finally I was able to get a prescription for hydrogen peroxide, which held the infection at bay without curing it and without deadening the pain. This continued for many months until finally I was able to have a root canal done while I was at the Addison County Jail in the custody of U.S. Marshals.

41

While deteriorating knees and teeth were certainly a distraction, I was more concerned with the deterioration of my domestic situation. My hopes for an early victory because of Dr. McMahon's transgressions had been dashed, and there was no particular reason for optimism although my appeal had yet to be decided. When I called home at night, frequently neither Katrina nor Lindsay was there and, although she had had a previous problem with alcohol, Katrina was out in the bars, supposedly drinking only ginger ale. Perhaps it was true for the moment, but that precarious situation wasn't likely to last without some reason for hope.

However, events were to prove that not every apparently hopeless situation was, indeed, hopeless. As I was fighting for my life in the federal appeals court, corrupt State Police chemists Brendan McMahon and Glenn Welker were plea bargaining their way into a state diversion program so that neither would have a criminal record. Federal charges certainly could have been brought, with draconian sentences to follow, but they were not. Washington County State's Attorney Terry Trono justified the scheme thusly: "We had here … not only serious drug cases, but cases where they analyzed blood in murder cases. We wanted to know whether they were tampering…We needed the immediate cooperation from those involved and we needed to get those people out of the lab as quickly as possible."[51]

While Mr. Trono might have personally wanted to know if "they were tampering", he surely didn't want anyone else to know. Besides my case, the chemists had done literally thousands of tests, all of which would have been suspect if there was admitted tampering in just one. The consequences would have been horrific, with the courts paralyzed by hundreds of motions challenging convictions, followed by the inevitable civil actions for wrongful incarceration. A similar problem had been solved in the past by granting dozens of gubernatorial pardons to victims of corrupt "supercop" Paul Lawrence.* This time, however, there were federal cases involved, and the pardons would have to come from the President of the United States. Clearly what prosecutors really wanted to

---

* Governor Thomas Salmon granted 75 pardons to Lawrence victims.

120

do was to sweep the whole matter under the rug as quickly as possible, and this is what they did.

In contrast Massachusetts authorities, recently confronted with evidence falsified by crime lab chemist Annie Dookan, performed a proper investigation even though over 30,000 cases were implicated. Ms. Dookan was sent to prison. However in Vermont Glenn Welker's lack of a criminal record allowed him to once more find employment in a position of trust until he was busted again in 2002, this time for prescription fraud. According to the *Rutland Herald* of April 20, 2002, Welker, as a nurse at Central Vermont Medical Center in Barre, had taken prescription pads from the hospital and had forged the signatures of CVMC physicians to again illegally obtain painkillers. To show they really meant business this time, prosecutors negotiated a plea deal for one to six years, all suspended except for 60 days. The article just above the Welker article in the *Herald* related that another man from the Barre area was looking at 20 years of federal prison time for possession of another painkiller, heroin, with (supposedly) intent to distribute. Apparently it paid to have friends in high places.

42

I was not aware of the scheduling of my appeal in the Second Circuit Court of Appeals in New York City, and David Gibson left me completely out of the appeal writing process. He didn't even bother to send me a copy of his brief, and the first time I saw it was on March 31, 1993, when my father brought the papers to Ray Brook. Gibson mailed the appeal to the court on April 2, precluding any comments or questions from me. Ten copies of the appeal and appendix were required by the Second Circuit and, due to the usual length of these documents, most lawyers sent appeals out to be copied and bound. This meant that by the time I got the appeal, it had already gone to the printers, and was already cast in stone.

Conspicuous by their absence were any appeal issues relating to the government's withholding of Mark Malmros's exculpatory testimony, or the lack of immunity for defense witness Sharon Stickney. I was to discover a couple of years afterwards, when I had the complete trial transcript, why the Sharon Stickney issue was never raised: Mr. Gibson had never done any legal research on the question and was unable to give Judge Billings any legal authority to grant immunity. Under the circumstances, there was nothing to appeal.

As to Mark Malmros, I never received any explanation of why that issue, of obvious importance, was never raised. I learned years later that Mr. Gibson had been given Mark's testimony prior to sentencing but, for his own reasons, Gibson had decided to keep this knowledge a secret and to make no protest despite the fact that there was still time to file a motion for a new trial for the government's deliberate withholding of exculpatory evidence.

In place of the Malmros and Stickney issues was a guaranteed loser: Gibson's contention that the conviction should be overturned because some of the evidence supporting the search warrant was "stale". Considering Mr. Gibson's abysmal performance at the suppression hearing, any appeal of that matter was going to be dead on arrival.

Notwithstanding Judge Billings' ruling on the McMahon matter, I thought I had a chance on appeal, not fully appreciating at the time that Gibson had used the wrong legal standard and that it had been vital to use my findings that McMahon's tests were fatally flawed. However, I quickly realized that I might have serious problems when I obtained the government's appeal brief. The government was arguing that Judge Billings had used the wrong methamphetamine tables in the Sentencing Guidelines, and that he should have used the "methamphetamine (actual)" tables instead of the "methamphetamine" tables. The practical effect was that the use of the "methamphetamine (actual)" tables multiplied any quantity of methamphetamine tenfold, with a correspondingly heavier prison sentence. Apparently Assistant U.S. Attorneys Gary Shattuck and David Kirby felt that ten years wasn't enough.

While I never researched the reasoning behind the two different methamphetamine schemes in the Guidelines, I assumed that it was to give a greater punishment for greater purity on the assumption that higher purity put one higher up on the supply chain. But in order to gauge the purity, one had to have a sample of the product. Since there had been no seizure of methamphetamine in my case, I couldn't understand how any guess as to how much there might have been could suddenly become "actual", and the argument seemed silly, but the potential downside was worrisome.

I should have been more worried than I was. I didn't start reading the government's brief until May 16, and Gibson filed his rebuttal on May 17 without showing it to me or even telling me that he was going to file it. A copy arrived on May 21 via my father's office, and the argument regarding the "methamphetamine (actual)" was not what I wanted or expected. I had looked up "actual" in the dictionary and had found the definition as "existing in fact and not merely potentially". I assumed that

122

since no actual methamphetamine had been found (except micrograms of unknown purity in Dr. McMahon's alleged scrapings), any guess as to the quantity that might have been made by methods unknown would be at best potential.

Mr. Gibson never made this argument. Instead, he argued that the lower court had found that the methamphetamine produced would not have been pure, and therefore not actual. Notwithstanding the finding of Judge Billings the argument was, for all intents and purposes, nonsense. Since no chemical could ever be made 100% pure, Mr. Gibson's argument, if adopted by the court, would have stripped the word "actual" of any meaning in the Guidelines - an unlikely result. Gibson was treading on dangerous ground, but he wasn't the one in line to bear the consequences; the arrow had left the bowstring, and there was little more that could be done.

My father wrote to Mr. Gibson suggesting that he raise the issue of the concealed Malmros testimony and the "actual" definition during oral arguments, but I assume he did not as there was no mention of either in the Second Circuit's eventual decision. My father must have had some misgivings about the outcome of the appeal, as he sent me a note along with Gibson's rebuttal brief indicating that he and Will Hunter were going to check again on the mysterious absence of Rutland jurors for my trial.

43

On May 26, 1993 I finally received the transcript of Dr. Brendan McMahon's trial testimony. Since the trial was over in April of 1992, it has always puzzled me as to why it took so long to prepare the transcript, but that seemed to be the pattern. My original sentencing date of November 3, 1992 had to be put off because DEA chemist Fasanello's testimony was essential, but not yet transcribed. Finally court reporter William Currie, III had prepared an advance version on December 4, just days before the hearing, but too late for me to have a copy to analyze beforehand. The official transcripts for both Fasanello and McMahon weren't prepared until February 14, 1993 and it took David Gibson another three and a half months to send me a copy of McMahon's, although he certainly knew of my interest. After finally receiving the transcript I began reading it at once and made an astounding discovery: Mr. Currie had either mistranscribed a portion of Dr. McMahon's testimony or had deliberately changed it: the testimony about the color of the Marquis reagent.

Dr. McMahon had described a screening test for methamphetamine using a test solution called the Marquis reagent. The reagent was applied to a test sample and, if it turned the proper color, further tests were performed to confirm the presence of methamphetamine. Conversely, according to McMahon, "[i]f you don't get the positive screen reaction [for methamphetamine], it's not there."[52]   My notes showed McMahon's testimony to have been that the positive screen reaction was "bright yellow", but according to the forensic literature I had been reading at Ray Brook, the proper color was orange. The significance of this was that McMahon was wrong about the color of his own screening test, and it called into question whether he had performed it at all. However, the transcript had Dr. McMahon describing the reaction as the correct "orangish color, very characteristic color".[53]

David Gibson's cross-examination of DEA chemist Jack Fasanello suggested that my notes, not the transcript, were correct. Fasanello testified that the Marquis reagent turned orange with methamphetamine, but Gibson went on to ask what turned it a yellow color.[54] There would have been no reason to ask about the color yellow - and only yellow - had Dr. McMahon not mentioned it previously. Furthermore although it was not in my notes, I recalled McMahon had stated that, in addition to methamphetamine, diphenhydramine (Benadryl) would also turn the Marquis reagent yellow. Both Fasanello[55] and the forensic literature also gave yellow as the proper color for diphenhydramine.

On May 28, two days after receiving the McMahon transcript, I called my father to report that the color had been changed and that the diphenhydramine testimony had been deleted. He, in turn, called David Gibson. Years later I obtained some of Gibson's personal notes from my client file. One was entitled "Bloomer- Misc. Notes" and was dated 5/28/93, the same day as my call. The notes mentioned the call from my father, and referred to the section of the transcript with McMahon's color testimony. They went on to show:

> Marquis reagent ▶ bright yellow vs. orange
>   DAG's notes = "yellow color"
> Q by me → anything else ▶ ?
>   diphenhydramine
> answer deleted

David A. Gibson often referred to himself as DAG in his notes. It seemed, then, that he agreed with me on both counts – the color error and the deletion of the diphenhydramine answer. However, he did nothing about it. After some prodding from my father he finally wrote to Court Reporter William Currie, III two months later on July 27, 1993:

In reviewing the transcript of the testimony of Brendan McMahon, notes taken by me and also by the defendant, are in disagreement in one notable place. The testimony is transcribed in Vol. II, page 177, at line 23. In describing the color reaction between methamphetamine and the Marquis reagent, the transcript states that it will, "turn an orangish color."

Both my notes and those of Bob Bloomer, Jr., recorded McMahon as having said, "a bright yellow color", or "yellow color".The question naturally arises as to how such a difference could occur. I would appreciate whatever advice you may be able to give me in response to this question.

Curiously, no mention was made of the deleted diphenhydramine. If there was any response by Mr. Currie, it was not in my client file by the time I finally got it many years later, and Mr. Gibson would not respond to an inquiry by me from prison in April of 1997 as to what Currie's answer (if any) had been. Mr. Currie himself claimed to have no recollection at that time. Also missing from the client file were Mr. Gibson's trial notes in connection with his cross-examination of Dr. McMahon wherein mention of the diphenhydramine should have been made. Mr. Gibson numbered the pages of his notes before I got them and, following the numbers sequentially, the notes skip from the end of direct examination to re-direct with no cross examination in between. Mr. Gibson's written list of cross-examination questions for Dr. McMahon was likewise not in the file.

There was correspondence between my father and David Gibson as well as discussions as to the ramifications of the transcript error or errors and what should be done. One suggestion was to drop Count II of the indictment, the manufacturing count. After persistent questioning by my father as to what action Gibson intended to take, he responded on October 21, 1993 that:

We can have Bill Currie sign a statement concerning the inaccuracy of the transcript relating to the test results color. I do not believe this point to be of sufficient significance to raise as an issue before the Court at this time. Nor do I believe that omission of any portion of a statement of the Assistant U.S. Attorney prior to the

reading of the transcript of the [Spencer-Galarneau] tape
recording is of significance at this time.

The matter was never "of significance" to Gibson at any time, and he
never raised the issue. I found out from a fellow prisoner in 1996 that tape
recordings were made of federal criminal trials in Vermont and wrote to
Mr. Currie to determine where mine were. Currie's reply, dated February
26, 1997:

> Regarding your three numbered queries:
>
> 1) There is no policy in the District of Vermont concerning
> backup tape recordings of trials.
>
> 2) Recordings were made during your trial.
>
> 3) There are no extant recordings of your trial. Once a trial
> has been transcribed, the tapes are reused. This has happened with
> the tapes used in your trial.

Mr. Gibson, of course, knew or should have known that there were tapes.
When he was first advised of the problem, oral arguments had not yet been
made for my appeal, and the appeal was going to be decided, at least in
part, on the transcript. It certainly would have been suspicious if the tapes
had disappeared while the appeal was still pending. However, by the time I
found out about the recordings, it was not so damning that they had been
"reused".

Certainly Mr. Currie had every incentive to destroy the tapes as
soon as possible. Besides the color change and diphenhydramine deletion,
there were other problems. David Kirby's speech to the jury about why
informant Michael Galarneau had worn the hidden microphone at Robert
Spencer's home was also missing, and according to my notes, part of the
testimony of Vermont State Police Sgt. Robert Vargo was inaccurate. In
response to a question of why Sgt. Vargo had turned over some of my
books on explosives to DEA chemist Jack Fasanello during the raid on my
house, Vargo responded according to the transcript[56]:

> For some reason, he had an interest in them...

My notes showed:

126

Fasanello liked books on explosives, so gave to him.

The warrant was for alleged drug crimes, not explosives (for which I was properly licensed), meaning that there was very questionable authority to seize the books. They were never listed as potential trial exhibits, and they were never logged into the DEA lab along with the chemical samples that Fasanello had brought back, so the books weren't being retained as evidence, but neither had Mr. Fasanello returned them.

Regardless of Fasanello's integrity or lack thereof, if this many errors, changes or deletions to the transcript could have been proved with the trial tapes, at the very least Mr. Currie's career would have been in jeopardy. And there would have been some very interesting questions. Out of all the colors of the rainbow, how did Currie happen to mistranscribe the incorrect "yellow" to the correct "orangish", considering that he could have had no personal knowledge of the correctness or incorrectness of the colors? Many years later I had the opportunity to visit with another court reporter and learned that the shorthand reporters used was phonetic, making it even less likely that any such gross mistranscription was inadvertent. Perhaps the error was only an astounding coincidence, but assuming that it was no accident, only a conspiracy involving Currie, the U.S. Attorney's office and one of the government's chemists could account for the facts.

While I was waiting for Gibson to take action on the transcript errors, the Second Circuit ruled on the appeal on August 25. As to Mr. Gibson's various attacks on my conviction, the Circuit wrote[57]:

> On appeal Bloomer challenges numerous rulings relating
> to his conviction. His claims range from attacks on the
> sufficiency of the evidence of his conviction, to charges of
> error in certain evidentiary rulings. We have carefully
> examined all of these claims and find them to be meritless.
> We discuss only his challenge to the district court's failure
> to grant a new trial based on newly discovered evidence.

As to the newly discovered evidence, the Circuit agreed essentially with Judge Billings:

> Moreover, although the evidence may have impeached
> [chemist] McMahon's credibility, it did not serve to
> contradict any of McMahon's conclusions or statements of

127

fact. As we have previously stated "[t]he discovery of new evidence which merely discredits a government witness and does not directly contradict the government's case ordinarily does not justify the grant of a new trial."

The final result was that my conviction was upheld, but the sentence was vacated and remanded. The court had bought the government's argument that the hypothetical quantities of drugs proposed by the chemists were "actual" and that the "methamphetamine (actual)" tables in the Guidelines should be used to determine my sentence. Moreover, the court found Dr. Brown's testimony so confusing that it couldn't determine whether his errors affected the final quantity accepted by Judge Billings. Unless something dramatic could be done to derail the train, I was headed for a considerably longer sentence. This time I was determined to have a much more direct role in the strategy and the proceedings.

44

While the appeal had been uppermost in my mind, it wasn't the only thing, and an incident in May had caused me to doubt the wisdom of staying at a medium security facility like Ray Brook. During a weightlifting session at the outdoor weight pavilion, my gloves had become quite greasy from one of the machines. The two Colombians with whom I often worked out usually brought new gloves, as they worked at Prison Industries (Unicor) sewing them, and helped themselves to as many as they liked. After using them once, they tossed them up into the roof over the weight pavilion, and on this occasion I didn't ask for a pair quickly enough to prevent their discard. Although both Colombians promised to bring me new ones, I thought they might forget and stood up on a weight bench, vainly trying to locate any of the discarded gloves. The Colombians walked away, thinking me silly and, after they had put about 30 yards between us, I gave up and ran to catch them.

I was intercepted by a guard. "Hold that inmate," came over the guard's radio. Meanwhile, the perimeter truck had parked by the fence adjacent to the weight pavilion and a half-dozen guards went running down. They began to poke around in the roof with long metal rods, knocking down indiscernible objects. Apparently the truck patrol had seen me fishing around in the roof overhang and assumed I was up to no good. Of course, if I had been, I would also have been much more careful about who was watching.

"Jeez, I hope there's not a knife or something up there," I said to the guard, a plump female nicknamed "Fluffy" by the inmates.

"Too bad for you if there is, Bloomer," Fluffy replied. "Guilt by association."

Apparently no contraband was found, as I was released to return to my housing unit. However, the incident was a vivid reminder that life was a bit precarious in the higher security institutions. One could be in the wrong place at the wrong time and perhaps even pick up another criminal charge. There were legitimate security concerns due to the nature of the inmates at Ray Brook, and the obvious solution to me was a transfer to someplace with a lower security level, even if it meant fewer visits. My marriage was already on shaky ground, and at the time I did not believe that the potential for more visits would change the outcome one way or the other.

It was a mystery to me why I was designated to medium-security Ray Brook in the first place, as my crimes were not violent and my sentence was "only" ten years. However, I have often suspected that there was a secret note in my file from the U.S. Attorney's office expressing a desire that I be kept at Ray Brook. Asst. U.S. Attorneys Kirby and Shattuck were obviously well aware of what they had done to obtain my conviction, and were equally aware that their tricks would not work a second time. Under the circumstances any information they could obtain about me, especially a purported confession, would be valuable in a second trial. DEA agents from Vermont were frequent visitors at Ray Brook, debriefing cooperating inmates, and it would have been a simple matter to direct some or all of them to me.

At least one was so directed in July of 1993, a Jerry Brown, which may or may not have been his real name. Upon his arrival at Ray Brook Mr. Brown hung around the Education Department for a few days, and then was assigned to work in the same classroom as I was. He wasted no time telling me that he was a methamphetamine cook for the Bandidos motorcycle gang in New Mexico, had been caught in possession of $118 million in drugs, and was sentenced to twenty-six years. He also claimed to have read my case, which was curious as the appeal had not yet been decided, much less published, meaning that the only reading he could have done would have been materials provided by his handlers in the government.

Mr. Brown also wasted no time ingratiating himself with Ray Brook's outlaw biker fraternity and white supremacists. While white supremacy literature might legitimately have been confiscated as contrary to the good order of the institution, Mr. Brown nevertheless was able to get some to share with other members of the Aryan Brotherhood.

He accosted me on several occasions, trying to engage me in conversation about drugs, the operation of the prison, my plans, or whatever else that came to his mind. I became so concerned that I wrote to both David Gibson and my father, detailing the encounters and expressing my suspicion that Brown was angling to reduce his 26-year sentence at my expense. He had already been to at least three other federal facilities, which only bolstered my opinion that he was a virtually professional informer transferring from one prison to another, gathering all the information he could about his fellow inmates. And sure enough, following a work strike at Ray Brook, Mr. Brown was shipped to yet another institution along with dozens of strike participants, although Brown himself had had little or nothing to do with the work stoppage.*

Informers and schemers would always be a danger. However, while nearby law enforcement agents or prison officials were obviously eager to please Vermont prosecutors, agents in faraway states had their own agendas and loyalties, and would have been unlikely to expend much effort on behalf of the Vermont authorities, another good reason to seek a transfer from Ray Brook.

45

The hidden hand of the U.S. Attorney's office may also have been responsible for the persistent mail problems I had encountered at Ray Brook. In theory, and in the written program statements of the Bureau of Prisons, inmates were allowed confidential communications with their attorneys. A special form, BP-493, was provided to inmates to give to their attorneys, which stated in part:

> The Bureau of Prison Program Statement on Correspon-
> dence provides the opportunity for an attorney who is
> representing an inmate to request that attorney-client
> correspondence be opened only in the presence of the
> inmate. For this to occur, Bureau policy requires that you
> adequately identify yourself as an attorney on the

---

* Time often passed quickly for connivers like Jerry Brown. His 26-year sentence ended a scant year and a half later on 2/13/95 according to the BOP's internet web site.

130

envelope and that the front of the envelope be marked "Special Mail - Open Only in the Presence of the Inmate" or with similar language clearly indicating that your correspondence qualifies as special mail and that you are requesting that this correspondence be opened only in the presence of the inmate. Provided the correspondence has this marking, Bureau staff will open the mail only in the inmate's presence...

Legal mail was routed to each housing unit's correctional counselor. A notice of legal mail was posted, and the affected inmates then went to the counselor's office. The mail was opened in front of the inmate and inspected for contraband, but not read, and was then handed to the inmate. However, numerous legal communications to me had been opened out of my presence and delivered at the normal mail call, leaving me to speculate as to whether they had been copied and sent to the U.S. Attorney's office, which certainly would have been interested in any new trial issues or sentencing strategies.

My complaints caused the prison authorities to revert to their typical defensive posture. First, the complaints were ignored. Then came a nonsensical answer: read the appropriate policy statement and follow it. Finally, Warden J.W. Tippy wrote that in order to qualify for special mail, lawyers had to "clearly indicate their SPECIFIC NAME, ATTORNEY AT LAW on the envelope, usually above the Law Office/Return Address." The Warden went on to quote the Code of Federal Regulations and a 1986 legal opinion of the General Counsel of the Bureau of Prisons to justify his position.

Thus, according to Warden Tippy, the BOP form specifically intended to advise both inmates and their attorneys about legal mail requirements was, at the very least, inadequate, if not outright wrong. Interestingly, virtually the identical form with the identical language appeared on the Bureau of Prisons' internet website in 2005, twelve years afterwards. There was no requirement that the letter indicate, "SPECIFIC NAME, ATTORNEY AT LAW" on the envelope.

Certainly a part of the mail problem was Ausable Unit's correctional counselor, Harland Smith, who was probably wound too tight for what may have been the most stressful job in the prison. I was unaware of Counselor Smith's personality at the beginning of his career, but by the time I encountered him he was a habitual liar and slacker displaying telltale signs of alcoholism. While Smith made it very clear that he didn't want to be bothered with legal mail, he nonetheless opened

131

one of my communications, read it in front of me, and then demanded that I justify why I needed the enclosed (supposedly confidential) documents from my attorney before he would give them to me.

This deliberate harassment and the lack of confidentiality of lawyer-client communications were yet more reasons to seek a transfer, but my efforts ran immediately into a roadblock. My Case Manager, Ron Lewis, had scored my security level as medium (appropriate for Ray Brook) by giving me 4 demerit points for "serious violence". However, the Bureau of Prisons Custody Classification Manual (Program Statement 5100.04), the official manual for assigning inmates' custody levels, stated in boldface type that in order to assess points for a history of violence, **"There must be a finding of guilt."** Since my drug offense was not violent, and since I had no previous convictions for violence, Mr. Lewis was clearly wrong, but initially he refused to budge. Finally, the filing of a semi-formal complaint against him got the ball rolling.

On August 9, 1993 I was called back to my housing unit from my job in education to be informed that the points for violence had been removed, I was a minimum security inmate, and that I should choose a prison camp to serve the rest of my sentence. This was excellent news, as the camps were reputed to be much more desirable than Ray Brook, and at the very least there would not be Ray Brook's obsession with security. Camps had neither fences nor perimeter patrols, and inmates were largely on the honor system.

To whatever extent the rumors had been true previously about golf courses and a five-star lifestyle at the "Club Fed" Allenwood Camp in Central Pennsylvania, this was definitely not the case in 1993. However, some camps had the reputation of being more lax than others, and on that basis I chose McKean Camp in Western Pennsylvania. (Otisville Camp near Newburgh, New York would have been much closer, but was mysteriously unavailable to anyone I knew who had tried to transfer there.)

While I thought it would only be a short while until I was transferred, a month and a half went by. Then Mr. Lewis informed me that I wouldn't be going to camp after all, but might get a gate pass, a highly undesirable development. With the gate pass I would work daily outside the prison in the warehouse or maintaining the grounds, and be unable to do any work on my legal projects. Worse, I would still be living in the same housing unit within the prison and subject to the same security mania of the staff and the same machinations of schemers trying to curry favor with the Vermont authorities.

Less than a week later, on September 26, I got more bad news: Katrina announced during a visit that she wanted a divorce. While certainly not a welcome development, it was hardly a surprise. Our relationship had become more and more strained, and there was little reason to be optimistic. My new-trial motion regarding Dr. McMahon had been brushed aside, McMahon himself had received a very light slap on the wrist, I was looking at a significantly longer prison sentence, and the legal system appeared more and more to be rigged. Although I didn't know it at the time, David Gibson himself gave Katrina little hope, telling her at one point that the likely outcome of my resentencing following the Second Circuit's instructions might be imprisonment for "15, 20, 25 years". Adding to Katrina's burden, the previously well-adjusted Lindsay was now having problems at school and was frequently subjected to taunts from classmates due to my situation.

I hadn't much time to consider my divorce, as the next day Mr. Lewis informed me that I was going to camp after all. It took another month, but on October 25 my name appeared on the Callout for "Laundry" and the Change Sheet showed my job had changed from "Education" to "Unassigned" – sure signs of an impending transfer. I went to the prison laundry as directed and turned in all my prison issued clothes in favor of travel clothes – a gigantic one-size-fits-all pullover shirt, baggy pants a foot too long with an elastic waistband, and "felony flyers", rubber soled sneakers with elastic/canvas uppers. I also turned in my personal property to R & D and awaited my transfer.

The next day I was able to ascertain that a prison bus had left very early in the morning as it usually did, but of course I had not been on it. Inquiries to my housing unit administrative team produced no answers. I then had to make arrangements to be reissued prison clothing and to pick up my personal property, and I also wanted to preserve my desirable job in education. I had finally burned out teaching reading to students with severe learning disabilities, and had landed a job as clerk for the horticulture instructor. The job and my boss, Mrs. Robinson, were not demanding, leaving me with free time and, best of all, my own electric typewriter – a highly prized machine for anyone doing legal work.

Finally, on November 10, the mystery of my non-transfer was solved when two U.S. Marshals showed up at Ray Brook and took me to the Addison County Jail in Middlebury, Vermont to await resentencing. At the time, I thought the whole episode was a trick orchestrated by the U.S. Attorney's office, but it turned out to be innocent enough. I had, in fact, been designated to Lewisburg Camp in Central Pennsylvania and my personal property was shipped there in my absence.

Later I learned that two weeks after the Second Circuit's mandate, Judge Billings had issued a writ on October 4th ordering the U.S. Marshals to produce me in court on November 29th for resentencing. It's possible that the marshals were advised of my impending transfer and put a hold on me, or the timing may have been coincidental. Either way, the marshals certainly preferred to transport me from Ray Brook to the court in Rutland rather than from Central Pennsylvania, a trip that would likely have required one of the marshals' "con air" flights.

46

The transfer to Addison County Jail did not interfere with my resentencing preparations, as I had already done about everything I could do. Nearly a year before, I had typed up an extensive set of questions intended to discredit DEA chemist Jack Fasanello, and had sent them to David Gibson. I had also written to Gibson stating my fear that I might receive a much longer sentence and, by letter of September 6, 1993 laid out four avenues I wanted pursued.

My preference at the time was to try to make a deal with new U.S. Attorney Charles Tetzlaff to leave my sentence at ten years "in that my risk exposure [wa]s so high". I made it clear to Gibson that "[a]t this point I have absolutely no faith in the legal system, and prefer not to risk the rest of my life on arbitrary rules and wild conjecture", and I thought Tetzlaff might go for it in the interest of fairness considering all the shenanigans that had gone on in my case. U.S. Senator Patrick Leahy had publicly expressed his disapproval of former U.S. Attorney George Terwilliger, and Leahy had been instrumental in the appointment of his successor, Mr. Tetzlaff, who was ostensibly going to correct the abuses of the Terwilliger administration. Tetzlaff had only recently been sworn in on August 16th.

If a deal couldn't be reached, I proposed three other avenues to keep the sentence low: show my chemicals were used for something else than drug manufacture, "attack McMahon's testing as unreliable", and "exploit ambiguities in the sentencing guidelines concerning methamphetamine, methamphetamine (actual), d-methamphetamine," etc.

At my request Bob Firpo had contacted Mark Malmros and he was willing, if not exactly eager, to testify about using various chemicals for the polyacetylene project. Clearly if they had been used for that purpose, they would have been unavailable for any other, and this would have confounded any attempt by the court to estimate the amount of methamphetamine that might have been made from my chemicals. I had wanted to talk with Mark myself, but thought it unwise to discuss exactly

134

what his recollection was on the tapped prison phones, and relied on David Gibson to follow up with Mark. He never did.

Also, Gibson still hadn't brought my evidence that Dr. McMahon's chemical testing was at least flawed, if not rigged, to the attention of the court, and I thought this was an excellent time to do so, as the sentencing schemes for stimulant drugs varied widely. If Dr. McMahon's testing was flawed, how could he be sure that he had correctly identified the drug residues as methamphetamine instead of the very similar phentermine, which carried a much lower prison sentence?

In retrospect the resentencing hearing was probably not the place to raise the question of the accuracy or integrity of the chemical testing as the case had been remanded for a narrow purpose, and probably the proper avenue would have been to bring the matter to the attention of the court by motion. However, at the time Gibson had not discussed his resentencing strategy with me, and I was ignorant of the correct approach. But regardless of the approach, Dr. Brown was going to be needed again for resentencing, and this time I was determined to discuss my chemistry concerns with him personally, instead of using David Gibson as an intermediary. Consequently, when Gibson wrote to Dr. Brown on November 8, 1993 he asked that Brown arrive in Vermont a day early so that he could meet with me at the Addison County Jail; Gibson indicated that he also "want[ed] to be on hand" for our meeting.[58]

Again looking backward, my final suggested strategy might have been the best to use at resentencing: exploit inconsistencies in the Sentencing Guidelines regarding methamphetamine. The reality of the federal courts was that claiming actual innocence was the strategy least likely to be successful, with the courts preferring to grant new trials or reduced sentences on technical procedural issues, and the Guidelines had some glaring inconsistencies concerning methamphetamine.

The essence of the argument was that methamphetamine existed in two isomeric forms, d and l, and the Guidelines treated the l-isomer more leniently than the d-isomer. Absent any chemical testing demonstrating which isomer was the drug in question, the judicial rule of lenity required that a criminal defendant receive the lesser of two possible sentences when the situation was ambiguous. In my case, no testing had been done on the alleged residues to identify which isomer was present, and Dr. McMahon had destroyed his test samples before trial, meaning there was no way that the isomers could ever be identified.

A fellow inmate at Ray Brook had given me a case in Virginia where his codefendant had raised the d/l isomer issue, and it was so compelling that the U.S. Attorney had capitulated without an argument. I

135

had included relevant materials from the case with my letter to Gibson, including the U.S. Attorney's response. Using the l-isomer tables, and assuming that Judge Billings again guessed the quantity of methamphetamine involved in my case to be about 500 grams, my base offense level would have been a Level 8, instead of a Level 26 or higher. Adding 2 points for the abuse of a special skill, my offense level then would have been 10 with a recommended sentencing range of 6 to 12 months, a definite improvement over the 10 years I had been previously been given and the possible life term I faced.

The d/l question eclipsed the "methamphetamine (actual)" question in that the new inquiry became: what actually was the methamphetamine - d or l? The Third Circuit Court of Appeals decided a New Jersey meth manufacturing case with essentially the same issues as mine in late 1994, and resolved the conflicts in the Guidelines by declaring that methamphetamine (actual) meant d-methamphetamine.[59] Even this result, while not as favorable as the Virginia case, would have cut the quantity of methamphetamine in my case in half.

I was unaware of the d/l issue at the time of my earlier sentencing, and don't believe that the issue had been raised until afterward in any jurisdiction. It could therefore have been raised legitimately with Judge Billings at my resentencing as new law relevant to my sentence. There remained the question of the mandatory minimum sentence for methamphetamine, but it turned out that it, too, was flawed for different reasons. Under the circumstances even if the mandatory minimum applied, it would have been five years, not ten.

With all these alternatives I was cautiously optimistic about the outcome of the resentencing, and awaited a visit from David Gibson, as a visit was the only secure way to converse. The cellblock at Addison had a telephone hanging on the wall for collect calls only, but anyone could hear the conversations. Worse, the calls were most likely recorded, and one had to assume that they were. There was a plaque over the phones at Ray Brook informing users that the calls were monitored, and during my stay there a part of the library was walled off to permit the installation of state-of-the-art recording equipment for inmate calls. Calls at the state prison in Rutland were also monitored, and it would have been extremely naive to think that any prison telephone offered any privacy. For delicate discussions of strategy, a meeting was the only safe way.

I was not surprised that David Gibson had not rushed to Addison to see me, as sentencing was several weeks away. Then, on November 24, he filed a motion to postpone sentencing further as he was expecting a disclosure of information concerning my chemical orders pursuant to the

136

Freedom of Information Act, and in "order for the sentencing Court to have the benefit of all relevant information, it is respectfully submitted that the date for sentencing should be postponed for 30 days".[60] Judge Billings obliged by pushing the hearing back a month to January 4, 1994.

Finally, I thought, Gibson and I were on the same page. I knew that the government had not produced all the chemical orders, and I was anxious to see why, and what they might show. If there were something wrong with the government's evidence of the chemical orders, they could not be used as the basis for any laboratory capacity estimates, and the "methamphetamine (actual)" tables would have been removed from consideration, certainly a welcome result.

47

Although Gibson did not come to visit me, time passed quickly at Addison, and when I first I arrived my primary concerns were dental. I had endured considerable pain at Ray Brook with a severely infected lower molar, and that pain followed me to Addison. I had been scheduled for a root canal at Ray Brook, but that had been canceled, first because of my impending transfer to Lewisburg Camp, and then because of my transfer to Addison. However, considering the runaround Ray Brook's dentists had given me, anything but tooth extraction at that institution was pure conjecture.

My father had some influence with the U.S. Marshal, and arranged that I be treated at Addison while I was in the marshal's custody. Just two days after my arrival a sheriff's deputy transported me to the office of Dr. Harvey Green a few doors down from the jail but, since I was a federal prisoner, the sheriffs had to follow federal procedures. I was shackled hand and foot, not only for the brief trip, but for the examination as well. Dr. Green initially prescribed antibiotics and then, a month later, performed the long overdue root canal. Meanwhile there was enough to distract me from my dental problems.

My close proximity to Rutland, and the informality of Addison made it easy for people to visit and Katrina came a couple of times, not mentioning our prospective divorce. I also saw friends that I had not seen for some time. Any visitors at Ray Brook had to be on the approved visiting list, which in turn required submitting a form with personal information authorizing the institution to do a background check, and I suspected that this might have intimidated some people, especially those who knew the details of what had gone on in my case.

Although it might have been easier at Ray Brook, Addison did allow me to continue my investigation into the peculiar mail problems that I had encountered at Ray Brook in connection with my Freedom of Information Act requests to the Drug Enforcement Administration (DEA). I had filed my first request shortly after entering prison, but the result had been a stack of papers with more than half the items blacked out. On some pages, virtually everything was blacked out. However, during the summer the U.S. Supreme Court had decided a case[61] that had changed the landscape by ruling that the FBI (and by extension all federal law enforcement agencies) could not simply declare all sources of information to be confidential and thus exempt from disclosure. With that in mind, I had some hope that I might fare better with a new request. On the other hand, I doubted that the DEA would be brought to heel without a struggle, and suspected it would continue with its various tricks to delay the process and to avoid producing much information.

On June 9, 1993 I had sent out three FOI requests for myself (to the DEA, FBI, and ATF) and two DEA requests I had prepared for other inmates. By June 25th all had been acknowledged except mine to the DEA. On July 8th I sent another request, this time certified mail, return receipt requested. I did get a stamped receipt from the Ray Brook Post Office, but received nothing from the DEA - neither an acknowledgement of the FOI request, as required by law, nor the certified return receipt showing delivery.

I wrote the prison mailroom on July 22, asking what had become of my mail and, although I received no response, the return receipt was delivered at mail call on the 27th. While it appeared to be the original in my handwriting, it lacked a postmark, delivery date or signature, indicating to me that it had never left the prison.

Not hearing from either the DEA or the mailroom for more than a month, I wrote to the postmaster at Ray Brook on October 15 explaining my problem and asking if he "ever had the letter and, if so, exactly what was done with it and the return receipt." The reply was a scrawled, unsigned note at the bottom of my letter stating that I should ask the mail room for a "TRACER (PS FORM 1510)" I had sent a similar request to the mail room on the same date, and had received the reply of "Send out a Tracer Form".

I sent another letter to the postmaster on the 26th informing him that other inmates had experienced similar problems, and I requested the internal USPS logging procedures for certified mail so that I could request the proper documents. I also asked that he/she sign any further communications. Mr. Al Stans responded the next day that certified mail

138

was only logged at the last post office, and that a form 1510 could be sent there for proof of delivery.

I had sent Mr. Stans a completed 1510 on November 4, but was transferred before I received any response. However, I had directed the prison mailroom to forward any mail to my home address, and no response had arrived there either by December 20. I wrote again to Mr. Stans on that date from the Addison County Jail to inquire about my 1510, and asked that any further correspondence be mailed to my father's law office as "the latest problem fuels my suspicion that I am a victim of mail tampering."

In the meantime, I had discovered that anyone could file an inquiry as long as he/she had the certified number of the letter, and I had asked my mother to make an inquiry through the post office in Rutland, Vermont. Strangely, the reply had come from the DEA, and contained a purported copy of the return receipt showing delivery on July 13. Mother had gone back to the post office to ask why, if a question concerning mail was asked of the Postal Service, the DEA would respond? The answer was, "The Postal Service and the Justice Department work pretty closely together." That interesting comment made me more determined to pursue an answer through Mr. Stans and the Ray Brook post office.

My investigation dragged on a couple of more months, but I was able to discern that Mr. Stans received a response to my tracer from 1510 and mailed it to me at Ray Brook, which I never got at any time. After receiving my letter from Addison, Stans sent another 1510 and this time directed the answer to my father's law office. According to the form, my FOI request had been delivered on July 13th, and the person accepting my letter was "Jackson".

I hadn't much faith that prison officials would follow the law, but this episode caused me to doubt the integrity of the postal system itself. In the final analysis certified mail wasn't a guarantee of anything, at least if the mail was deposited in a prison's mailbox. This skepticism later served me well when the Second Circuit Court of Appeals began to play games of its own.

48

I had a final project to keep me busy at the Addison County Jail: responding to interrogatories in my suit against Pollution Solutions and the State of Vermont. My father had filed the suit on my behalf during the summer alleging, "on or about August 11, 1990 defendants converted to their own use many chemicals, laboratory equipment and glassware in

139

excess of $10,000 in value, the property of the plaintiff." The plan was to fight back where we could and, through the discovery process, obtain information that we had been unable to get through the federal system.

Shortly after the suit began, Pollution Solutions filed a cross complaint against the State claiming that it was "acting solely upon the express instructions of the State". The State then filed its own claim against Pollution Solutions alleging the "State at no time has ordered any of these seized items destroyed. All were to be stored pending the conclusion of the litigation which is presently ongoing, as an appeal of the criminal conviction is being resolved." From my point of view, the fact that the State and Pollution Solutions were fighting was to my advantage. And it was inescapable that, as I had been trying to recover my property, and as the state and federal government had been representing to the court that my retained property was necessary to the investigation, it was being systematically destroyed.

It would have been nice to have a little favorable publicity just before my resentencing, or at least some balanced reporting. Instead, on November 7, the *Burlington* [Vermont] Free *Press* published a Sam Hemingway column entitled "The Bloomers can't put case behind them". The column began:

> Maybe the venerable Bloomer family of Rutland is just suffering from a severe case of denial. Then again, maybe the reason for filing what has to be one of the more curious lawsuits in recent memory involves some indefatigable point of family pride or legal principle. Either way you look at it, the case of Robert A. Bloomer, Jr. vs. Pollution Solutions of Vermont and the state of Vermont, now showing in Rutland Superior Court, is a tragi-comedy in the making.

Hemingway went on the recap my conviction on drug charges, and went on to erroneously state as fact that the appeals court agreed that a "longer sentence was in order". He then included an astounding quote from Pam Linton, president of Pollution Solutions:

> "It's absolutely amazing," said Pam Linton, president of Pollution Solutions, a Williston hazardous waste disposal firm brought in by the state to clean up the mess. "He's guilty as hell, and he's trying to come after us, and we were the ones that protected that neighborhood from

140

blowing up." Linton estimated that beyond the illegal drug issue, there were enough explosives in the home to have blown up half a city block. "This was a very serious situation," she said. "It was as bad as any drug-related incident we've been involved with."

Hemingway ended the piece with "Or maybe the Bloomer clan just doesn't get it."

Actually, it was Hemingway who didn't get it. Pam Linton had greatly exaggerated the role of her company, which had only hauled away chemicals and glassware piled in my driveway by the police. Furthermore, there was nothing on the Pollution Solutions inventory about explosives, much less enough to "have blown up half a city block". Had Pollution Solutions actually transported explosives without listing them on the manifest and without using the appropriate hazardous materials placards, it would have been in violation of federal law.

Two and a half months after the Hemingway column, on January 18, 1994, Pollution Solutions itself was raided and "investigators from the EPA and U.S. Customs seized more than 100 documents" according to Hemingway's employer, the *Burlington Free Press*. The *Rutland Herald* ran a detailed article on January 22 stating that "an affidavit unsealed in U.S. District Court Friday alleges company personnel falsified records to mislead environmental officials, disguised hazardous waste as 'bookends' when they shipped chemicals to Canada and imported waste containing lead for illegal disposal..." The article further revealed that the company had received notices of alleged violation in 1991 and 1992, one of which was that "the hazardous waste inventory did not accurately reflect the waste in storage at the time of the inspection ".

(Despite a $60,000 fine, Pollution Solutions continued its errant ways until it was finally liquidated in 1998. According to the March 6, 1998 issue of the *Burlington Free Press* "Inspectors found pools of unidentified waste collecting in areas near the company's loading docks, corroding barrels, and barrels improperly stored. Inspectors also found hazardous material not labeled as such...". The mendacious Pamela Linton was barred from the industry for 5 years, but never went to prison.)

Without regard to the opinions of government stooges in the press, my suit against Pollution Solutions went forward, and one of the things I was supposed to be working on at Addison was a valuation of my property stolen, damaged or destroyed by Pollution Solutions and/or agents of the State. One way would have been to order various chemical and laboratory equipment catalogs, hope the companies would send them to a prison

141

address, and hope that the prison authorities would let me have them, or some variation on that theme with my father trying to order catalogs he didn't understand. At the very least this way was going to be time consuming, and it occurred to me that I could come up with at least a preliminary valuation by using the government's trial exhibits of chemical and equipment orders. In that regard, I had asked David Gibson for copies of the exhibits, and had received them.

The day after Christmas I was going through the trial exhibits of orders I had purportedly placed with Alfa Products, when an astounding anomaly jumped off the page. Although the shipping address for the chemicals was my company, Soron Engineering, in West Rutland, Vermont, the buyers of some of the chemicals were shown to be a D. Hapatunian or Harotunian in Danvers, Massachusetts and an M. Keefe. I did not know the mystery buyers, and knew no one at all in Danvers, although I did know that it was the location of Alfa Products.

A company records clerk, Vincent Ronayne, had testified at my trial about the procedure by which Alfa accepted orders, shipped them and generated documents. Nothing in his testimony explained how anyone but the actual buyer would be listed as the buyer, and nothing in his testimony described any process by which extraneous names would be placed on invoices. The company supposedly retained a copy of the invoice sent to the buyer as its record of the transaction. Certainly I had never received any invoices from Alfa showing anyone as the buyer but my company or myself, so these were not records of any transactions that I had made. It was thus inescapable that, to the extent that the invoices were supposed to represent my dealings with Alfa, they were not genuine.

The order for methylamine allegedly placed by Allan Hobson, d/b/a Vermont Solar Engineering, the chemical order that had ultimately determined my sentence the first time around, was similarly tainted. While the shipping address was that of Vermont Solar in Rutland, Vermont, the SOLD TO box on the invoice showed:

VERMONT SOLAR ENGINEERING, INC.
SEND INVOICE TO M. KEEFE
DANVERS   MA 01923

Vincent Ronayne had testified specifically in connection with this invoice, but again had given no mechanism by which the name of Keefe would appear as the buyer if he were not, in fact, the buyer. Of course, Mr.

142

Ronayne was never asked at trial about Keefe, and neither was Allan Hobson. I was never given readable copies of the documents prior to trial and was never shown the government's exhibits during trail, so I was unaware of the mystery buyers at the time. David Gibson asked to see the invoices at the time they were offered as evidence, meaning that either he didn't look at the them carefully, or he was aware of the discrepancies and decided to say nothing.

Although I had been at Addison for nearly two months, Mr. Gibson had not visited me and had given no time when he planned to visit, although my resentencing date was fast approaching. Under the circumstances I thought I had no choice but to use the telephone to advise Gibson immediately that the invoices were not genuine. His response was alarming. "Well, those are just those chemical orders," he said. "Yes," I replied, "the ones they're using to determine my sentence." I knew immediately that something was terribly wrong and returned to my cell to contemplate my next move.

I had another reason to doubt Gibson's competence, if not his loyalty. On December 8, without consulting me first, he had filed a motion for a new trial alleging irregularities in the jury selection for my trial. My father had hired private detectives to get statements from the jurors, and there was no doubt about what had happened. According to Gibson's motion some of the jurors from the Rutland area were not notified to appear for the selection of the jury, at least one was instructed not to appear, and one from North Clarendon reported for service even though she had not been summoned. "The name of the North Clarendon juror did not appear on the roster of potential jurors from the March 1992 panel and was not called during the selection process." Gibson concluded, "the inference may be drawn that prospective jurors of the areas of the City of Rutland, Town of Rutland, Town of West Rutland, and surrounding communities were deliberately excluded from the array of jurors from whom a jury was to be selected in this case."[62]

While it was certainly appropriate to bring the jury-rigging to the attention of the court, the timing could not have been worse as I was looking at what could have amounted to a life sentence, largely to be determined by the whim of Judge Billings. And Judge Billings, as Chief Judge, was required by law[63] to supervise and control the jury selection process. Gibson was therefore asking him to rule on a matter for which he had the ultimate supervisory responsibility, a matter going to the heart of the integrity of his court.

I have always been baffled as to why Gibson would provoke the wrath of Judge Billings just before my resentencing when there was no reason to do so, and it was all the more baffling why he would do so and not simultaneously ask Billings to remove himself from the case. Of course, the judge should have stepped down automatically under the circumstances, but he didn't.

The prudent strategy would have been to let Judge Billings pronounce sentence, and then file the motion alleging jury tampering. As it was, Gibson's motion was incompetent on its face. The motion had been brought pursuant to 28 U.S.C. §2255, which was an attack on my sentence, except that I didn't have a sentence because the Second Circuit had vacated it. It turned out that this was the least of my problems, although I didn't know it at the time. What I did know was that I was headed for disaster.

The same numbness began to set in that plagued me during trial. It was clear enough to me where things were going, but once again my attorney seemed oblivious to the obvious. On December 28, I wrote a letter to David Gibson in longhand to document my findings about the chemical orders and my instructions to Gibson, as I was quite sure that I was going to need it later. The sheriff's deputies at Addison made me copies, one of which I sent to my father's office to be preserved in case the others turned up missing. The letter read, in its entirety:

Dear Dave:

I would like you to file a motion immediately to postpone my resentencing on the basis that the DEA has still not provided any documents from my file. LaMoria's affidavit for the search warrant indicates that the file contains information relating to chemical orders placed by the Hobsons and myself. As you recall, the government is basing its guess as to drug quantity on these orders.

Also, I have just discovered that at least my copies of the Alfa (Morton Thiokol) billing invoices are forgeries of some sort. The early orders show SOLD TO: D. Hapatunian(?) Danvers, MA 01923. Later invoices show an F. or M. Keefe. The 1984 orders have a label of some sort pasted over the SOLD TO space with SORON ENGINEERING, etc. typed in much darker than the rest of the document. The Hobson order also shows M. Keefe, Danvers, MA.

I never knowingly stipulated that these documents with someone else's name on them were accurate. Also, I deny I ever received any billing invoices with some type of label pasted or stuck on them. [AUSA Gary] Shattuck apparently offered these into evidence as original documents (Tr. V P90) which they are not. Also, at least one order of

144

mine (I have the cancelled check) has been concealed along with, I
believe, one or more orders placed by the Hobsons.

If Judge Billings will not postpone the hearing, [Morton records clerk]
Vincent Ronayne should be subpoenaed, along with whatever records he
provided in connection with his Grand Jury subpoena. I think Gary
Shattuck should be subpoenaed also, along with the supposed original
documents used as evidence at my trial. Perhaps the Hobsons should be
subpoenaed to ascertain if they know anyone named Keefe, especially
since their document is labeled a "duplicate invoice".

I would like to visit with you prior to the hearing so that I can provide the
maximum amount of help to you, and therefore myself.

Sincerely yours,
Bob Jr.

     My recollection at the time was not completely clear regarding the
stipulations. I remembered that Gibson had sent mostly unreadable copies
of the chemical invoices and had wanted me to sign stipulations, but I had
refused. I also remembered that the chemical invoices were used at trial
pursuant to some kind of stipulation, but I had not seen it. What was most
confusing was that I believed that I had to sign the stipulations myself, and
yet I had no memory of having done so. It turned out that, after my
refusal, Gibson had signed them himself as my attorney, and had neither
informed me nor given me copies. It also turned out that the stipulations
Gibson had signed were different than the ones he had shown me while
seeking my consent, and in fact he had stipulated only to orders the
government wanted to use in the prosecution, omitting others useful to the
defense. Years later AUSA Gary Shattuck wrote in an affidavit that,
contrary to his statement to the trial court, the government didn't have the
originals of many of the invoices I claimed were forgeries, only copies.
But the question remains to this day, copies of what? And where did the
copies come from?
     David Gibson now had a serious problem. He had defied the
express wishes of his client and secretly stipulated to the accuracy of
documents that were obviously not genuine. And the documents affected
not only the sentencing, but also the trial itself. The proper course for
Gibson to follow would have been to withdraw immediately from further
representation. With another attorney, the matter could have been fully
presented to the court, and the court could have taken the appropriate

action. However, this would have almost certainly led to a civil action against David Gibson for incompetence or worse, and possibly a disciplinary sanction.

I spoke to David Gibson on the telephone on December 30 regarding my sentencing, but didn't get into much substance because of my distrust of the prison phones. I had told him both verbally and in writing that I wanted a meeting, and we had a lot to talk about, but I waited in vain for a visit from Mr. Gibson. Neither did he file anything with the court regarding the chemical orders.

Doctor Brown showed up alone at the Addison County Jail on the afternoon of January 4, 1994. Despite Mr. Gibson's previous written indication to Dr. Brown that he "want[ed] to be on hand" for the meeting, Gibson never arrived. I had a discussion with Dr. Brown regarding Dr. McMahon's testing, and he was not impressed. In particular he agreed with me that if Dr. McMahon had done his gc-ms testing the way he had testified, he would have obtained no result at all for methamphetamine. I had also wanted Dr. Brown to explain to the court about d and l methamphetamine in connection with the argument I expected David Gibson to make to the court. However without Mr. Gibson there, the conversation was futile as neither Dr. Brown nor I could make the presentation alone.

I began to panic after a while, and more so after I couldn't reach Mr. Gibson at his home or office. In desperation I called my father, and he was eventually able to contact Gibson, who claimed to be unable to attend the meeting due to automotive transmission problems. Whatever car trouble Gibson might have had seemed to vanish as soon as my meeting with Dr. Brown was over, as Gibson met with Dr. Brown in Rutland, a scant thirty miles south of Addison County Jail, that very evening. Given that I was facing a potential sentence of life in prison, Gibson's excuse was ridiculous. Not only could he have borrowed or rented a car if necessary, but my father or one of my brothers would have driven to Brattleboro to pick him up if no other way could have been found to get him to Middlebury.

49

The next morning it was the same story. The marshals transported me from Addison to the courtroom in Rutland and placed me in their holding cell across the hall from the courtroom. I was there at least a half hour before the hearing, but Mr. Gibson never came to see me. Our first encounter was in the courtroom as the hearing was beginning and there was no time to talk.

David Gibson called Dr. Brown to the stand, and for a moment I had a glimmer of hope as he was actually eliciting some testimony about the d and l forms of methamphetamine, but that hope was very short lived. Gibson had filed no sentencing memorandum with the court or otherwise brought to Judge Billings' attention the inconsistencies in the Sentencing Guidelines concerning the isomeric forms of methamphetamine, so that Dr. Brown's testimony on the subject was no more than gobbledygook with no apparent connection to sentencing issues. The court would have been bound to at least consider legal precedent in the form of the Virginia d/l case, but it was not obligated to decipher irrelevant chemical testimony, and by all outward appearances it did not. Gibson moved on, and that was the end of the issue, but not because he had some other winning strategy.

It quickly became obvious that Dr. Brown was essentially going to repeat his earlier testimony, a strategy virtually guaranteed to get me a much longer prison sentence, as much of what Gibson elicited was a rehash of his purity arguments that had already been rejected by the Second Circuit. It was equally obvious that Judge Billings considered the question before him as very narrow, and that he had pretty much made up his mind before the hearing. Finally, since Gibson had given Judge Billings no reason to change his preconceived notions, it was obvious that I was going to be hammered. Katrina knew it, too, after talking with David Gibson, and didn't attend the hearing to see the gory details of exactly how badly I was going to be beat up.

Things weren't headed in a favorable direction by the morning recess, and Gibson spent most of that brief respite talking with Dr. Brown about his upcoming testimony. The whole proceeding was pretty much locked up, and there was little I could do to change it. Judge Billings announced that he was not going to revisit the question of which method I had used to produce the methamphetamine; he was going to stick with his earlier finding of the aluminum amalgam method. The only real question left was the same one at the original sentencing: what ratio of methylamine to P-2-P had been used? And that refocused me on the utter absurdity of the whole exercise. The ratio was impossible to know in any case, and it was even impossible to guess with any degree of confidence without a sample of the methamphetamine product, and yet this indulgence in pure speculation was going to determine my prison sentence.

It seemed as though Asst. U.S. Attorney David Kirby was aware of the d/l issue, because he asked of Dr. Brown: "So that can you tell the

147

Court whether, in your opinion, under the guidelines there is in the determination of actual methamphetamine, that there is any relevance of whether it is d or l methamphetamine?"

Before Dr. Brown could answer, David Gibson objected: "Your Honor, we would object. We think that that's a question for the Court." The Court overruled the objection and Dr. Brown answered: "With all certainty, I don't know what the correlation is between d and l and actual and a mixture of that stuff, meth."[64]

So, not only had Gibson failed to make the legal argument regarding the d/l issue, he hadn't spent any time preparing Dr. Brown to provide the expert chemical underpinnings either. I wasn't surprised when Gibson didn't spend any part of the lunch recess discussing the hearing with me, but I was certainly disappointed that he didn't use the time to coach Dr. Brown regarding the d/l matter.

When court reconvened after lunch, it was already snowing hard, and Judge Billings announced that after Dr. Brown concluded, he would recess until the following day. David Kirby resumed his cross-examination regarding the effects of the purity of the starting chemicals on the eventual yield of methamphetamine, and soon took an interesting direction. He had marked as exhibits 1, 2 and 3 some of my alleged chemical orders to Alfa Products for benzyl chloride, and had Dr. Brown look at them to confirm that the purity had been listed as 97%. I never saw the hearing exhibits but, assuming that Kirby was using the government's exhibits from trial, some had to have shown the buyers to be the mysterious Keefe or Harotunian.

This would have been a perfect opportunity for Gibson to have "discovered" a problem with the invoices, as court procedure allowed him to examine documents and object before witnesses were questioned about them. He never asked to look at them, never made any objection, and never notified the court despite the fact that my written instructions to do so were barely a week old. Neither did Gibson revisit the d/l question with Dr. Brown although, again, he had the perfect opportunity to do so on redirect because of David Kirby's question.

After Dr. Brown finished, the Court recessed until 9:30 the following morning, and I was taken back to the marshals' holding cell across the hall from the courtroom. Through the second floor window I could see an accumulation of several inches of snow, and the storm was still going full force. I had expected that Mr. Gibson would stop to see me immediately following the hearing, but he hadn't arrived as the marshals were preparing to move me.

148

"I've got to wait for my attorney," I told them. "You saw how it went today. I've got to talk to him before tomorrow."

Paul Whelton replied, "We have to move you right away. This storm is getting worse. I'll go look for Mr. Gibson."

Five or ten minutes later Whelton returned. "Mr. Gibson is not in the building," he said. "I even went down to the first floor. We've got to leave right now."

Although I had assumed that I would be going to the Addison County Jail, instead I went only the half-mile or so separating the court from the Rutland state lockup where I had had problems before. I told Paul Whelton, "I don't think this is a good idea. You know what happened before." The marshals didn't answer, and I was dropped off at the prison.

This time things were a little different, undoubtedly because of the lawsuit. The guards were very friendly, and I was placed alone in a large holding cell with two bunk beds facing the intake desk. There was some occasional activity at the desk, and the lights were on all night, but otherwise it was quiet and I was left alone. The next morning I was allowed to shower and shave without harassment, and the marshals returned me to court. Once again, David Gibson didn't visit me before the hearing began.

Gibson opened with a curious sideshow: the Mark Malmros grand jury testimony. According to Mr. Gibson, it had been offered as an exhibit at my previous sentencing, but for whatever reason, the court didn't have it, and Judge Billings made it clear by his comments that he had no recollection of it either, in spite of the fact that it had been used, at least in part, to enhance my sentence for my special skills in chemistry. Gibson then went into an overview of Mark's and my association with the polyacetylene project, and then began to read portions of the grand jury testimony, much of it with little or no applicability to the proceedings. Judge Billings interrupted and questioned the relevance. Gibson answered:

> So the relevance, your Honor, is that these chemicals had
> many different uses; that they were, in fact, used in
> connection with the work that was done with Mr.
> Malmoros [sic] by Mr. Bloomer at his lab at his home in
> the period of time from 1980 through 1984...[so] that it
> does indicate other uses for some of the chemicals for
> which the government is taking the position, if you
> consider that they were all used in the manufacture of
> methamphetamine, then it comes up with this maximum

149

figure. And what we think the Court should consider in determining the quantity is the reasonable other uses that were made of these same chemicals in order to try to determine fairly what quantity might have been manufactured regarding the methamphetamine.[65]

This argument was fine as far as it went, but it never went far enough. The court was relying on the quantity of methylamine, allegedly ordered not by me but by the Hobsons, to ultimately determine the sentence, and Gibson made no presentation in that regard. Had he contacted Mark, as I had assumed he would, he might have been able to make a relevant showing.

It would have been necessary to go back to DEA chemist Fasanello's chart from trial showing the different ways I might have made methamphetamine, single out an essential chemical, and present testimony from Mark that it had, in fact, been used for the polyacetylene experiments. This would have limited the amount of P-2-P theoretically available to react with the methylamine, and undermined the court's analysis. Without this showing, Gibson's presentation was just so much blather that looked good from a distance, but meant nothing.

Gibson's second exhibit, documents from the Pollution Solutions case, was likewise completely meaningless. The argument was that, since the chemicals had been destroyed, there was no way to tell what had been in stock in my laboratory the day of the police raid, and therefore no way to make a showing that those remaining chemicals had not been used for methamphetamine. To make such an argument, Gibson must have hoped that either the judge or I, or both, were imbeciles. The evidence before the court was not the chemicals themselves, but rather the inventory of them prepared by the police when they were seized. As long as the inventory was accurate, it made no difference if the chemicals had been destroyed or not. Of course, Gibson knew the inventory was not accurate, but had failed to point it out at trial, and it was too late now.

David Kirby then engaged in a brief examination of his expert, Mr. Fasanello, wherein he largely and briefly repeated his earlier estimates. During cross, Fasanello demonstrated to me that either he was completely incompetent, or was deliberately lying, but even so, David Gibson made no serious attempt to discredit him in spite of having a list of his errors for more than a year. In any event it made no difference, as Judge Billings was paying no attention. Instead, he was flipping pages in the Sentencing Guidelines Manual, and taking notes. As for me, a nearly complete numbness had set in, and I had become detached from the proceedings as if I were watching them on TV.

150

At the end of Fasanello's testimony both sides made arguments to the court, which then recessed for lunch. Upon our return, Judge Billings launched into his standard tirade against the Sentencing Guidelines as to how he thought they were unfair and unconstitutional. (Ten years later the U.S. Supreme Court finally agreed with him.) Given the option, he said, he would sentence me to 60 to 84 months. However, he was bound by the Guidelines and the sentence was 188 months, almost 16 years, followed by another 5 years of supervised release. If I were lucky and got the maximum amount of good time, I would finally be free of the system at age 62. The hearing ended and I was led away by the marshals. That was the last time I was to see Mr. Gibson for five years.

The snowstorm had ended and I was taken, not back to Rutland, but to the Addison County Jail, easily my preference of the two. On the way, the marshals told me not to get too comfortable, as I wouldn't be staying long. After I arrived a guard gave me the message that Katrina had called, and I returned it by the phone on the wall of the cellblock. She was headed to Burlington with friends, was passing by the jail, and thought to stop. There were no visiting hours that day, and I would have needed to get special permission, which I was loathe to do, since there was really nothing to talk about. Our life together was, for all intents and purposes, over.

Generally the marshals liked to make their jobs as easy as possible, which meant waiting to transport a vanload of prisoners rather than just one at a time. Perhaps they thought that the thrashing I had taken in court might provoke me to an act of desperation, as they obviously didn't want to leave me at Addison with its lax security. I spent only one day there before I was taken alone to Ray Brook.

50

The problem with leaving prison and returning is that things are never the way you left them. The money in my commissary account, including money for the inmate telephone system, had been sent to Lewisburg Camp. However due to my new, longer sentence I would not be going there anytime soon, as camps were only for those with less than 10 years left to serve. In addition, there were no two-man cells available, so I was assigned to a small, cramped 4-man punishment cell at the end of the tier. The original intent was apparently to leave them empty except to administer a sanction short of sending someone to the Disciplinary Segregation Unit, aka The Hole. However, prison overcrowding being what it was, these cells were pressed into service for ordinary inmates.

For me, it was a form of punishment in that it put me in what I considered too close proximity to dangerous idiots. The ringleader of the bunch had apparently held up several banks and armored cars at gunpoint. The latest crime was, according to other inmates from his hometown, an armored car hijacking gone wrong. The thieves had successfully overpowered the driver and sped away in the car, with two guards remaining locked in the back with the money. The plan was to bury the car and its contents in a pit dug for the purpose, and to come back much later to blow it open. The conspirators had neglected to consider that the guards had radios, by which police helicopters were able to locate the car as it was being entombed, and arrest the perpetrators.

Another of the armored car codefendants was also at Ray Brook, but resided in another housing unit. This one was nicknamed "The Cat" for supposedly surviving nine bullet wounds, and a gnarly scar on his neck gave considerable credence to the story. Prison hadn't done anything to deter these two, and they were already planning their next heist, more than a decade away. One proposed plan was to park a crane with a magnet on an overpass, and to snag the armored car as it passed beneath.

By jailhouse standards, my cellmates were salt of the earth. They hadn't snitched on anybody and despised those who had, but the problem was their utter contempt for the system. Their long sentences made them immune to most of the prison's disciplinary measures, and also made them careless, as a trip to the hole or the loss of a few days good time just didn't make any difference. As a result, they were involved in various activities ranging from hashish smoking to a gambling operation to a nightly tattoo parlor run in the cell, with an artist from another unit brought in to do the actual work.

It was not that I cared what they were doing, but rather that I didn't want to bear the consequences of Ray Brook's "guilt by association" investigative methods. I was still eager to go to a camp, and certainly picking up another drug charge in prison was not the way to get there. I had been gradually learning about the system, in part through my own efforts to lower my security level, and in part though my activities as translator/advisor for some of my relatively uneducated foreign friends. What I concluded was that the prison's disciplinary system was the worst kind of kangaroo court, and guilt by association was a very real danger.

An illustrative case involved a middle-aged Colombian drug dealer with a 35-year sentence (later amended to life) who spoke virtually no English. With such a long sentence, Javier had tried to settle into prison, taking his pleasures as they came. From time to time on a Friday or Saturday night, he would partake of some - or more than some - hooch, or prison moonshine. On one occasion a guard passed by the open door of Javier's cell, smelled an overpowering odor of alcohol, and discovered the highly intoxicated Colombian. A disciplinary report followed.

Inmates were not allowed to attend other inmates' disciplinary hearings, much less represent them, so Javier was given a staff "advisor", a female guard of Philippine descent who spoke a few words of Spanish. She had Javier confessing to everything, and he was sent to the Hole.

Later, he showed me the paperwork and was incensed at his purported confession. While he freely admitted consuming the hooch, he vehemently denied making it, although that's what his confession showed. Moreover, the guard's incident report indicated that the hooch had been tested for alcohol, and tested again 15 minutes later at which time the concentration had doubled, a clearly impossible result. I suspected that the guard had actually tested the inmate, not the hooch, with one of the small breathalyzers guards sometimes carried around on weekends, but that's not what he wrote in his report.

Javier had already been to the hole, but was angry about the incident, so I prepared a grievance for him and he turned it in. Not surprisingly, it was rejected. The real problem was not the guilt or innocence of Javier, but reputation of the guard who was obviously incompetent. Still not satisfied, Javier appealed to the BOP's regional office in Philadelphia, aka "Region". The response this time was angry and accusatory, containing the interesting phrase, "... and now you claim you don't speak enough English to confess...". Javier and I laughed when we saw it, because of the contortions Region went through to avoid addressing what were clearly the issues. Just to complete the process, we sent the final appeal to the main BOP office in Washington and never heard anything. The Ray Brook mailroom staff could have simply removed the appeal from the mail, as it was certainly capable of doing, or perhaps Washington just didn't want to deal with it and threw it away. So the net result was that even an innocent inmate had a great deal to fear from the prison disciplinary system, and the best strategy was to do everything possible to avoid it.

51

I had only been back at Ray Brook a couple of days when an inmate work strike began. The organizers had posted thugs at the doors of the housing units during morning work call, advising other inmates that it would be a bad idea to go to work. Almost all agreed and returned to their cells, although a few toadies thought it more important to ingratiate themselves with their captors than avoid the very real possibility of violence at the hands of their peers, and foolishly reported to work. They need not have bothered, as they were quickly returned to their housing units. The institution then locked down for three days until the ringleaders of the strike could be identified and shipped out.

There was no political problem for me, as I had not yet been reassigned to my job in education, and there were no other problems after I persuaded my cellmates to open the window to vent the hashish smoke out of our cell during the lockdown. When staff questioned me as to my sympathies, I stated truthfully that I didn't have a job yet, and that was the end of the interview. Winston Birbal was similarly situated, but was even more angry and bitter following his indictment on heroin charges. He answered that he didn't have a job, but if he had had one, he wouldn't have gone. He was taken promptly to the Hole.

After the lockdown was over prison life returned to normal, and I found out from speaking with my father on the phone that my motion for a new trial had been denied by Judge Billings on January 12. My father had had a great deal of faith that the motion would be successful, and his voice was cracking on the phone. His understanding, based on a conversation with David Gibson, was that any challenges to the jury had to be brought within seven days of trial. Gibson had quoted the law, and Dad had checked it. "Stupid law," he said.

Regardless of what the statute said it was inconceivable to me that an officer of the court could rig a jury, and that the supervising judge could subsequently claim I had received a fair trial. It turned out that while the law did, in fact, specify a seven-day period to challenge a jury, there was a way around it: bring the motion directly under the Constitution.

Much later, after I had learned the criminal law, I saw that absolutely nothing had been done correctly. First, the motion had been brought as an attack on my sentence when I didn't have one. Second, the basis of the motion was entirely without legal foundation. Third, Mr. Gibson defaulted on the motion and then failed to appeal.

Gibson proffered that the Sixth Amendment to the U.S. Constitution required an impartial jury, and "the Supreme Court ruled that the impartial jury requirement may be complied with only where a fair cross section of the community comprises the pool of jurors." However, Gibson was "not aware of any case that has held that the absence and apparent exclusion of prospective jurors from a given town or area denies a defendant right to an impartial jury..."[66] In other words, Gibson was making a pitch to the court with nothing to back it up. Unfortunately for me, and much worse, there was plenty of legal authority that Gibson's

154

position was wrong, as the courts had ruled that the lack of an even geographic distribution of jurors did not deprive a defendant of a fair trial. While the motion looked good to someone unfamiliar with the law, it was worthless.

Ultimately Judge Billings never even got to the merits, dismissing the motion on procedural grounds. The government, in its opposition, had demanded a cause and prejudice showing and Gibson never responded at all, thus defaulting. Judge Billings wrote:

> ...Defendant has shown neither cause nor prejudice
> sufficient to excuse his delay of nearly 20 months, and
> thus is procedurally barred from making the claim now.
> Consequently, defendant's motion to set aside and order a
> new trial is hereby DENIED.[67]

The courts were concerned with what they called the "finality of justice", that is, they didn't want defendants returning over and over again to challenge their convictions or sentences. As a result, the courts made one jump through some hoops if an issue wasn't raised at the earliest possible moment. One manifestation of this requirement was the so-called cause and prejudice test, making it incumbent on the movant to demonstrate actual prejudice, as opposed to hypothetical, and to list a valid reason why the issue wasn't raised before.

The prejudice part of the test was easy enough. One way could have been to show that the number of jurors secretly excluded by the clerk far exceeded the number of peremptory challenges allowed the government, thus giving it an unfair advantage. The cause was a bit more problematic, as it was plain to see in the courtroom that no Rutland area jurors were available for the jury draw and, although it was unknown to the court, my father had mentioned it specifically to Gibson at the time. The cause, then, was my attorney's incompetence, which would have met the test. However, it was unrealistic to expect that David Gibson was going to admit his incompetence and leave himself open to the consequences, especially under the circumstances.

It is inescapable that Gibson knew exactly what he was doing in connection with the motion. Assuming that he had once again failed to do adequate legal research, Asst. U.S. Attorney Gary Shattuck laid out the cause and prejudice matter with great clarity in the government's opposition to the motion, and Gibson had had an opportunity to respond, but chose not to.

It is equally inescapable that at some point Mr. Gibson's instinct for self-preservation kicked in as his previous mistakes, whether accidental or deliberate, were coming back to haunt him. Within at most two days of receiving the government's opposition, Gibson had also received my letter from Addison County Jail informing him that the documents he had stipulated to against my wishes were forgeries. Gibson's personal interest, then, was not only to leave me in jail, but for a very long time. Owing to other court decisions, as long as my conviction remained valid it was going to be virtually impossible for me to bring any malpractice suit against him.

Given the consequences to me of Judge Billings' ruling on the new trial motion – a huge sentence increase - it was inconceivable that Gibson would fail to appeal the ruling, but no appeal was ever filed. Or rather, Gibson filed an appeal two days after Judge Billings' decision, but it didn't include the jury-rigging issue, only the sentence.

While he told me nothing at the time, there was no doubt that Gibson had told my father that he had appealed the jury issue. Immediately after the decision Dad had written to Gibson on January 17, 1994 stating, "...I understand that you have taken the appeal and have filed appropriate papers to do it in Forma Pauperis...."[68] Since the sole topic of the letter was the jury matter, the appeal mentioned could have referred to nothing else. Also, by letter of March 1, 1994 Dad again asked Gibson, "...Please keep me posted on the appeal relative to the jurors..."

While I didn't realize it then, Gibson's failure to adequately present the jury issue to the court most likely foreclosed it forever. The Sixth Amendment to United States Constitution guaranteed a defendant's right to counsel, and the U.S. Supreme Court had interpreted that to require that counsel be effective, that is, do an adequate job. Strangely, the guarantee extended only to trial and direct appeal, and the courts were explicit that defendants ran the risk of ineffective assistance in later proceedings. Had I attempted to revive the jury issue, the government would have howled that I was making a mockery of the process or, more technically, that a second petition was an "abuse of the writ". In this event, I would have been out of luck as the only "cause" for failure to properly put the matter before the court was Mr. Gibson's incompetence - or deliberate betrayal, which I would not have been able to prove. As the Second Circuit wrote in another appeal I filed years later: "...ineffective assistance of counsel does not constitute cause sufficient to excuse an abuse of the writ."[69] That left the victim to bear the consequences of incompetence or treachery on the part of his attorney.

52

I didn't realize at the time that David Gibson had not appealed the jury issue, and in theory there was a glimmer of hope, but as a practical matter I was overwhelmed by the enormity of my situation and the seeming hopelessness of it all. My attorney had at least abandoned me if not sold me out, and the courts had slammed the door on issues I had thought were sure winners. No other moves occurred to me at the time, and I drifted about for a few weeks in a haze.

Apparently the prison's investigative apparatus decided to see what they could get out of me in a moment of weakness, as I was harangued at length one morning by a fellow inmate employee of Ray Brook's education department seeking information or a confession. I was certainly off my game, as I spent about a half-hour arguing with him instead of immediately questioning his motivation and purpose. It wasn't advisable to call someone a snitch to his face, even if it were true, but a pointed comment or question generally worked wonders.

My father was also off his game, and part of it surely was that his view of the world had been shaken. While quick to admit that things weren't perfect, he had believed that at its core the American system was sound, but now he was disillusioned. I thought at the time that depression had weakened his resistance a little, and that the flu-like symptoms and respiratory problems that evaded a definite diagnosis were attributable in part to that cause. There was some speculation that he might have been exposed to a bird virus in filthy barracks in World War II, or exposed to some other toxic agent during the war. There was other speculation that he might have contracted the tick-borne Lyme disease, for which there was no definite test. His doctor put him on antibiotics for months, and eventually the symptoms subsided. What the doctor overlooked was that something was eating away at his lung, something that would eventually kill him.

53

I hadn't been at Ray Brook long when the question of my security level arose again. I now had more than 10 years left to serve in my sentence and was ineligible for a camp placement, so Lewisburg was out. My security level had been raised from minimum to low, which was still inappropriate for the medium security Ray Brook, and some action was indicated. Had the situation been the same as the previous year, the institution might have continued its games with the security forms, adding a "management variable" or something similar to keep me there.

However, the mission of the institution had changed, and so had its population.

Due to the Sentencing Guidelines, mandatory minimum statutes and the federal prosecution of what had once been considered state crimes, the federal prisons were full to the point of overcrowding, and something had to be done to relieve the pressure. One of the solutions had been to convert part of the abandoned military base at Fort Dix, New Jersey, into a low security prison, primarily with a labor force of minimum-security inmates moved there from other institutions. A double fence like Ray Brook's had been thrown up around the institution; some, but not all, of the asbestos had been ripped out; and the old barracks buildings were mildly customized. The modifications consisted primarily of removing a half wall in each of the rooms and patching the floors. While the rooms were intended to house eight soldiers, four on each side of the wall in single beds, six bunk beds were now packed in along with 12 large military lockers. A quick coat of paint was splashed on, and the place was ready for occupancy. Busses soon began to roll from other institutions all over the Northeast.

Fort Dix mania had struck at Ray Brook, and a staff member informed me that 300 inmates were to be transferred in the very near future. Given the realities of the federal system, the transfers were unavoidable. The high security penitentiaries were also full, but there was a long lead-time and considerable expense to build more, meaning that the only real option in the near term was to reclassify some of the high security inmates as medium security, and send them to places like Ray Brook. To make room, some of Ray Brook's inmates had to be reclassified and sent to lower security institutions like Fort Dix.

If one were going to cram inmates into a large institution like Fort Dix, it was essential that they be as low risk as possible. That obvious requirement notwithstanding, a few desperados apparently slipped through the cracks. A fellow education worker had held up twenty-one banks in the Boston area at gunpoint, with shots fired during at least one of the robberies. Despite his strenuous objections, he was transferred to Ft. Dix, perhaps because of his Harvard degree in economics.

Another odd transferee was a dentist, also from the Boston area, who had been a lookout during an armored car robbery. Although the lookout himself was unarmed, the conspirators were deadly serious, having amassed a collection of machine guns, and they had planned to take on the crew of the armored car. Fortunately for the guards, a snitch betrayed the robbers prior to the holdup, and police averted the shootout.

158

While some violent people had been shipped out of Ray Brook, many more had been shipped in, and the prison had changed very noticeably in the two months I had been gone. Most obvious was the shrinking percentage of white inmates, with their replacements younger, rougher and tougher. The newcomers were often arrogant, with a general disdain for everyone and everything.

One manifestation of the new attitude occurred in the mess hall. Following the meal, inmates passed through a corridor and handed their cafeteria trays through a window to the dishwashing crew. The plates and dishes were quickly cleared of food, the plastic utensils separated, and the items passed on for loading into the dishwasher. There was a minimal delay, even if a crowd of inmates all arrived at the window at the same time. Even this slight inconvenience was too much for the new arrivals, and they simply threw everything on the floor and left. By the end of the meal there was an immense pile of dishes, trays and uneaten food on the floor in front of the window, making it impossible to walk through without tracking the discarded food around. The people responsible for the mess surely realized that it wasn't the warden who was going to be cleaning up, but rather their fellow inmates.

A few guards, and even an old lieutenant, openly admitted that they didn't like their new charges, and it was a poorly kept secret that unit staff was spending much of its time dealing with violence. It was a good time to leave, and I put in a request for a transfer to a low-security institution at either Fort Dix or Loretto in Central Pennsylvania.

Time passed quickly as I waited to see what the institution would do. I resumed my work as clerk of the horticulture department and continued to tutor two severely disabled students in reading. I also continued to ghost write college papers for some of my fellow inmates. College credits were offered through the prison's education department under the auspices of North Country Community College, and some of Ray Brook's students were far more interested in the credits than the knowledge presented in the courses. Consequently, I had been hired by two inmates to do much of their course work for them. My writing skills were a little rusty at the beginning, but after a while I was able to crank out their papers with little effort. This writing practice served me well later when I began to represent myself in the legal system.

With so much going on, a couple of months passed without much notice. Katrina knew I was likely to be transferred, but had not come to visit, although she did inform me that she intended to move out of our West Rutland house, which apparently had some problems. I had known before reporting to prison that the heating system, an old coal-to-oil conversion, was on its last legs and there were some other loose ends as well. However, we had already spent considerable time and money on renovations to the benefit of the new owner, Attorney General Janet Reno, and it made no sense to spend any more until the ultimate fate of the house was decided. Given my predicament I saw little chance to save my half of the property, and assumed that it would be sold. I also assumed that Katrina could recover the value of her half under the innocent owner defense. At the time I had no idea of the extent to which the property had deteriorated, and no one told me, undoubtedly to spare me the anguish of a situation I was powerless to change.

54

So it was with blissful ignorance I read the callout on March 16, 1994 ordering me to report to the laundry the following day to turn in my prison issue clothing. I also packed up my personal property and turned it in to R & D for shipment. About 3:00 a.m. on the morning of the 18th, I was awakened and told to dress. Other inmates also being shipped out that morning assembled by the door of the housing unit, and a guard then led us to the mess hall for an early breakfast. From there, it was only a few steps to R & D for processing, which consisted mostly of strip searching everyone and shackling us. Fortunately, with the exception of a sole Jamaican, the twenty or so of us awaiting transfer wore no leg irons. The Jamaican also sported a so-called "black box", or special sheet metal enclosure for his handcuffs to make picking the locks virtually impossible for the wearer. The rest of us had only the standard handcuffs, thoughtfully attached to a chain belt. We boarded a prison bus at about 5:00 a.m. in Ray Brook's parking lot, and off we went to Lewisburg Penitentiary in central Pennsylvania, about 30 miles south of Williamsport.

We weren't going to arrive at Lewisburg until after lunch, so we were issued bag lunches sometime around noon in the moving bus. The bag contained a primitive sandwich, a can of soda, potato chips, a candy bar and an apple. I had certainly seen worse, especially during lockdowns, but having one's hands tied to one's belt made eating difficult. As it turned out we had plenty of time - two or three hours - to struggle through the meal before we were greeted by the penitentiary's forbidding wall topped with gun towers. Unlike Ray Brook, the interior of the prison wasn't visible from outside the wall and it wasn't until the gigantic gates opened that we got a glimpse of the place. We were quickly unloaded and ushered into Lewisburg's version of R & D for processing.

I had assumed that our paperwork went with us on the bus, and in-processing would be perfunctory at best, but I was wrong. More papers had to be filled out and questions answered. During the lengthy process I noticed that the heavily shackled Jamaican had a wild look in his eye, and the other inmates were giving him a lot of space. I thought, "How dangerous can this guy be in this environment", and went over to talk to him. It turned out that his crime wasn't murder or mayhem, but illegal entry into the U.S. for the second or third time, and he was being transferred to a deportation center. I couldn't imagine why he had warranted extra security, except that he might have tried to escape in the past.

After our processing was complete, we were taken to the old hospital section of the penitentiary that had been converted into a dormitory. The interior of the hospital was like a stone castle with a seventy-five foot long corridor down the middle perhaps fifteen feet wide and twenty feet high. At the end of the corridor was a small TV about ten feet off the floor blaring unintelligibly at ten rows of church pews, echoing off the stone walls. Behind the pews were shelves of well-read paperbacks, many shredded beyond usefulness. On either side of the corridor were long, narrow rooms with bunk beds packed in only a shoulder width apart. The bathroom consisted of two rooms, one with a row of fully enclosed stainless steel shower stalls and a toilet more or less in the middle of the room. The other room had urinals. Inmates had strung some sheets to afford a little privacy to toilet users.

The Bureau of Prisons used a hub and spoke transportation system like the airlines, and Lewisburg Penitentiary was the hub for the Northeast Region. Inmates were thus brought there from all over the region to be accumulated until there were enough of them to justify a bus trip to another destination. Like any place housing exclusively transients, the old hospital tended to be filthy. There were no privileges to be taken away, and as a practical matter the guards lacked any meaningful sanctions to be used against those who did a poor job cleaning the place. I learned to my horror that some inmates had been there for weeks, and hoped that my likely destination, Fort Dix, would be sufficiently popular that I would only be in Lewisburg a short time.

There was nothing to do but read and watch TV. The old hospital had only a single telephone, and one had to sign up the day before for a short time slot, but there was such frenzy for the phone that I only used it once to tell my parents where I was. The only other possible excitement was the occasional flood from above.

Tens of thousands of Cubans had entered the United States illegally during the Mariel boatlift in 1980, but most had been successfully integrated into South Florida. Some, however, had been deemed undesirable, and Castro had refused to take them back, meaning that they were going to be locked up indefinitely. Those confined at Lewisburg expressed their frustration from time to time by plugging the drains in their cells and running the water, resulting in a cascade into the beds and everything else below in the old hospital.

Despite the ever-present possibility of inundation, boredom set in almost immediately, and easily the high points of the day were our guard-escorted trips to the mess hall. The institution was scrupulous about keeping transients, some of whom were being shipped to camps for short sentences, separated from the penitentiary's high-security inmates, although we would encounter the occasional orderly mopping the floors on our march from the old hospital to the mess hall. (It turned out some years later that even this security was inadequate, as a transient was killed by a designated inmate during the short march. After that, transients never left the old hospital, encountering only Lewisburg's guards.)

As a result of the safety and security concerns, breakfast was at 5:30 a.m., lunch was at 9:30 and supper was at 2:30 in the afternoon. We were given only a half-hour to eat. Upon exit from the mess hall we were thoroughly pat searched, allowed to carry only a single piece of fruit, and marched back to the hospital.

The meals themselves were actually quite good, as they had to be at a penitentiary. High security inmates usually had very long sentences, perhaps the majority were violent, and most had little to lose in a prison uprising. One of the few things that could unite inmates across ethnic and racial divides was poor food, and for that reason the institution took pains to serve a good meal. A guard behind the serving counter watched each portion carefully, making sure all were the same, thus removing another potential source of conflict. There was even a self-service soft ice cream machine in the middle of the mess hall near the salad bar.

After I had eaten the fruit from our mid-afternoon supper, it was a long wait for breakfast, but there was one consolation: the Jamaican I had befriended in R & D brought me a cup of hot coffee every morning, an astounding feat. Apparently he had friends of his own on the upper floors of the penitentiary, and was able to communicate with them either by shouting through holes in the ceiling bored for utility pipes, or by notes on a rat line, dental floss running along the sides of the pipes. Either way, individual packets of coffee came down to the Jamaican each morning by the lines. Under the circumstances, coffee was a real luxury, and only the two of us had any.

After the coffee, there was a long day ahead with little to fill it. I couldn't understand a word from the TV, and most of the paperbacks were missing pages, a most frustrating experience. This left plenty of time for socializing, and I made a fortuitous acquaintance at Lewisburg, an acquaintance that was to teach me the skills I needed to fight back: Tony LaRosa*. I was to learn much more about Tony as time went on, but at the time knew that he was a lawyer and businessman from the Boston area that had found himself in trouble over some kind of real estate deal. Tony had come on the bus with me from Ray Brook, and I recognized him as having worked in the law library there, but otherwise knew nothing else

Although the law library was part of the Education Department, I had never spent much time there. First, I had an attorney, David Gibson, who was more knowledgeable than I, and he was supposedly looking after my interests. Second, the library appeared to be the hangout for delusional incompetents believing themselves to be legal experts. It was bad enough that some were writing worthless motions for themselves, but vultures falsely touting their prowess were charging other inmates for equally worthless papers. All in all, it seemed a good place to avoid.

Tony LaRosa, however, was on his own mission as a library clerk. His practice in the street had been centered around tax and business matters, and he was giving himself a crash course in the criminal law so that he could attack his own eleven-year sentence. In the process, he was a genuine help to those desperately seeking help in the library, and he was going to be helpful to another desperate litigant: me. In the four days we were at Lewisburg we had considerable time to get to know each other, especially since Tony was much more comfortable with white Americans than blacks or foreigners. While I was still very guarded concerning details of my case, I was starting to take an interest in the law and Tony was certainly knowledgeable.

Luckily we had to endure the torture of Lewisburg for only four days before being shackled and loaded again on a bus. After passing through Harrisburg and Philadelphia, Pennsylvania, we crossed the Delaware River and arrived a while later at the Federal Correctional Institution at Fort Dix, New Jersey.

---

* Not his real name.

55

It took six and a half hours to process a busload of inmates at Fort Dix R & D, a painfully long time, and a ridiculously long time considering that a half-busload was processed into Lewisburg in somewhat less than an hour. From my first moments there, Fort Dix reeked of incompetence and confusion, and that set the tone for the rest of my stay.

The facility was actually two separate institutions, Fort Dix East and Fort Dix West, which shared only the top administrators like the warden and his staff, the warehouse for food and supplies, and the motor pool. It turned out that each facility had a distinct character, with mine, Fort Dix East, being the more easygoing of the two.

Each prison was huge by Ray Brook standards, with a perimeter of nearly a mile and, while ordinary guards had to negotiate the compound on foot, anybody who was anybody on the staff had a golf cart. Inside each of the two facilities were six three-story brick housing units, which were the former military barracks, as well as two mess halls and separate buildings for medical, R & D, education, visiting, gymnasium, and the prison police.

While there was adequate security to protect the public in the form of a double fence and armed perimeter truck patrol, security within the institution was extremely lax. Unlike Ray Brook, neither the housing units nor the rooms within them locked, supposedly because of the lack of sprinkler systems, and there was no controlled movement of inmates on the compound with the result that hundreds of them were milling about during much of the day and evening. Prisoners were pouring into the institution so fast - four busloads during the week I arrived alone - that there simply wasn't the manpower to fully supervise them all. Fort Dix East rapidly swelled to 2,400 inmates, and accountability was spotty at best, although there were the mandatory inmate counts at 4 p.m., 10 p.m., midnight and several times during the night.

Some work details maintained a strict count of their workers but the two biggest, yard work and labor pool, did not. While perhaps a hundred inmates would show up and sign in for the morning yard cleanup crew, within a few minutes all but a handful would drift away, some to the gym, some back to bed, and others to wherever. The institution would make an occasional stab at a lockdown census count, but at least half the inmates weren't where they were supposed to be.

On one occasion Tony LaRosa and I were both out on the compound when we should have been in the education building, and we had to duck into the paint shop as the compound closed. Inside it was strangely dark, and as our eyes adjusted we could see other inmates stretched out on long shelves probably meant to hold paint. Rather than a workshop, the place had the appearance of an opium den. The paint foreman's first question was, "OK, how many of you guys work for me?" It turned out that not only was the foreman unfamiliar of his own crew, but fully half of us trapped in the paint shop were supposed to be on other details. The foreman dutifully recorded the names of those admitting they worked for him, the compound reopened, and the rest of us walked out without further inquiry.

As a practical matter, little could be done. Fort Dix had no disciplinary segregation unit and an infraction had to be serious to justify transporting an inmate over an hour to The Hole at FCI Fairton, New Jersey. Not only that, but Fairton couldn't begin to accept a thousand disciplinary cases from another prison because they had deserted make-work prison jobs.

(Generally speaking, at Ray Brook every inmate could be accounted for in ten minutes during a lockdown census, although there was at least one notable exception. During a mock escape drill in 1991 or 1992, an inmate actually turned up missing. In its zeal to participate in the exercise, the unit staff of Ausable Unit had rushed out of the unit offices to take their positions for the drill, inadvertently locking an inmate inside. After yelling and pounding on the door for a few minutes, the inmate decided that nothing further could be done and made good use of his time reviewing boxes of greeting cards donated to the institution by Hallmark.

Despite the prison's boast that any escapee could be identified in five minutes, the reality was that the process inexplicably took about an hour. When the identity of the missing inmate was finally determined, someone remembered having seem him in the vicinity of the unit offices, and there he was, reading greeting cards.)

Escape from inside the institution at Fort Dix was probably as difficult as it would have been in Ray Brook, but the same could not be said of the outside work details. The agreement the Bureau of Prisons had made with the Army for the use of a small corner of the sprawling base was that more than a hundred inmate laborers would be supplied to mow laws, pick up papers and do other menial work on the base in minimally supervised work crews. Although Fort Dix was theoretically a secure, low security institution, a large cadre of minimum/out security level inmates had to be included in its population to service the contract with the Army.

Normally the BOP handled similar situations by building minimum-security satellite camps outside the main institutions, but for unknown reasons this had not been done at Fort Dix. The result was a security nightmare with hundreds of inmates passing out the rear gates of both Fort Dix East and Fort Dix West in the morning and returning in the afternoon, Monday through Friday. Not only could the inmates themselves smuggle contraband into the prison, but they could also easily conspire with friends inside the institution to introduce whatever they wanted by throwing it over the fence and having it quickly picked up. It was common knowledge that drugs were coming in by this method, and there were rumors one inmate had a 9 mm pistol. Given the security situation, the lack of a satellite camp was all the more puzzling considering that vacant buildings identical to those inside the prison could be seen just outside the fence.

Equally puzzling was the BOP's rationale for including deportable aliens in the outside work cadre, and apparently the plan was for them to work several years on the honor system at Fort Dix awaiting a near-inevitable deportation. Surely it occurred to some of them that it made little sense to wait for years when they could deport themselves immediately, and a few disappeared. Two years after I arrived at Fort Dix enough had left to interest the local newspaper, the *Burlington County Times*, which printed an article with the headlines "Escaping jail is a quiet walk in the park" and "Jail breaks just a walk away". (May 19, 1996)

56

By chance Tony LaRosa and I were assigned to the same twelve-man room in housing unit 5751, but Tony immediately saw that he didn't belong there, and began to figure a way to change quarters. Fortunately for me, Tony had experienced several prison transfers (although none quite like Fort Dix) and advised me to immediately turn in my telephone list to the Correctional Counselor. We went together to the Counselor's office, but since the inexperienced counselor hadn't been given explicit instructions, she was unsure what to do. Tony said, "I've been to Schuylkill and Ray Brook. All you have to do is turn in our lists to ITS [Inmate Telephone System] and they'll turn on our phones."

The counselor quickly shot back a comment that reverberated through my time there, "I don't care how they do it in Schuylkill. I don't care how they do it in Ray Brook. This is Fort Dix!" Without meaning to, our counselor had hit the nail directly on the head. The staff at Fort Dix reserved the right to ignore common sense and to run the most fouled-up institution in the entire system. This was to have its benefits, but few were apparent in the first couple of days.

166

What was apparent was that if I didn't move quickly, I would be assigned to a work detail that I probably wouldn't like much. The day after my arrival at Fort Dix, I went down to check out the education department and ran into an old acquaintance from the Ray Brook department who urged me to submit a request to work there. Figuring the devil I knew was better than the devil I didn't know, I acquiesced. However, the following day I found I had been assigned to the yard cleanup crew, and I also found out that working at the library was more desirable than teaching. At the time it looked like my prospective teaching boss hadn't acted on my request, and I thought I should get the machinery moving for the library position as soon as possible. I submitted a request for the library job, and for the next couple of days I simply wandered around, waiting for action on my request.

However, after the two-day vacation I started teaching at the request of the instructor even though I was still assigned to the yard crew. In the morning I signed in with the yard foreman, and then left for the school. After a week of this, my boss at education told me that I couldn't teach anymore until my job change was officially entered in the computer, which at a place like Fort Dix might have meant never. Worse, the yard crew had recently been assigned to remove asbestos-laden tiles from one of the buildings with, of course, no protective equipment. Since I had been teaching instead of working on the yard crew I was not a familiar face, and I was able to sneak away from the hazardous detail, but it was imperative to push for the library job.* A week later my persistence paid off, and my job transfer was official.

My library job consisted of processing new books into the library, which entailed making a card and affixing a spine label. Like almost everything else at Fort Dix, there were no clear performance standards, and I spent most of my time reading the books rather than working on them. I also had easy access to the typewriters that were in the leisure library, and across the hall in the law library, and I quickly settled into my new position.

Apparently the lack of standards also appealed to many of the guards. Ray Brook was in a sparsely populated area of the North Country with no large industries, and most of the guards were country folk

---

* The asbestos project came to an abrupt halt after inmates pointed out to the guard/foreman that he, too, was being poisoned by the institution. An outside crew of professionals with special equipment then had to be brought in to finish the job.

supporting their families in a situation with few alternatives. Fort Dix, on the other hand, was near both metropolitan New York and Philadelphia. With such abundant opportunities, clearly the applicants for prison jobs were those who needed to work at a place where, for all practical purposes, it was impossible to fail. Unfortunately for the inmates, this guaranteed a level of incompetence and indifference that was truly difficult to imagine.

Things that took a day or two at Ray Brook, like approvals of a visitors list, took weeks at Fort Dix. Normally an exception was made for immediate family members, but one inmate in my unit waited more than a month to have his wife approved. I wasn't expecting too many visits at Fort Dix, but nonetheless wanted to keep the possibility open, and returned numerous times to my counselor's office to prod him into action. On one occasion, I was told he would be gone several days for "training" - a bad sign. After repeated complaints he was transferred to the adjacent housing unit to begin again, but despite the new start the result was the same. The situation finally resolved itself when the counselor left the BOP entirely after receiving a part in a TV soap opera in New York.

There were more annoyances in Fort Dix than incompetent staff. An overwhelming percentage of the inmates had cooperated in some manner with prosecutors during their criminal cases, and some actually saw themselves as members of the government. Institution staff did nothing to dispel this notion, and cooperators in big cases were given obvious special treatment. The result was that these people did pretty much as they pleased, which often included an extreme disrespect for their fellow inmates.

One of my roommates, a Manny somebody from Philadelphia, was a tall black kid in his mid-20s. He was supposedly the kingpin of a large crack cocaine ring in Philly, but despite this status he had apparently earned the gratitude of the government by turning in his underlings. He had no prison job and slept all morning, but thoughtfully played his radio all night for the benefit of those of us who had to get up. On several occasions, his homeboys from another room came to visit at midnight although our lights were off. They turned them on, pulled up chairs, and started hollering. Such incredible rudeness would have been dealt with quickly and effectively at Ray Brook, which is perhaps why Ray Brook had two-man cells instead of twelve-man dorms. However, at Fort Dix these people had the protection of the institution, and if any harm befell them there was little doubt that the perpetrator would be facing disciplinary action or additional criminal charges.

Tony LaRosa had seen immediately that our room was not for him, and pestered his counselor for a few days until he was given a new

168

room assignment. I decided to stick it out, as there were definitely rooms worse than mine, with inmates yelling and playing cards all night almost every night. My patience was rewarded about a month later when Manny had a stomachache.

Medical care at Fort Dix was perhaps the worst in the federal system, involving long lines and long waits for very questionable services. Given the large number of inmates, the small medical staff, and the fact that a majority of the inmates were from the third world, the situation was probably impossible, but the considerable difficulties were compounded by a numbing indifference - except in Manny's case. Despite a seemingly minor ailment, he was transported from the housing unit to the infirmary in a golf cart chauffeured by a guard.

It turned out that Manny was seriously ill with an intestinal blockage, and had to be taken to an outside hospital for care. When he returned, he was housed in a special room in Fort Dix's hospital, and it was there that he threatened a guard for not catering to his whims with enough zeal. This time Manny had finally pushed the institution too far and was summarily shipped out, but he returned briefly to our room to change his clothes before one last Ft. Dix visit from his mother and wife. While he was lying on his bed the unit manager, Belinda Avalos, came in to see him, and Manny began to complain immediately about his treatment at the hospital. Ms. Avalos replied in the sweetest voice, "Well, you tell them that when you get where you're going." And then, thank God, he was gone.

57

While Manny and his crew were certainly an annoyance, I had a more serious threat at the library. My sole coworker on the book-labeling detail, an ethnic Albanian that had played tennis with one of my cellmates at Ray Brook, was engaging in a ham-handed attempt to obtain information or a confession from me. Although we had barely spoken at Ray Brook, he offered me an expensive pair of sneakers upon my arrival at Fort Dix. Then, he apparently thought us good enough friends that he could ask how much I had paid my lawyer, and what quantity of drugs I had left for my wife. He had seen her in the visiting room at Ray Brook, he said, and could tell immediately that she was a drug addict, so I must have left her some drugs. He also asked in a loud voice in front of other inmates which country I would go to if I escaped from prison.

This was certainly a dangerous situation, as we were surrounded by people who knew well the benefits of cooperating and informing. All that needed to happen to permanently end my hopes for a camp placement was for another informer to overhear the one-sided conversation, and report that I was planning an escape. This was not a paranoid delusion, as one didn't need to look far at Fort Dix to find people that had turned in their friends and their brothers, and two had supposedly turned in their mothers. I found out later for certain that one fine young man had implicated his father, a police officer, in an armored car holdup and the father had subsequently committed suicide.

As time went on I became more and more convinced that there was an organized network of informers, probably run out of the Lieutenants' office. While some at Fort Dix were certainly compulsive tattlers, others seemed to be receiving direction from somewhere, as I seemed to have been singled out by more informers than the Albanian. I probably never spotted the more surreptitious of them, but a few were so obvious at to be laughable. One afternoon as I sat alone at a table on the lawn outside my housing unit, a scruffy, middle-aged man with rotten teeth and a moth-eaten ponytail sat down next to me. "Can you tell me how to make explosives?" he asked. I directed him to the library and suggested that he try the encyclopedia. A few weeks later, the same character was craning his neck to overhear a conversation I was having with another inmate outside the library. When we went outside to avoid him, he soon peeked out the door to see what we were doing. A similar cooperator had presented me with a hand-scrawled, misspelled list of chemicals at Ray Brook, asking what I knew about them.

Surely it was more than coincidence that someone I had never met, one of my codefendant's drug associates, appeared at the library asking for me within a day of arriving at Fort Dix. How would he have known that I was at Fort Dix? Or that I worked at the library? And surely it was more than coincidence that, out of the hundreds of rooms at Fort Dix East and West, he was reassigned to my room a short time after his arrival.

There didn't seem to be any sense of shame at Fort Dix. One of my previous roommates had been out several times to testify against codefendants, and went to the unit offices daily just to say "hi" to staff. And the pettiness of it was astounding. A man down the hall from me turned in one of his roommates for hiring someone to mop the floor rather than doing it himself, which didn't violate any prison regulations. Two lieutenants that had transferred to Fort Dix from a high-security penitentiary summed it up during a conversation at one of the mess halls. One said, "What an old ladies' joint! They're telling on each other for everything!"

170

"Yeah," replied the other. "They're telling us stuff we don't want to know."

At night as Tony LaRosa and I walked around the compound, a half-dozen or so inmates could usually be seen through the window of the Lieutenant's office, sitting in a row of chairs. While some were undoubtedly summoned for a urine test or were otherwise there unwillingly, we were quite sure that others were there to volunteer information. "Take a number," Tony would say.

Although I liked the job in the library, I endeavored to find something to separate myself from the Albanian as soon as possible, as it was certainly peculiar that he was in a low security institution like Fort Dix in the first place. He'd been a member of a vicious Albanian organized crime group in New York City, and was involved in the "Balkan Connection" heroin case. During the investigation and prosecution the gang allegedly targeted an Assistant U.S. Attorney and a DEA agent for assassination, and the matter was sufficiently important to U.S. Attorney (later New York mayor) Rudolph Giuliani that he showed up in person for sentencing to see that justice was done. According to the *Wall Street Journal* of September 9, 1985 "[Trial] Judge Broderick remarked during the trial that the case involved the most reckless disregard for human life that he had ever seen."

My understanding was that the Albanian working in the library with me had a sentence of 40 years, but the Journal had the sentence at 80 years. In either event, desperation must have prompted him to try his hand at informing, but the reality was that he was going nowhere. With a powerful enemy like Rudy Giuliani determined to make an example of him, the Albanian wasn't going to get parole anytime soon regardless of whatever prison snitching he might do, but reality didn't seem to enter into the equation.

My opportunity to extricate myself from the situation come at the end of August, 1994, when a position opened up for a tutor in the English as a Second Language (ESL) class on the floor immediately above the library. In theory I was perfect for the job as the majority of the students were Hispanic and my Spanish was, by that time, quite good. In reality, I only lasted a week. Virtually all the Hispanic students requested me for their tutor and the other tutors became jealous, creating what could have been, at most, a minor headache for the instructor. Apparently even a minor headache was too much, and I was abruptly fired without warning. So, not only was failure impossible at Fort Dix, success wasn't going to be allowed either.

Actually, things worked out for the best. I returned to a different, even easier job at the leisure library, minus the Albanian.

58

Boorish inmates and treachery were inherent to the prison experience - all part of the punishment, I sometimes remarked - and, while stressful, didn't distract me much from my numerous projects. I had polished my writing skills somewhat at Ray Brook ghostwriting college papers, and was ready for a more difficult task. My stepdaughter, Lindsay, had been asking me to tell her about some of the characters I had met in prison, and I began to write about them shortly after arriving at Fort Dix. Within a month I had written several short stories, and sent them off.

Fort Dix also gave me a fresh start with a new unit team, and an opportunity to clean up my central file. Considering the security level problems I had encountered at Ray Brook and the obstinacy of the staff, it seemed prudent to begin the process immediately even though I would not be eligible for a camp for at least 2 years. Without too much effort, I persuaded my case manager to give me minus 3 security points for my personal recognizance bail during my trial, and later minus 6 points for my self-surrender to the marshals for transport to prison. This left me with an overall point total well into the minimum security range and camp eligible as soon as the time remaining on my sentence dropped below 10 years.

Although an appeal was pending, I had little confidence that it would be in any way successful. Despite the opportunity to do so, David Gibson had failed to raise any substantive issue during resentencing, and there was little to appeal regarding the sentence. As to the jury-tampering issue, Mr. Gibson had given no legal authority for his position that a geographically non-representative jury panel denied me a fair trial, and I assumed that the appeals court was going to deal with it the same way Judge Billings had - a denial of the new trial motion. I was, however, interested to see how Gibson was going to present the clerk's misconduct to the court, and if the court would state any opinion on the matter of corruption in the district court regardless of its ruling on a new trial. In light of what had happened already with the first appeal, and in light of David Gibson's performance, it seemed prudent to consider this one lost also, and I surely would have considered it lost if I had realized at the time that Gibson didn't appeal the jury issue at all.

Regardless of the outcome of the appeal, I certainly wasn't going to rely on Mr. Gibson again, and consequently began to work on the case myself. In the evening I often walked around the compound with Tony

LaRosa, picking his brain about what I needed to do to challenge my conviction. Although I was not particularly receptive to the idea, Tony was emphatic from the outset that I would have to study the law. His advice in a nutshell was: "Nobody knows your case like you do, and nobody can do it for you. Go to the law library and find some winning cases, then see if you can adapt the facts of your case to any of them."

While I wasn't yet ready to begin an intensive study of the federal criminal law, I was ready to find out everything I could pertaining to my case, and in that regard I filed a Freedom of Information act request with the United States Attorney's Office, which was forwarded to Executive Office for United States Attorneys (EOUSA) for processing. On May 18, 1994 I was given a full denial of my request. Not one page was produced. The exemptions from the law cited to justify the denial were that any disclosure "could reasonably be expected to interfere with enforcement proceedings" and "material reporting investigative efforts pertaining to the enforcement of criminal law including efforts to prevent, control, or reduce crime or apprehend criminals, except records of arrest". (It later turned out that among the thousands of pages withheld were over 100 pages of newspaper clippings about my case and over 1000 pages of photocopies of published legal cases from the Federal Reporter, which was not only available to the general public, but was available in every federal prison law library.) I appealed the decision and waited.

I had a little bit better luck getting papers from David Gibson, although he, too, delayed and withheld some materials. I learned much later that the client file, generated by a lawyer during his representation of a client, actually belonged to the client, the exception being the lawyer's work product, i.e. the lawyer's personal notes, legal research and similar materials. A lawyer had, thus, no legal basis to deny the client his file or documents from the file, and actually had an affirmative duty to respond to the client. This was spelled out clearly in the Vermont Code of Professional Responsibility (a code of ethics or conduct for lawyers adopted by the Vermont Supreme Court) and decisions of the Supreme Court in disciplinary cases.

By letter of June 3, 1994 I asked Mr. Gibson for my trial transcripts, and to determine whether court reporter William Currie, III had recorded the final arguments at my trial. Finally, I wrote, "I would like to know who you retained to look over [State Police Chemist Dr. Brendan] McMahon's work, what materials were provided, and what opinion was rendered." The trial transcripts arrived after a time, but Gibson was silent on the other inquiries. I wrote a follow-up letter on July 11 stating, "I never received any report, oral or written, concerning a review of

173

McMahon's work. I need this material immediately for use in the Pollution Solutions case." This time I heard nothing at all, and wrote yet again on August 8th. I again asked for the material, reminding Mr. Gibson that I had been inquiring about the final arguments for "about a year", but this time I supplemented my earlier requests with a request for "a copy of the appeal brief filed in connection with the jury tampering". Mr. Gibson had sent me copies of his appeal brief in April, but there was nothing about the jury tampering matter. It was inconceivable to me at the time that he wouldn't appeal what to me was an obvious new-trial issue so, ignorant of exactly how the courts worked, I assumed that there was another appeal relating to the jury. My father also thought that Gibson had appealed, as he wrote about the jury matter to David Gibson on January 17, 1994. Part of the letter read, "I understand that you have taken the appeal and have filed appropriate papers to do it in Forma Pauperis."[70] Finally, on August 25, David Gibson responded by sending Freedom of Information Act materials that had been provided to him by the DEA and the report of Dr. Karen Sentell, the chemist that he had hired prior to trial. Nothing was mentioned about the jury tampering appeal or the final arguments. However, it now seemed that Mr. Gibson was determined to interject himself into my prospective divorce as his letter contained questions from Joan Wing, Katrina's attorney.

Katrina had notified me of her intentions a month before during her first and only visit to Fort Dix. Lindsay had accompanied her to New Jersey, but had decided at the last minute to stay in the motel, undoubtedly to avoid what could have been a very uncomfortable situation. It would be another five years before I was to see Lindsay.

Katrina had indicated her desire for a divorce some time before and, given the circumstances, I had no particular objection, but I wanted to postpone the divorce until after the forfeiture proceedings against our West Rutland house had concluded. There had been some new developments in the federal law about property forfeitures and double jeopardy, and I had at least a slight chance of overturning my convictions on double jeopardy grounds. If Katrina were awarded the property in the divorce, as I thought likely, that would complicate, if not compromise, my claim.

Katrina seemed determined to press on with the divorce, as evidenced by Joan Wing's letter. In spite of Mr. Gibson's sellout at the resentencing debacle, and in spite of his failures to fulfill my document requests, he was now presuming to represent me in the divorce. I wrote back on August 31st stating, "It may be appropriate to inform Atty. Wing that you have not been retained to represent me in any divorce action, and she is free to write me at Ft. Dix." I also wrote, "Since no appeal was

174

enclosed concerning the jury tampering, I am assuming that none was taken and I would like to know why not." I didn't get an answer to that question for six years, well after I had been released from prison.

59

David Gibson clearly didn't want me to have the closing arguments from trial, probably because he had no idea what I intended to do with them, although he no doubt assumed that whatever the reason, it would not be good for him. My father began to pester him with a series of letters and finally, on October 3, Dad wrote to Gibson threatening to sue the reporter, William Currie, III. Surely Dad suspected, as did I, that the fault lay with Gibson, not Currie, but it was more diplomatic to blame Currie. This rather drastic step finally bore results, and I got the government's closing arguments. It took months more prodding to get the defense closing arguments.

A day after Dad's letter, I wrote again to David Gibson, and he could certainly see the direction things were headed. I asked for several items, but the most ominous were copies of the stipulations that Gibson had signed behind my back prior to trial, and the chemical orders admitted into evidence pursuant to the stipulations - the same chemical orders I had described as forgeries. While I truthfully said that I needed the material for the pending Pollution Solutions case, Gibson must have realized that he was one of the targets of my investigation. The effect was that there was no response to my letter.

I wrote again on October 31st, more threatening this time:

I have not yet received any response to my letter to you of October 4. In the matter of the chemical orders, I do not have the luxury of waiting more than a year for the materials as I did with Currie and the final arguments...I never stipulated the accuracy of chemical orders that were sold to someone unknown to me in another state, and I don't understand what happened, but I'm certainly not going to concede that they are genuine. Since some of the documents are obvious forgeries and others have been withheld, I may repudiate all the stipulations until such time as the documents can be verified by the companies involved if, in fact, they can be verified...It may seem to those on the outside that, once a person settles into prison, time ceases to have much meaning. At least in my case,

just the opposite has happened and I become more
frustrated and angry each day. Please indicate at your
earliest convenience whether you intend to supply the
materials I requested and, if so, when I might expect
them...

David Gibson sent me a letter on November 8th with a copy of the court's
denial of the appeal. A handwritten note on the bottom said,
"Disappointing, but not unexpected." As to my specific requests, he said
only, "I will be in touch with you shortly to address your various
correspondence of late." He wasn't.

The Second Circuit had disposed of the appeal in a little more than
a page, in part by refusing to consider Gibson's best argument. The
argument, while technical, was legally interesting. Basically it said that
the Sentencing Guidelines regarding methamphetamine had been amended
without due care, and were now inconsistent with the criminal statute.
Unfortunately, according to the Court, "Bloomer did not raise this
argument before the district court, however, and has presented no
reasonable excuse for his failure to do so. The argument is therefore
waived."[71]   The court had nothing to say about the jury tampering, as
Gibson had not appealed that matter or otherwise brought it to the court's
attention. The criminal matter was now over, with only the house
forfeiture remaining. That matter had been dormant for some time, but
with the conclusion of the appeal it was sure to be reactivated soon.

In retrospect, I should have asked Mr. Gibson for my entire client
file relating to the criminal case then and there, instead of pursuing
particular documents. Not knowing any better at the time, I wrote to
Gibson again on December 27, 1994:

I am saddened and somewhat mystified at your lack of
cooperation concerning my requests of October 4, 1994.
Certainly the trial exhibits of chemical orders ...should
have been provided as a matter of routine. This is
especially puzzling in light of the fact that you have been
aware for some time of discovery deadlines in my case
against Pollution Solutions and my need for the chemical
orders in that regard. I cannot allow your lack of diligence
to jeopardize my suit, and therefore plan to take your
deposition in the near future...My patience is exhausted
and I will not wait indefinitely for the other material
before taking appropriate action...As for those who have

breached their legal or ethical duties, let them suffer the consequences.

Although Mr. Gibson was not to respond to my requests for many months more, my letters apparently had an unintended effect: at some point Gibson contacted his malpractice insurance carrier to notify them that I would be suing him. Of course, Mr. Gibson did not advise me of this contact, but rather continued to represent me.

If my previous experiences in the courts were any indication of how things were going to proceed, challenging my convictions was going to be a slow process, and I realized that the more things I could do simultaneously, the better. After finally receiving her report more than two years after it was generated, I began corresponding with our trial chemical expert, University of Vermont chemistry professor Karen Sentell. My Dad continued pestering United States Senator James Jeffords, a personal friend, about the government's failure to follow its own laws regarding Freedom of Information disclosures, and I slowly began to familiarize myself with the federal criminal law, especially as it concerned the rapidly evolving area of double jeopardy.

As 1994 drew to a close, I had settled into Fort Dix and manipulated the system as much as I could for my own benefit. My job was not demanding, leaving plenty of time to pursue my legal case or other interests, and I had finally transferred into a satisfactory eight-man room where all of my roommates were Hispanic and none of the beds were bunked. A friend from Vermont had come to visit, as had my parents and my brother, Tom, who lived about two hours away in New York.

60

Nineteen ninety-five began with a dramatic incident: my uncle, John Bloomer, was killed in a car accident on January 4th on his way to the state capital. When my father had retired from the Senate, my uncle had run for his position and had been elected. He had also succeeded in occupying my father's old positions as president pro tem of the Senate and chairman of the Judiciary Committee.

I first learned of the accident from a friend in the library, who had seen an item in the *New York Times*. Later I was summoned to the office of my case manager, as my father had called from Vermont with the same news. She said, "I don't think I can let you go to the funeral because it's not immediate family, and you have more than 10 years left in your sentence." This was the first I knew that it was even a possibility, and it warranted further investigation since there were some questions about my father's health.

It turned out that there were two possibilities: an escorted trip and a furlough. The escorted trip involved at least two guards, at least one armed, and shackles unless the inmate had minimum/out custody according to the relevant Program Statement. I would never have considered showing up at any family event in irons with armed escorts, and this made it all the more imperative to work on reducing my custody level. Minimum/out custody was also a requirement for the second alternative - a furlough, or unescorted absence from the prison. Furloughs were rarely granted but were, nonetheless, possible.

61

Barely a week after my uncle's death I received another bombshell in the form of a letter from David Gibson dated January 10, 1995 concerning the forfeiture action against my house.[72]   Rather, the letter was a copy of one Gibson had written to Asst. U.S. Attorney James Gelber with the handwritten note "Bob, For your info. Dave" at the top left. The letter contained the astounding comment, "Finally, I expect to file in the next few days a motion to have the forfeiture proceedings dismissed on grounds of double jeopardy."

Considering Gibson's refusal to meet with me prior to resentencing and the result, his continuing failure to supply me with documents from my client file and my increasingly hostile letters, it was incredible that he could think I'd want him to represent me. Moreover Gibson's proposed motion, had it been successful, would have left me in jail to finish my 188-month sentence while preserving the real estate for my soon-to-be-ex-wife. I immediately called Gibson's office and left word that I did not want the motion filed.

I had been studying the double jeopardy matter in Fort Dix's law library with a little help from Tony LaRosa, who thought that the double jeopardy argument might help his case also. The essence of the argument was that the Fifth Amendment to the United States Constitution forbade double jeopardy, stating specifically "...nor shall any person be subject for the same offense to be twice put in jeopardy of life or limb..." Several U.S. Supreme Court decisions, taken together, seemed to indicate that a civil forfeiture (such as the one pending against my house in West Rutland) and a criminal prosecution based on the same facts would constitute double jeopardy, and the second punishment would be barred by the first. Prisoners immediately flooded the courts with petitions to have

178

either asset forfeitures or criminal convictions overturned on double jeopardy grounds.

While double jeopardy was a simple proposition on the surface, problems arose immediately, particularly over the question of when jeopardy attached in the various proceedings. It appeared to be reasonably settled law that jeopardy attached in a criminal case when the jury was drawn for a trial or when a guilty plea was entered. However, in the civil matter things were less clear. The government was using what were essentially maritime statutes in forfeiture cases like mine, and under those statutes title to the property passed immediately to the Attorney General of the United States upon the issuance of a warrant of forfeiture by a judge or magistrate without input from the defendant property or its owner. A letter from Deputy U.S. Marshal Jeffrey Payne to the West Rutland Town Clerk on January 23, 1992 left little doubt as to who owned the property as of that date, more than two months before my trial. The letter read in part:

> The United States Marshals Service has seized 96
> Clarendon Avenue in your town owned by Robert A.
> Blomer [sic] pursuant to an order of the United States
> District Court...Property owned by the United States
> Government is exempt from taxes pursuant to Vermont
> Statute...no property taxes will be paid that are assessed
> after the date of the offense that gives rise to the forfeiture.

While the property could be defended later, ownership in the meantime was by the Attorney General. Since the penalty was the loss of the property, it could be argued that jeopardy attached when title first passed to the government. In spite of this, some district courts were ruling that jeopardy didn't attach until the forfeiture was final, even though the owner had actually lost it some time before. There were actually quite a few possibilities as to when jeopardy might attach, and the rulings varied widely from court to court. Eventually, the Supreme Court would have to sort it all out.

Few, if any, prison inmates with long sentences preferred to serve the time rather than give up their property. Under the circumstances, then, the prudent course was to argue that jeopardy had attached first in the civil case and the criminal penalty was barred. Even if the district court judge disagreed, the argument would be preserved pending the final resolution of the question by the Supreme Court. Apparently David Gibson was not planning to even make the argument that I should be released from jail.

I had told Mr. Gibson rather bluntly that he was not representing me in the divorce, and had directed him not to file any double jeopardy motion, and therefore thought the matter was closed. However, I discussed the situation with my father during a visit my parents made on January 21st, and he thought I should write to Gibson and state explicitly that I did not want him to represent me. Indeed there was absolutely no reason for Gibson to continue on the case. My father was handling the divorce, and Will Hunter was still an attorney of record for the forfeiture. In addition, my father had entered a special appearance in the forfeiture on January 20th as he didn't think my interests were being adequately protected.

Dad had received a copy of David Gibson's January 10th letter to James Gelber, and became concerned about Gibson's reference to Gelber's letter of December 29th mentioning the unpaid mortgage for the West Rutland house. The terms of Katrina's and my tenancy agreement with the U.S. Marshals included a provision that the mortgage be paid, and the government was threatening to terminate the agreement immediately without waiting for the forfeiture hearing. Apparently several notices had been sent to Katrina, but none had been sent to me although I had also signed the agreement and had a co-interest in the real estate. I still had a considerable amount of personal property at the house, and certainly didn't want to give it to the government by default for sale or disposal.

Although my father diplomatically blamed the government, he was not pleased to learn that neither Will Hunter nor David Gibson had sent me anything regarding problems with the mortgage, and thought that by entering a special appearance at least he would be receiving copies of relevant documents. There was no need to do anything else as I had planned to craft my own double jeopardy motion, either to be filed by my father or by myself pro se at the appropriate time. Meanwhile it was my intention to let the forfeiture proceed, as I didn't want the government to give back the property and then claim that I had no double jeopardy issue. Katrina had retained counsel to represent her in the divorce, and I assumed that the same attorney could look after her interests in the forfeiture.

In my mind there was no particular urgency to write to David Gibson, and I got around to do so on February 28, 1995. The letter began: "There seems to [be] some miscommunication between us and I am writing at the suggestion of my father to clarify a couple of things. First, I do not wish you to represent me further in any matter whatsoever." That seemed clear enough, and I saw no need to belabor the point. I went on: "Second, I have not yet received any of the materials I requested in my

180

letter of October 4, 1994 in spite of pointed follow-up letters on October 31 and December 27, 1994."

Consistent with my wishes at the time, federal Magistrate Judge Jerome Neidermeyer issued a report and recommendation on April 11, 1995, that my interests in the West Rutland property be forfeited. On April 21, nearly two months after he was fired, David Gibson sent a motion to the court for an extension of seven days for time to file objections to the report and recommendation. Under his signature on the motion, Gibson described himself as "Attorney of record for Robert A. Bloomer, Jr." The cover letter for the motion indicated that copies were sent to AUSA Gelber, Will Hunter, my father, Joan Wing (Katrina's attorney) and S. Stacy Chapman, the lawyer for the mortgage-holding bank, but Gibson sent no copy to me. Neither did he advise the court that he had been fired.

When I received copies from my father, I went wild and called him immediately. I practically yelled into the phone, "What is it about being fired that Gibson doesn't understand? That idiot is going to foul up my double jeopardy claim!" I also said that apparently Mr. Gibson wasn't going to listen to me, and I asked my father to call and explain in no uncertain terms that he was fired. This time Gibson got the message, because on April 24th he wrote the court again, withdrawing his motion, but he never notified the court that he had been fired, nor did he ever withdraw as my attorney. U.S. Judge Fred Parker issued an order adopting Magistrate Neidermeyer's report and recommendations and granting the motion for forfeiture of my interest in the West Rutland property on May 31, 1995, clearing the way for a double jeopardy claim.

62

The actual forfeiture of the property took a while longer, as Katrina's interest had to be dealt with. I had thought that she would contest the forfeiture of her one-half interest using the innocent owner defense and, since the government had conceded earlier that Katrina was not a target of the investigation, she was in a perfect position to assert that defense. The property would have most likely been sold, especially since Katrina didn't want to keep it, but she could have recouped at least the cash value of her interest - something around $50,000 based on the town appraisal. Even if she had to pay off the mortgage, there was only a balance of about $5,000, which would have left her a considerable sum.

I didn't realize at the time the extent to which the house had deteriorated. Katrina had moved to Rutland in the fall of 1994 and I was later told that the unoccupied house had become a popular teen party spot. No one who saw the house later could easily find words to describe the mess, but clothing and other personal property mixed with trash were knee-deep in much of the house. "Churned" and "rototilled" were two words that came up in connection with what was on the floor. Deputy marshal Paul Whelton described it as "trashed". In addition a pipe had frozen and burst in the basement, spraying water on an accumulation of garbage, and producing a rotting, bug-infested mass and a thousand-dollar water bill.

I heard later that the coils in the refrigerator had been punctured so the Freon could be inhaled. In the process the icemaker apparently sprang a leak, because supposedly there was a huge block of ice in the middle of the kitchen about three feet on a side during the winter. It was my understanding that the water had been shut off, so perhaps the partygoers had turned it back on to use the toilet. In any event, the damage was considerable, and contrary to the terms of the tenancy agreement. The result was that the government threatened to back charge Katrina for all the damage to the house.

I was not fully aware of the deplorable condition of the property until May 25, 1995, when my Dad inspected the premises to determine how best to remove my effects. The marshals, continuing with their highhanded tactics, had padlocked the house sometime in late 1994 or early 1995 with no notice to me, trapping my personal property inside and, because of the pending divorce, they would permit nothing to be removed without Katrina's consent. Her attorney was not returning telephone calls, and Katrina herself was unavailable for one reason or another over a period of months. The marshals finally agreed to an inspection as long as nothing was taken away. During the inspection my father recognized a Japanese sword hanging on the bedroom wall as one that had been my grandfather's, brought back from New Guinea after World War II, and he also recognized a .22 rifle in the gun cabinet as one that he had had as a boy. Although the partiers at the house left a mess, they didn't appear to have stolen anything of much value.

Finally it was agreed that moving day would be on July 7th, perhaps in part because the Judgment Order and Decree of Divorce had issued on June 26th. My father, mother, brother and several friends showed up, along with Katrina, Lindsay, their professional movers and the obligatory U.S. Marshals. It was discovered immediately that the back door to the house had been broken open, and the sword and whatever guns

182

had been in the house had been stolen. Perhaps other items were missing, but the house was in such disarray that my father couldn't clearly recollect what had been there previously except for the sword, the .22, and two or three other guns that he could not describe by make or model.

While the marshals were visibly upset, their discomfort apparently produced only a certain amount of hand wringing. Although breaking into federally owned property was ostensibly a federal crime, the only investigation I was aware of was conducted by the Vermont State Police, and it appeared that only a minimum of effort was expended. A New Jersey State Trooper came to interview me at Fort Dix regarding the missing guns, but I never heard anything more from the police. The bottom line was that I had been prevented from recovering my property by the marshals in whose custody it had been for months and, now that it was gone, it was my tough luck.

The sword, in particular, may have been quite valuable. A customer for whom I had done machine work made reproductions of medieval arms and armor for renaissance fairs, and he had estimated its value at $20,000. According to him, it was several hundred years old, and he had described in detail the primitive processes by which it had been made.

The loss of the sword was certainly a disappointment, but the surprising thing was that most of my tools survived, although not in the neat order that I had left them. No rational process could be imagined to account for how my garage came to look as it did. Like the house, tools and trash had been mixed together and strewn about. While some things were gone or unaccounted for, many of the expensive items remained. "Real master mechanics," observed a friend at the scene, an automotive professional. "Steal the hammers and leave the [costly] torque wrenches behind." The same friend moved my tools to a semi-trailer he had behind his garage, with the balance of my personal property deemed worth saving going to my parents or another friend. My brother, Rick, even took my small racing hydroplane that I'd had since I was 15 and placed it in storage where it remained until I resurrected it several years later.

In all it took three trips to move everything, the last being on September 1. While many, if not most, prison inmates left with the clothes on their backs and little more, thanks to family and friends I would have tools, clothes, and other items of personal property with which to start again.

Katrina was not inclined to fight with the government anyway, but under the circumstances apparently didn't want to risk what could have been a very substantial liability if she lost her claim. She struck an

183

agreement (filed with the court as a stipulation) to relinquish any claim she had to the property in exchange for a promise from the government that it would not charge her for any damage, and she just walked away. The property was, ironically, awarded to me in the divorce. The final order of forfeiture by Judge Murtha was filed on July 24, 1995.

At the time, the courts were in such turmoil over the double jeopardy matter that it made no sense to file anything until some of the issues had been sorted out. As I was waiting and reading the cases from around the country, a decision by my own trial judge on September 27th rocked the system from coast to coast. Judge Franklin Billings, Jr. released Brian Brophil from prison on the grounds that his property in Glover, Vermont had been forfeited prior to his criminal prosecution, invalidating the latter on double jeopardy grounds.

While this was certainly exciting news, it remained to be seen if Brophil would be re-jailed by a higher court (which is what eventually happened). However, within three weeks of the Brophil decision an article appeared in the *Rutland Herald* of October 13th giving me a much better new trial issue than double jeopardy: the convictions of my acquaintance from Ray Brook, Winston Birbal, had been reversed due to erroneous instructions given by Judge Billings to Birbal's trial jury. The bad instructions, quoted in the newspaper, were identical to the instructions Judge Billings had given in my case. It was time to shift gears and carefully research and prepare a motion for a new trial - this time myself with a little help from Tony LaRosa.

63

I was not otherwise idle as the house forfeiture and double jeopardy matters moved forward, but rather was gathering such information as I could and trying to make good use of my time. Incredibly, the prison had consented to offer a private pilot's course through the Education Department, with none other than Tony LaRosa as the instructor. In his previous life, Tony had been a pilot with his own single-engine plane and an interest in a small commercial aviation company. The course was even offered in Spanish, with a former pilot for the Dominican national airline as the teacher. I had more confidence in Tony, as Hispanic inmates were joking that the Dominican company had been banned from the United States for a poor safety or maintenance record.

184

Surprisingly, the local airport was quite excited about the project and planned to send a certified examiner to the prison to administer the FAA test. Of course, actual flight training would have been necessary to get a license, but ground school was a necessary and significant part of the process. Unfortunately, the Fort Dix staff member charged with making the arrangements dropped the ball, and by the time he finally contacted the airport to set a date certain for the tests, the FAA had switched to an examination given exclusively by computer. The mere mention of the word "computer" struck fear into the BOP, and there was no way that inmates were going to be allowed access to any computer connected to the outside world, so the test was never given. The course was, nonetheless, interesting and attracted, besides dilettantes like myself, a couple of smugglers with wild tales of landing on clandestine airstrips in the Caribbean and South America.

While Tony's pilot's course was entertaining, he made a move in January of 1995 that would fundamentally change my direction. Apparently he figured that things would be better for him working for religious services rather than the education department in the law library. The problem was that the director of libraries, universally known as Miss O, was not inclined to let him leave without finding a suitable replacement, which turned out to be me.

Tony LaRosa, as a real lawyer, was actually irreplaceable, but he somehow convinced Miss O that I could take over for him in the law library. Perhaps it was because Fort Dix East was accustomed to a relatively low level of education; out of about 2,400 inmates there were only three lawyers I knew of, one dentist, two engineers, and a smattering of self-proclaimed foreign doctors with dubious credentials. And certainly Fort Dix was accustomed to a low level of competence among staff and inmates alike. Whatever the politics may have been, I was transferred without warning or consultation from the leisure library to the law library. At the time I was quite angry with Tony for what I thought was a cheap trick, but it turned out that Tony knew exactly what I needed to do.

The work consisted mostly of going to the shelves and getting books that the inmate patrons requested, and there was no requirement that any of the library clerks actually help with another inmate's legal work in any way, although some did. Updated material arrived weekly which had to be filed, but it didn't take long. In the process of filing, the library clerks were the first to see the latest laws and court decisions, a great benefit in a system where there was frequently squabbling over the order in which people saw the new material.

Another advantage was that I was actually among the books and had ready access to the indices. Everything one really needed to pursue a federal legal claim was in the prison's library, but the research tools, while adequate, were rudimentary. There were no research computers, and there were never going to be. Neither were there tools often found in lawyers' offices such as West's Key Number Digest. However a determined inmate could look at the key numbers in the back of each volume of Federal Reporter if he were so inclined, a process made immeasurably easier when one could simply stand there and take the books off the shelves one by one without having to sign them out.

At last I was among people who really knew the federal criminal law. Of course, some of the library patrons were imbeciles and some of the imbeciles were actually charging other inmates for their work, but a few of the library's habitués were probably more knowledgeable than most criminal lawyers in the street. These people could quickly focus one's efforts on promising post-conviction remedies without the necessity of a general study of the law. In addition, Tony LaRosa was teaching a legal research course and, although I didn't attend, Tony gave me the course material as well as some private tutoring. So as I kept abreast of the double jeopardy issue, I was also on the lookout for other avenues that might produce results.

64

Another great benefit of the law library was the availability of typewriters. With a typewriter I could continue to gather information about my case, and prepare the appropriate legal papers if the opportunity presented itself. Theoretically I could have written letters longhand, but realistically I had trouble reading my own writing, and a scrawled note or motion from an inmate surely received less consideration than a professional appearing document.

Unfortunately the typewriters were only homeowner models and began to wear out after a year or two of intensive use. To keep them in service I had to repair them with primitive tools on several occasions. Since the machines were purchased at the same time, the failures came all at once, and at one point, about half the daisy wheels had failed, making those machines useless. While any business would have stocked adequate spares of expendable parts, Fort Dix had only a few extra wheels, which were quickly used up. Inexplicably, it took weeks to obtain more, causing a genuine problem for those facing court deadlines.

My typewriter problems were solved entirely on October 8, 1995 when I changed jobs from law library to chapel clerk. Apparently Tony LaRosa thought I had passed my crash course in the law, and had arranged for me to join him in the chapel as a clerk. The job had few responsibilities and involved minimal contact with other inmates, but came with an electronic memory typewriter and frequent access to a photo-copier, both highly desirable for a prison litigator.

There were, of course, typewriters in the libraries (when they had print wheels), but a memory writer was more powerful - almost a word processor. And theoretically there was a copier in the law library for inmate use, but it was an old, worn-out machine haphazardly maintained by an outside vendor, and it often didn't work. Repair times were unpredictable, and if something had to be copied without delay the only alternative was to pay a premium price to a group of Miss O's clerks for copies made more or less clandestinely on her office machine. The chapel copier solved this problem almost completely, and promised to be available indefinitely as long as the privilege wasn't abused.

Another benefit of the chapel job was that the boss, head chaplain Father Pete Literal, was one of the true gems of the Fort Dix staff. Born to a Phillippino correctional officer Father Pete had become a Catholic priest and had himself pursued a career in corrections. Tony LaRosa had been active in the Fort Dix Catholic community, and had first encountered Father Pete at that time, although he had misread the priest. Initially Tony had considered him just another overly officious BOP employee and derisively referred to him as "God's cop". However as Tony began to know Father Pete better they became friends, and Tony saw that Pete had a deeply humanitarian side.

Perhaps Pete's empathy could be attributed in part to the fact that a prisoner had donated a kidney to him, or perhaps it was part of his calling, but regardless he wasn't much of a taskmaster. He was always ready to give an inmate the benefit of the doubt, but reacted decisively when his trust had been abused. I was present on one occasion when an indigent inmate begged a free (and expensive) telephone call to Africa, supposedly because of a family emergency. When it became clear that the call was for business, Pete reached across the desk and unceremoniously hung up the phone. The inmate never bothered to ask for any favors again.

Of course, religious services didn't have a mission vital to the operation of the prison like the medical or facilities departments, which explained in part its more relaxed style. However it did seem to be a popular hangout for inmates that might have had something to fear from their peers. A young Haitian with a compulsion to spy overtly on other inmates, and to tattle about trivia, was a frequent visitor. The grapevine said that he had been transferred to Fort Dix for more or less protective custody after severe beatings at another institution.

Fort Dix seemed to have an odd mission in that regard, as it was also loaded with child sex offenders. They couldn't be housed at a high security facility because of the probability of violent retribution, and they couldn't be placed at a minimum-security facility because they were considered dangerous predators. To the question, "Well, then what would you do with people like that?" the answer seemed to be, "Put them in Fort Dix." Indeed, one mousy-looking gentleman seen in frequent tête-à-têtes with Father Pete behind closed doors had made the front page of the *Baltimore Sun* as a kiddie porn filmmaker.

One expected to find unsavory characters throughout the prison system, and the fact that some of them inhabited religious services hardly made any difference to me. Tony and I each had our own desks with typewriters in the religious library, which was normally quiet and empty except for the occasional Bible or Koran reader. At one point free greeting cards were dispensed once or twice a week from the library, but a group of Latino inmates had more or less taken over the franchise and moved it down the hall, so we were spared the frenzy that sometimes accompanied that operation. (Hallmark and perhaps others donated surplus cards to the prison system, which were then given to inmates. Someone had to handle the distribution, and at Fort Dix it was religious services.)

Sometimes there were not enough of the most popular cards to go around, leading to accusations of favoritism. At one point a Jewish inmate stole a carton the size of a banker's box of the best Christmas cards, and then sold them to Christians. Someone repaid the favor by stealing a case or two of the very expensive kosher grape juice used for Jewish services, no doubt to make some excellent prison wine. The crime was never solved, and even the glass bottles that contained the juice disappeared completely, no mean feat in a prison where "recycling" meant sorting through all the trash and separating the recyclables under the supervision of guards.

Tony and I were glad to be out of all that nonsense, and stuck to our minimal duties and our legal work. Tony was trying to reduce his eleven-year sentence, and in the meantime was doing legal work for other inmates, perhaps for pay although I never inquired and he never said. I picked up a little extra money typing legal work for others, charging a dollar a page and cleaning up the spelling and grammar in the process.

Father Pete was surely aware that Tony and I were doing legal work, and no doubt suspected that we were making legal copies, but said

188

nothing. One day he got a call from the Lieutenant's office advising him of our activities, but told the amazed Lieutenant that he already knew and that we had his permission, and that was the end of it. He then came to us and said, "You can continue with your legal work, but just keep it down a little." Nothing more was ever said.

It seemed that a real estate swindler from Philly, the same Jewish inmate responsible for stealing the Christmas cards, had decided to take over all the legal business in the prison with a little help from his friends in the Lieutenant's office, notwithstanding the fact that he had absolutely no legal skills. We learned later that he had stolen the volume of the United States Code most used by inmates trying to get out of prison, 28 U.S.C. § 2255, and had all the law library clerks fired on apparently no more than his word that they were doing legal work for money, a common but prohibited activity. (It was all right to do it for nothing.) It looked like he intended to have Tony and me fired also, but the plan failed thanks to Father Pete.

One of the former law library clerks was always at the typewriter typing religious screeds, but never to my knowledge legal work. When I ran into him on the compound, I said with a smile, "Hey I hear you got fired for doing legal work." His reply was angry, "That's a lot of bullsh*t. I had to pay somebody to do my own 2255 [new trial motion]."

It turned out that the Jewish swindler was trying to substitute pure chutzpah for legal expertise. He had a Dominican shill that was charging Hispanic inmates for the privilege of having "the Jewish lawyer" work on their cases, and business must have been good as the Dominican had a spare locker jammed absolutely full of food and other items from the commissary. Tony and I were later told by a reliable staff source that the missing law book had been found in the "lawyer's" locker, but there were no consequences whatsoever that we were aware of for what was arguably a criminal act.

The swindler's case had been covered in some detail in the Philadelphia newspaper, and appeared to have been a one-man show. That seemed to leave only informing on other inmates, perhaps untruthfully, as the only way to curry such favor with the authorities. With such unabashed treachery afoot, Tony and I were glad to be where we were.

65

I wasn't sufficiently confident with my newly acquired legal skills to accept responsibility for the fate of others, and it was a heartbreaking business besides. There were some real hard luck stories, and most of the prospective litigants hadn't even a slight chance of overturning their convictions or reducing their sentences. Nevertheless, there was no shortage of hucksters willing to sell blue sky to people desperately searching for a way out, although I was determined not to be one of them.

Lawyers in the street wanted thousands of dollars for their services, leaving inmate lawyers as the only option for most prisoners, but there was certainly no guarantee that even if one paid a real lawyer, one would get good representation in return. I had had my own experience with David Gibson, and had heard dozens of stories of equal or worse incompetence or treachery. One of the most egregious was the case of one "Chino" Ramos, with whom I was acquainted at both Ray Brook and Fort Dix. After paying a string of real lawyers more than a quarter of a million dollars, he finally succeeded in getting his sentence increased from 18 to 30 or 35 years.

While I was reluctant to represent others, there was no doubt in my mind as to who was going to be my attorney for the new trial motion based on the erroneous jury instruction identified in the Birbal case: me. However, there was never any question that I would solicit the services of the highly experienced Tony LaRosa, and he began to research the matter as soon as I gave him a copy of the court's Birbal decision in mid-October. An agonizing three weeks followed.

Tony had often complained to me that his clients were always pestering him to hurry, and his response was, "Do you want it done quickly or done right?" With that in mind I said nothing, although I thought at the time that he was working for others instead of me despite our friendship. It turned out that he was doing an extremely thorough job, looking at all the angles, and that had I filed the motion the way I had originally intended it most likely would have been blown quickly out of the water. As it was, we had all the bases covered, and the motion for a new trial was filed in the court in Vermont on November 9, 1995.

The Second Circuit had already found Judge Billings' jury instruction on reasonable doubt to be constitutionally deficient, and Supreme Court precedent took care of the rest. My motion listed three grounds for relief, any of which alone could have reversed all my convictions: 1) my right to due process of law was violated by the deficient instruction, 2) my Sixth Amendment right to a verdict of guilty beyond a reasonable doubt was violated, and 3) my attorney gave ineffective assistance by failing to object to the deficient instruction.

I was now giddy with excitement. From a legal point of view, it didn't get any better than this. Considering all that had gone on before, and the highly questionable integrity of both the U.S. Attorney's office and
190

the federal courts, I should have realized that it was going to be a long, dirty fight. Instead I naively thought that I'd be home for Christmas, 1995.

66

As I waited for my new trial motion to work its way through the courts, I looked back with some satisfaction at the loose ends I had tried to tie up, and the progress I had made on issues that might come up at a new trial. I had spent several months, on and off, accumulating documents and making copies for use in a prospective malpractice suit against David Gibson. Dad had taken the depositions of Pollution Solutions president Pamela Linton[73] and former Vermont State Police chemist Dr. Brendan McMahon[74] in connection with the civil suit against Pollution Solutions and the State of Vermont.[75] Considering that Ms. Linton and her company had themselves been the subjects of an investigation into improper handling of hazardous waste, it wasn't surprising that she was evasive and had a poor memory.

The McMahon deposition was more interesting. Although the police inventory of my chemicals had been introduced into evidence at my trial through the testimony of Dr. McMahon, Dad established that he really knew very little about how it was prepared and certainly couldn't vouch for its accuracy. And he nailed down the fact that "probably in the neighborhood of 20"[76] onsite tests were performed for methamphetamine, all of which were "negative" or "not positive". Also, according to Dr. McMahon, the chemists at my house had no geiger counter.[77] I hadn't expected anyone to bring one, especially since the chemists had failed to bring enough collection bottles to take samples of unknown chemicals before having them destroyed, and I thought it preposterous when DEA chemist Jack Fasanello testified at trial that they had tested a bottle of purported thorium nitrate at my house with a geiger counter to confirm its radioactivity. Given what I had discovered about chemist Fasanello, I was confident that he could be discredited at any future trial. However, I also discovered that I might have to discredit my own chemist, UVM professor Karen Sentell. After finally receiving her report from David Gibson indicating that she could find nothing wrong with Dr. McMahon's testing I thought I should find out exactly what information Gibson had given her, and how she had reached her conclusion. In that regard I wrote her directly at the University of Vermont on September 1, 1994. The letter stated in part:

I am presently serving a prison sentence for methamphetamine manufacture and related charges. I have
maintained my innocence throughout this ordeal, and am
continuing my legal fight. I was represented by Attorney
David Gibson and, although I was aware that he consulted
chemical experts on my behalf, I have only recently
learned your name and been provided with your report
dated April 15, 1992 (copy enclosed) ... Since there were
no methamphetamine residues from any activity of mine,
and since Dr. McMahon admits that he committed serious
crimes related to his work, I am scrutinizing his results
with great care. To that end, I would appreciate it if you
could elaborate on certain portions of your report. To
begin with, I would like the results of your extensive
literature research on March 27-29 and the materials from
Mr. Swartz ... While I am indigent, I'm sure that my
parents can be relied upon to pay reasonable copying fees.
Thank you for your cooperation.

On October 6 my father also wrote to Dr. Sentell as my attorney
asking for a copy of whatever she sent me. A month went by with no
response, so I wrote again on October 3:

To date I have received no response to my letter to you of
September 1, 1994. I am presently involved in a legal
action where Dr. McMahon is expected to be a witness,
and I have already taken his deposition without the benefit
of your materials. I regret any inconvenience it may
cause, but time is of the essence and I would appreciate a
prompt reply to my query. I have no explanation as to
why I was not made aware of your report and research
work much earlier but, having apparently paid for it, I
believe I am entitled to it at this time."

This time Dr. Sentell replied within two days (on October 5th) enclosing
her report, her billing statement, the materials from a professional
colleague concerning forensic drug testing, copies of excerpts from the
Proceedings of the International Symposium on the Forensic Aspects of
Controlled Substances, as well as a cover letter laying out the chronology
of her involvement in my case and contacts with David Gibson. The letter
closed with:

The above as well as enclosed materials are everything
tangible that I can send you with regard to your case, and
more than encompass the work that you 'paid for and are
entitled to' from me, as stated in your letter of October 3.
I say more than encompass, because I have used a
considerable amount of my own time today in
photocopying these materials (at my own expense),
replying to your letters, and sending copies of the above to
your current legal counsel. I wish you luck in your current
legal actions.

I suppose that I should not have been surprised that Dr. Sentell was a little
prickly as it surely occurred to her that she might have overlooked
something in the work of a scientist who was admittedly dishonest. For
my part, I thanked her promptly and began to digest what she had sent.

One thing jumped out immediately from Dr. Sentell's enclosures.
She claimed to have "spent a great deal of time carefully scrutinizing the
material before formulating [her] professional opinion". However, her
billing statement showed only .50 hours for an "Initial review of Brendan
McMahon's lab report" and 1.75 hours for an "Extensive review of
Brendan McMahon's lab report", a mere two and a quarter hours total.

According to Dr. Sentell, the material which she had scrutinized
had been faxed by David Gibson and included " grand jury transcripts,
analysis sheets and GC/MS reports of Dr. McMahon's analysis..."[78] At the
time I had no way to know exactly what David Gibson had faxed, but the
available relevant material consisted of at least Dr. McMahon's 25 pages
of grand jury testimony, 5 pages of his reports, 5 pages of log notes, 2
pages of IR spectra, 19 pages of gas chromatograms and 22 pages of mass
spectra, as well as whatever David Gibson had related to Dr. Sentell
verbally about McMahon's trial testimony. Gibson may also have sent
Jack Fasanello's 22 pages of grand jury testimony as Dr. Sentell used the
plural transcripts in her letter. I thought it unlikely that Dr. Sentell had
thoroughly digested all that material in 2 hours, especially considering that
she had missed the changing reference values for methamphetamine.

Of concern to me was her statement that she was to "give [her]
professional opinion on whether the analyses were carried out according to
standard analytical practices and as to whether there was any ostensible
reason to doubt their reliability." She further wrote that her "professional
opinion on the above two points as an expert analytical chemist [was] fully
elaborated on and entirely contained in [her] April 15, 1992 report", i.e.

193

she found nothing wrong and she wasn't going to change her opinion. I had to assume that the government already knew her opinion, and I thought that it might be a problem at a second trial, but decided to do my own research before challenging Dr. Sentell.

An article in the excerpts from the Proceedings of the International Symposium provided by Dr. Sentell referred to a DB-5 gas chromatographic column for drug testing, and the description matched Dr. McMahon's description of his column at trial. In addition, McMahon's printouts contained the entry LIBRARY = DB5 @ 15 C/MIN, which I interpreted to mean a DB-5 column heated at 15 degrees per minute. I had my mother order a complete copy of the Proceedings to see if anything else relevant might be in there, and wrote to J & W Scientific for a catalog to get more information on the DB-5.

The information I got confirmed what I had already strongly suspected and discussed with Dr. Brown: if Dr. McMahon had actually performed some of his tests the way he testified, he would have obtained no results at all for methamphetamine even if some had been present. Had Dr. Sentell been in the courtroom for McMahon's testimony, she would ostensibly have come to the same conclusion, but for unknown reasons David Gibson didn't have her in court.

It was time to confront Dr. Sentell with my findings. I wrote her on January 9, 1995 indicating that I had read the Proceedings in their entirety as well as the material she had supplied, and some of Dr. McMahon's protocols seemed at variance with those specified in her sources. More ominously, I asked:

> Since you stated that 'McMahon's conclusions ... were scientifically solid, and Prof. Sentell could think of no sound basis on which these conclusions could be challenged' I assume that you concur with his findings. I have only a partial mass spectrum (up to 120) with no reference data whatsoever to support McMahon's identification of N-formylmethamphetamine. On what basis did you confirm McMahon's identification of this substance?

I suspected that David Gibson had never mentioned the n-formylmethamphetamine to Dr. Sentell, and neither was it mentioned in any of McMahon's reports, but I was nonetheless interested to see her response. She may have hoped her best defense was to put her head in the sand, because I heard nothing.

194

On August 18, Dad wrote her a short letter as my attorney, indicating that if she was not going to respond, "give me some dates which will be convenient for you to give your deposition." This apparently unhinged the good doctor, because she put the letter back in its envelope, resealed it with Scotch tape, and hand wrote "refused - return to sender" on the envelope. The post office was unable to explain to my father why it accepted an opened letter for delivery without additional postage, but it was delivered.

On August 28th Dad wrote Dr. Sentell back, this time saying that if he didn't hear within a few days he would notice her deposition. Again the letter came back, more emphatic this time: **REFUSED** **Return to Sender**. A subsequent inquiry to the University of Vermont revealed that Dr. Sentell was no longer there, but had moved to Georgia. A friend in an Atlanta suburb was able to find her address in nearby Alpharetta, and Dad wrote again, enclosing a copy of his previous letter. This time, she was willing to visit by telephone.

Dad followed up on November 17th indicating that I had several questions I wanted answered, either by letter or deposition. Instead of generating a letter of response, Dr. Sentell handwrote various comments on Dad's letter. She double underlined the word "deposition" and added the notation "not at all necessary See below: ", and in the bottom margin were additional scrawled comments. She apparently was of the belief that since her opinion wasn't used at trial, it was irrelevant, and we should not "persist in bothering [her]".

Dad was willing to take Dr. Sentell's deposition in Georgia, but wondered if the time and resources might be better spent on other projects. My new trial motion had already been filed for a month at the time Dad received the response to his letter, and we let the matter drop for the time, figuring that I would be able to deal with Dr. Sentell myself in the near future if it proved necessary.

67

While the chemists were certainly more important to new trial issues, the government's failure to return my property continued to bother me. Back in 1991 Vermont Judge Silvio Valente had ordered the State to return to me "any materials seized on August 11, 1990 from 96 Clarendon Avenue, West Rutland, Vermont which are not necessary or material to the criminal investigation." In 1995, not only was the investigation over but the criminal case was over as well. In spite of that fact, nothing had been returned since 1991. Particularly galling was the theft of my explosives books by DEA chemist Fasanello.

My property was in an interesting legal limbo. The seizure of the property had been made under the authority of a state warrant, but the federal government had used some of it in a federal prosecution without any authority from the State that I was aware of allowing them to take possession. My house had been the subject of a forfeiture action, but the rest of my things had not. Perhaps the feds could have filed another forfeiture action against the cash found at my house, but there was no proof that any of it was the result of illegal activity, and 500 dollars of it wasn't even used as evidence at trial for unknown reasons. In addition another forfeiture action would have, at the time, raised double jeopardy questions as well as given me an opportunity to extensively question police officers myself without the bumbling David Gibson to limit the scope of the inquiry.

In the end, it may have been simply pragmatism that motivated the government, at least regarding my glassware. The Vermont State Police had rented a storage garage to keep it, and may have been sick of paying the rent. Whatever the reason, the glassware and 6 of the 7 chemicals that had gone to the police lab were returned to my father on April 11, 1995. (The 7th chemical, described on the inventory as "MENHZ 25g", disappeared, although the inventory showed a sample was sent to the DEA lab.) I didn't get to see the items personally for several years, but Dad had brought along a professional photographer who had taken a lot of pictures, and they were subsequently sent to me at Fort Dix.

Following the police raid on my house, it took over a year to develop sufficient evidence to bring a criminal indictment. In spite of that fact, the police apparently had no intention of returning my glassware or chemicals from the beginning. Several pages of the inventory of my chemicals were labeled "Chemicals for Destruction" and these were turned over to Pollutions Solutions of Vermont, a hazardous waste outfit. The glass, some of it both intricate and delicate, was carelessly loaded without any packing into 55-gallon drums, and also given to Pollution Solutions. A lot of the glass was broken, either in packing or transportation, but the surprising thing five years later was how much of it wasn't broken. Also surprising was that even my cylindrical furnace and the metal drip tray from my fume hood, which had been used as evidence at trial, were returned. What wasn't surprising, knowing the government's chemists as I did, was that some of the glassware was missing.

Even items that were badly smashed left pieces by which I could identify them, but my vacuum regulator, which had a massive glass top,

196

was entirely gone. Also gone were all my teflon stopcock valves for several items as well as glass and teflon stoppers. My suspicion was that DEA chemist Fasanello had taken them for analysis and, finding nothing incriminating, either stole or destroyed them without generating a report.

Although the police were supposed to have prepared a detailed inventory of what they seized, dozens of pieces of glassware were listed only as "6E ASSORTED gl[sic]ASSWARE" and "2 beaker". (The so-called beakers were actually two automatic pipetters.) Under the circumstances a claim for missing or stolen glassware was going nowhere, especially considering what had occurred regarding Katrina's missing gynecology records. However, there were a few loose ends, and I decided to pursue those.

On August 15, 1995 I wrote to Asst. U.S. Atty. Gary Shattuck beginning:

> I had thought that my former attorney, Mr. David Gibson, might have taken care of the following items but since he apparently has not, I'm writing you directly in hopes of avoiding a more formal proceeding.
>
> I believe you were present during the raid on my home August 11, 1990 during which a great deal of my property was taken. One of the items inventoried by the police was:
>
> #31   Explosive and propellants
>   Military Explosives
> books
>   Explosives and Demolition
>   Landmine Warfare (papers)

According to Sgt. Vargo of the Vermont State Police, these books were given to DEA chemist Jack Fasanello because, "For some reason, he had an interest in them." (Trial VI P37, L3) It was never clear to me what authority a federal agent had to take any of my property during a state raid, especially since it was unrelated to either the probable cause or the charges under investigation. Also, at all times relevant I had a valid Vermont Blaster's License permitting me to purchase, possess, use, etc. explosives. In any event, Mr. Fasanello has kept my property for more than five years, it was never used by the government as evidence at trial, and I would like it returned immediately.

I also asked for the return of my cash, some of which had not been used as evidence, and an accounting for it. Finally, I asked for copies of government exhibits 49, 50, 51, and 52 which were the stipulations relating to chemical orders allegedly placed by me because "I [had] asked Mr. Gibson for these stipulations repeatedly, but he tells me he is unable to find them."

I sent copies to Gibson, my father, and new federal judge J. Garvan Murtha who had taken office in March. Judge Murtha had a reputation as a straight shooter, and I thought it couldn't hurt to let him know that there were a few oddities in my case. Had I realized at the time that he was a former prosecutor (serving as a deputy to State's Attorney Jerome Diamond in Brattleboro) I wouldn't have held out much hope of any curiosity on his part regarding government or attorney misconduct.

As it turned out Judge Murtha would be little more than an arm of the U.S. Attorney's office, but perhaps Gary Shattuck didn't know it at the time as he responded in a week to my letter.[79] He enclosed copies of the stipulations and indicated that "[i]nquiries are being made" into my books, papers, and money and that I would "be contacted at a later date."

Any lingering doubts I might have had regarding David Gibson's loyalty were dispelled by the stipulations. He had signed them himself the day before trial while I was waiting for him at my father's office, and had failed to either mention the stipulations or give me copies at our meeting only minutes later. Gibson's professed inability to find his copies was yet further proof, especially considering that the stipulations were trial exhibits. (When I obtained a portion of my client file several years later, there was a folder entitled "Government Trial Exhibits".)

My father made arrangements with Lieutenant Steven Miller to pick up my money at State Police Headquarters in Waterbury on October 25, 1995. While all the money was there, it was loose in an envelope although at least one of the two trial exhibits of cash (29A and 31A) had been stapled together. I wrote Gary Shattuck again (with copies to Judge Murtha and U.S. Attorney Charles Tetzlaff) a month later[80] inquiring again about my books and inviting Shattuck to explain the missing staple in my money. He never responded.

Finally, following a telephone conversation between my father and Mr. Shattuck on February 26, 1996, three books purporting to be mine arrived at my father's office. The problem was that the books returned

198

were not the same at those seized. The books described (correctly in this instance) by the inventory were Explosive [sic] & Propellants, Military Explosives, and Explosives and Demolition. What had been returned were Modular Explosives Training Program and two copies of the same book, Explosives and Demolitions. Subsequent inquiries by my father to Gary Shattuck never produced any explanation for the inconsistency, and letters from my father to DEA chemist Fasanello were never answered. While my father eventually dropped the matter, the government's careless handling of my property would, some months down the road, give me a pretext to challenge the integrity of Judge Murtha.

68

It was just as well that I filed my new trial motion when I did as the situation was beginning to deteriorate, both at Fort Dix and in the federal government. Fort Dix had been hastily thrown together to relieve severe overcrowding in other federal institutions, and it was inevitable that there would be problems. The buildings were old, and the occupancy rate was much higher than the design contemplated, which led to a general crumbling and deterioration. Steam billowed from several manhole covers, indicating leaks in underground steam lines; hot water systems in the units failed; bricks fell out, and many of the windows were covered with plywood like a housing project in an urban ghetto.

With so many inmates and so much glass, it was certain that the windows in the housing units would be broken, but no one breaking a window, accidentally or otherwise, wanted to report it, so the obvious solution was to take one from somewhere else to replace the broken one. A downstairs bathroom in my unit had been a frequent source of glass until all the windows had been removed during the winter. Our unit manager did nothing, no doubt figuring that frostbitten inmate appendages or inmate butts frozen to the toilet seats would send a message to the perpetrators.

The policy, however well intentioned, was proved to be shortsighted during the first cold snap. The pipes froze and cracked during the night, spraying water everywhere. An emergency crew was then finally dispatched with plywood to cover the windows (which was still there when I left some years later) and another crew had to fix the pipes.

A more significant problem arose across the street in the mess hall, with a strange smell around Thanksgiving of 1995 giving the first warning of impending disaster. The odor got progressively worse until finally the overpowering stench of rotting sewage forced the closing of the mess hall just before Christmas. Apparently after several weeks someone had decided to check the basement as a possible source of the smell and had discovered a broken pipe and a basement full of sewage.

The institution never posted any notice detailing the precise situation in the mess hall, probably to deny inmates documentation for a lawsuit against the prison, but assurances from the warden of a quick fix began almost immediately. First, it was going to be a matter of days, then weeks, and the building briefly reopened, only to be closed again. This time it remained closed for many months, meaning all the meals for the 2,000 plus inmates had to be served in the one remaining mess hall. Instead of requiring an hour or two, it now took twice as long.

The nights that chicken was served were particularly bad, as it was particularly popular with Fort Dix's large Latino population. Even before the sewage leak, chicken nights were a problem as inmates released first to eat went through the line several times to get more chicken such that it ran out by the time the last housing unit was released. This situation was now exacerbated by the long wait, and the assignment of only two guards to each housing unit guaranteed that people would try to game the system. On chicken nights inmates could frequently be seen jumping from the back windows of their housing units and running to the mess hall before their units were called to eat, meaning just that much longer a wait for those obeying the rules. The last of the six housing units often wasn't released to eat until eight o'clock, which also interfered with evening leisure time activities.

Something clearly had to be done, so the institution opened a sandwich shop of sorts in a Prison Industries warehouse offering unhealthy fare, but short lines. A representative meal was hot dogs and potato chips, with a Fort Dix original soup recipe: puree the soup left over from lunch, dilute 10 to 1 with water, and add sliced carrots. Even with this menu, there was never any doubt in my mind, or the mind of Tony LaRosa, as to where we were going to eat during the madness of chicken nights.

Unfortunately, the same incompetence that led to the mess hall disaster also pervaded the prison hospital. As a general matter one expected such things in prison, but when the same tooth that had given so much trouble at Ray Brook began to hurt again, my problem became more personal. I went to the hospital and signed up for a dental appointment, which meant a wait of at least weeks if not months. The only thing one could do was wait and watch the callout, a computerized list of appointments posted in the housing units. The only problem was that inconsiderate inmates would take the callouts, perhaps to save roommates the walk to the guard's station, and not return them. Even though there

200

were several copies for each unit, they were often gone by the time I got back from work. On one of those days, my dental appointment was listed for the next day, and I missed it. The stated penalty for such an offense was a yearlong wait for another appointment.

Since I was in considerable discomfort I persisted at the hospital and was finally given an appointment. Upon examining my tooth, the hygienist exclaimed, "Oh, no, this is terrible, " and began to pace the floor. It turned out that an x-ray from at least a year previous had shown a crown failure on that tooth. It had gone untreated, and now the tooth was badly decayed. At that point I asked to see my records, and discovered that the x-ray from Ray Brook showing the infection had been removed from the file, and the records had been doctored to imply that I was a complainer without much in the way of justification.

Finally I had a solid basis for a medical malpractice suit, and thus the basis to obtain treatment. The head dentist, a man of rare competence at Ft. Dix, devoted quite a bit of time to repairing the bad tooth and installing a new crown, as well as identifying some incipient problems with other teeth and fixing them also. As I was sitting in the chair, an associate warden came in with a sheaf of papers and informed the dentist that his proposed budget had been rejected. A short time later he wisely transferred to an institution in California.

69

As the living conditions at Fort Dix deteriorated, there were ominous changes in the federal law as well. In January of 1995 the Republicans took control of the U.S. House of Representatives for the first time in 40 years, and wasted no time bringing up a favorite topic: crime. One of the first bills introduced was the so-called "No Frills Prison Act" which denied federal money to state prisons that offered too many amenities to prisoners. While there may have been five-star jails of the type described by the bill's sponsors, I hadn't seen or even heard of any.

The "No Frills" bill didn't pass, but its provisions lived on and were passed into law affecting federal prisons through the infamous Zimmer Amendment to the Appropriations Act. Kathleen Hawk, Director of the Bureau of Prisons issued a memorandum on November 15, 1995 to implement the amendment. While some of the provisions had little to do with Fort Dix, other had a profound impact: no more R-rated movies, no more speed or heavy bags for boxing practice, no more bodybuilding or weightlifting equipment of any sort, and no more electric musical instruments. While the instruments were to be sent home forthwith, the movies could run until the contract expired with the cable or rental company that was providing them, and the weightlifting equipment was going to be allowed to wear out as long as no money was spent to repair it.

Rep. Zimmer apparently thought only weightlifting equipment was a frill, as Director Hawk instructed that "Institutions are encouraged to utilize alternatives such as fitness courses or equipment which enhances aerobic fitness...however, institutions should not purchase equipment that gives the appearance of belonging in a health club (e.g. exercise bikes that have computerized displays)." So, exercise bikes and treadmills were OK, as long as they looked appropriately shoddy for inmate use. In fairness to Director Hawk and the Bureau, it was made very clear that these new rules were opposed by the BOP and, at least at Fort Dix, efforts were made to repair the equipment in violation of the directive.

Perhaps these changes made sense to someone in Washington behind a desk, but they made no sense to anyone in a prison setting. There was a tremendous amount of stress inherent to the jail experience, and it was beneficial to the guards as well as the inmates to offer ways to alleviate that stress or, better, redirect it in a positive direction. Inexpensive entertainment in the form of HBO or other movie channels, musical instruments owned by the inmates themselves, and weightlifting equipment provided time-tested ways to do that. Indeed, a large number of inmates had nothing in the street, but had spent hours a day in the prison gym sculpting their bodies into something of which they were justifiably proud.

The biggest of the effects of the Zimmer Amendment were going to take several years to manifest themselves at Fort Dix, but were immediately apparent at the new institutions. Two inmates were thrown in the Hole for doing pushups at the newly opened FCI in Elkton, Ohio, and the population responded by burning much of the prison. Transfers of new inmates, in full swing at the time of the fire, had to be suspended for months until repairs could be made.

Rep. Zimmer (New Jersey) ran for the Senate in 1996 and lost, and tried to regain his House seat in 2000, losing again. Ironically in March of 2005 a sponsor of the original "No Frills" act, Rep. Randy "Duke" Cunningham of California, was himself sentenced to 100 months in federal prison for accepting bribes from defense contractors, but these events were only footnotes to the real performance: the Republicans and Democrats were engaged in a fierce fight as to who could be the toughest on crime.

Probably the frenzy in Congress had been caused mostly by the Republican ascendancy, but certainly an additional force had been the bombing of the federal building in Oklahoma City by a homegrown

202

terrorist, Timothy McVeigh, as just a year after the bombing President Clinton signed the Antiterrorism and Effective Death Penalty Act (AEDPA). To some of us closely following criminal issues in Congress, it soon became apparent that much of the legislation had been drafted long before Oklahoma City, and was waiting for the appropriate incident to bring it forward.

It was hardly surprising that the new law had additional provisions relating to explosives, but restrictions on habeas corpus had nothing to do with Oklahoma City although they obviously were part of someone's agenda. Habeas corpus was the common law right of a prisoner to challenge the legality of his confinement and dated back at least to the Magna Carta in 1215, or arguably before. (For most purposes federal habeas corpus was exercised through 28 U.S.C. §2255, the statute under which I had filed my new trial motion.) Among the changes were the requirements that a second or subsequent challenge had to rely on a new Constitutional rule announced by the Supreme Court or had to claim actual innocence. The federal appeals courts were to be the gatekeepers of the new system, and had to approve any second or successive petition before it could even be filed in the lower courts.

The new rules applied even if the claim could not have been made earlier with the exercise of due diligence. This provision seemed designed to encourage prosecutors to withhold evidence, because if it were eventually discovered later, it probably couldn't be used. And while the innocence requirement seemed reasonable at first glance, in reality it was an exceedingly difficult standard. Without any changes to the law, claims of actual innocence were least likely to be successful in the federal courts, with most of the winning cases involving procedural issues, i.e. "technicalities" like my pending motion based on a defective jury instruction. And proving a negative - that you didn't do something - was obviously more difficult than to present evidence of guilt. In my own appeal regarding the corrupt chemist, Dr. McMahon, the appeals court had said, in essence, "well, yeah, this guy was a crook, but somebody else said you're guilty, so we won't disturb the conviction." The effect of this legislation on me was that if I didn't prevail on my jury instruction motion, it was going to be virtually impossible to get back into court on any of the other issues I had been working on.

As Congress was making it more difficult to challenge the validity of one's confinement, the U.S. Supreme Court was doing its part to keep prisoners from ever obtaining consideration of their claims. Since the Court's 1977 decision in Bounds v. Smith[81], it had been a given - in at least the federal prison system - that inmates would have access to adequate law libraries, but this suddenly changed in 1996 in the Lewis v. Casey[82] decision. The Bounds court had recognized the considerable difficulties attending litigation from prison and the absolute necessity of some method of apprising inmates of the rules and the law to frame their legal issues properly for consideration by the courts.

Such concerns were sarcastically dismissed by the Lewis court, which declared that "Bounds does not guarantee inmates the wherewithal to transform themselves into litigating engines capable of filing everything from shareholder derivative actions to slip-and-fall claims." Justice Scalia, writing for the majority, indicated that certain statements in Bounds "appear to suggest that the State must enable the prisoner to discover grievances and to litigate effectively once in court...and we now disclaim them." Law libraries were specifically not required in prisons, and the Lewis Court encouraged experimenting. "One such experiment, for example, might replace libraries with some minimal access to legal advice and a system of court provided forms...forms that asked the inmates to provide only the facts and not attempt any legal analysis."

In my own case, the statute (28 U.S.C. § 2255) prescribed a form, and I had filled it out. Under the Supreme Court's new theory, all I would have had to do was state: "The Second Circuit already determined in the Birbal case that Judge Billings' jury instruction on reasonable doubt denied him a fair trial. Since my instruction was the same, my convictions should be reversed, as were Birbal's." The reality was to be much different. Ultimately the decision would involve a complex analysis of several highly technical legal questions including abuse of the writ, the cause and prejudice test, what constituted ineffective assistance of counsel, and whether counsel's effectiveness or lack thereof was even relevant given the procedural posture of my case. Without access to a law library I never would have been able to respond to the government's opposition to my claims, and the claims undoubtedly would have been dismissed on technical grounds without ever reaching the question of whether I had received a fair trial.

70

The increase in government power and the related ratcheting up of criminal punishment also filtered down through some less obvious channels. In mid-1995 my unit team notified me that I was a "violent offender" for purposes of the Violent Crime Control and Law Enforcement Act of 1994. The only immediate effect that I was aware of was that I would have to display "exemplary compliance with...institutional disciplinary regulations" to receive my 54 days of good time, which meant that the 54 days could be easily denied on a pretext like a disorganized locker or poorly made bed. Worse, I was sure that this was only the beginning, with more restrictions to follow. Certainly the prohibitions for convicted felons continued to increase, regardless of the nature of the underlying crime.

Of even more concern was the fact that the government's definitions seemed to metamorphose over time into something quite different than the original, commonly accepted meaning. While "Saturday Night Special" originally meant a cheap handgun of low quality, it came to mean any small handgun or even a larger one without certain features like adjustable sights, and a similar process was already at work to broaden the definition of violent offender. A Bureau of Prisons Memorandum dated November 15, 1995 defined several pages of offenses that constituted crimes of violence. Some, like 18 U.S.C. 36 (firing weapons into a group of persons) and 18 U.S.C. 1111 (murder), seemed obvious enough, but others seemed so far afield as to be laughable like 16 U.S.C. 773e (violation of Northern Pacific Halibut Act), and 7 U.S.C 473c-1 (offenses in relation to the sampling of cotton). While the latter offenses were not inherently violent, they could be deemed violent in the discretion of Bureau of Prisons staff even if there had been no conviction for violent behavior.

An immediate thought was that I might be denied a halfway house as a supposed violent offender, a legitimate concern as one of my room-mates was denied such a placement for a nonexistent sex offense. He and his girlfriend, both juveniles, had been caught having sex, and originally the authorities thought to bring charges but, since both participants were underage, they were unsure of what charges to bring and let the matter drop. I saw the paperwork myself, and there were no convictions for sex offenses, but my roommate was still denied the halfway house on suspicion.

Through persistence I was able to determine that my "violent offender" status was based on the recommendation of an enhanced sentence for weapons possession in my Presentence Investigation Report. However, my case manager had failed to read further to where Judge Billings had specifically found that any weapons I might have possessed were unrelated to my drug offenses, and he had declined to follow the recommendation in the PSI. After going around and around with the case manager, my "violent offender" classification was finally removed.

71

Yet another disquieting event was the police raid on Will Hunter's home law office. The court finally lifted the stay of the proceedings in Bloomer v. LaMoria on March 24, 1995, a case in which Will was representing me. On June 7th federal agents, some wearing bulletproof jackets, woke the Hunter family at three in the morning to serve a search warrant. Unnamed informants had supposedly claimed that Will, as an attorney for convicted drug dealer Frank Sargent, was involved in laundering Sargent's drug profits. The agents were there to seize legal files relating to the alleged scheme, which were presumed to be in Will's home office. The reason given for the early morning raid was to prevent Will from destroying evidence, but surely it could have waited for daylight, and just as surely the real intent was to terrorize the family and to send a message to others willing to challenge the system.

A week after the raid, in what was termed a coincidence, the Vermont Professional Conduct Board brought ethics charges of its own. Barely a month before, Will had sued the Vermont Supreme Court, which controlled the Board, on behalf of attorney Vince Illuzzi. In yet another coincidence, the Asst. U.S. Attorney who had signed the motion to seal all the Hunter search documents, and the ostensible lead prosecutor in the Hunter case was Gary G. Shattuck, my own prosecutor with whom Hunter had tangled on my behalf.

Even the prosecution-friendly Magistrate Jerome Niedermeier had been a little queasy about issuing a warrant for a lawyer's office given the privacy interests of clients totally uninvolved in the alleged laundering, like myself, and had put in place what he thought were safeguards. In theory, an Asst. U.S. Attorney supposedly not associated with the investigation was to review all the client files, and decide which were to be turned over to the police. In practice, the prosecutor kept Will at bay for several hours as a half-dozen agents ransacked his files. According to Will, he overheard one agent say my name, and that he had been involved with my case. The agents took only a few paper files, but took two computers with their associated hard drives and over one hundred floppy disks, one labeled "Bloomer".

Ultimately the money laundering charges failed to materialize, and Mr. Sargent pled guilty to not only drug charges, but to perjury. Clients and friends rushed to Will's defense, and his case made national news. Perhaps unwisely, Will's wife was very persistent and vocal in his defense, and had made it very clear that she intended to sue DEA agents for making false statements to the press, meaning something had to be done. After leaving Will twisting in the wind for two years, meanwhile retaining his business records, the government brought an indictment for 10 counts of mail fraud and one count of bankruptcy fraud.

While conceding that his records were in disarray, and that he had failed in some of his ethical duties to clients, Will nonetheless maintained that there had never been any criminal intent, and that he had never profited from any of the alleged crimes. After trying futilely to have the improperly-executed search warrant suppressed, Will decided that the certainty of four months house arrest was better than the risk of winding up with a sentence like mine, a distinct possibility since the indictment made clear that the government intended to link Hunter to Frank Sargent. Under the "relevant conduct" provisions of the Sentencing Guidelines, it wasn't necessary to convict Will of any crime with Sargent to sentence him for the weight of Sargent's drugs. All that was required was to show a connection by a "preponderance of the evidence", i.e. Frank Sargent said so.

Subsequently, Will Hunter's wife (April Hensel) and several clients sued the government over the illegal confiscation of their files and records. After the matter languished in the courts for several years, the suits were thrown out by judge William Sessions, formerly the lawyer for my codefendant, and formerly the campaign manager for U.S. Senator Patrick Leahy. No jury ever heard the evidence. Will Hunter no longer practices law.

72

The jail experience itself was sufficient reason to want to leave, but the changing political and legal climate gave new urgency to my pending motion. It was my understanding that the motion would be assigned to Judge Billings, and that would have been a golden opportunity to expose the jury tampering scheme, as I intended to file another motion to have Billings removed for bias, in the process laying out the history of the jury matter. This time, without David Gibson, I was going to be sure the news media had copies of everything.

Procedure in the federal courts was governed by a maze of rules, and there were even special rules for 2255s, appropriately named Rules Governing Section 2255 Proceedings for the United States District Courts. My assumption that Judge Billings would hear my motion was based the fact that he had heard my previous motion alleging jury tampering, and on Rule 4, which provided in pertinent part that the "motion shall be presented promptly to the judge of the district court who presided at the movant's trial and sentenced him...". Prisoners didn't care much for this rule in that often it was the judge's rulings that were under attack, and it was hard to believe that a judge could dispassionately decide that he had made a mistake sufficient to warrant a new trial or resentencing. The reasoning behind the rule was given in the Advisory Committee's Notes, quoting a 4th Circuit Case:

> Complaint is made that the judge who tried the case passed upon the motion. Not only was there no impropriety in this, but it is highly desirable in such cases that the motions be passed on by the judge who is familiar with the facts and circumstances surrounding the trial, and is consequently not likely to be misled by false allegations as to what occurred.

I wasn't initially concerned about the court being "misled by false allegations", although that was exactly what happened. At the time I wanted the motion assigned to Judge Billings for my own political reasons, but he was in a peculiar position.

Judge Billings could have simply retired as a federal judge, but instead on September 9, 1994 he went into a semi-retirement known as senior status. As such he was available to conduct court business, and did so. Among the cases with which Judge Billings was involved since opting for senior status were Wilbur v. Toyota[83] (Billings order issued on May 27, 1995); the landmark double jeopardy opinion in U.S. v. Brophil[84] (dated September 27, 1995) barely a month before my motion was filed; U.S. v. Resnick[85] (judgment issued on November 9, 1995, the very day of my motion) and the sentencing in US v. Halpin[86] on May 16, 1996, months after my motion was filed. Perhaps most telling was the motion filed by Joseph "Jay" Schneider on the same day as mine seeking to have his indictment dismissed. Judge Billings ruled on the motion January 9, 1996.[87]

Given the explicit language of the rule, the reasoning behind it, and the obvious availability of Judge Billings I expected that I would be hearing from him soon, but I didn't. Instead, Magistrate Judge Jerome Niedermeier ordered the government to respond.

Although I was unaware of it at the time, the District of Vermont had adopted its own Local Rules in apparent contradiction to the 2255 Rules:

(5) Prisoner Cases Under 28 U.S.C. §§ 2254 and 2255

(A) A magistrate judge may perform any or all of the duties imposed upon a judge by the rules governing proceedings in the United States Courts under § 2254 and § 2255 of Title 28, United States Code. In so doing, a magistrate judge may issue any preliminary orders and conduct any necessary evidentiary hearing or other appropriate proceedings and shall submit to a judge a report containing proposed findings of fact and recommendations for disposition of the petition by the judge. Any order disposing of the petition may be made only by a judge. "

The rule was, of course, internally contradictory as well, first saying that a magistrate "may perform any or all of the duties imposed upon a judge", but then saying that only a judge could dispose of a petition.

Perhaps if Judge Billings had been given my new trial motion he wouldn't have acted any differently or any more quickly than Judge Niedermeier, who took more than a week after the motion was filed to order the government to respond. The government then waited 28 of the 30 days given to it by Judge Niedermeier before filing a motion for an extension of another 10 days[88], which was granted.

It seemed that AUSA David Kirby had to "participate in a significant fashion in preparing the response of the United States to [my] motion", but had "reinjured his back in another sport related accident" and was "suffering from sciatic pain in his left leg which prevent[ed] him from completing his normal schedule at work."[89] I had to giggle reading Kirby's affidavit, imagining how such a claim would have been treated at the Fort Dix hospital, and remembering that crutches for my knee injuries at Ray Brook had not been "medically indicated" even though I wasn't trying to get out of my "normal schedule" at work.

Of more concern to me than Mr. Kirby's alleged bad back was the government's assumption that it's motion for a delay would be granted. Judge Niedermeier didn't send me a copy of his order to the government, but according to the docket sheet it was filed on November 17th, and the "gov't shall file answer within 30 days." By my calculation, this meant that the response to my motion should have been filed by Monday December 17th, but it was not. However, the judge's order granting the delay wasn't issued until Thursday, the 21st.

It would have been a serious matter for the government to fail to respond in the time allotted by the court, and technically this would have constituted a default. Because of this only three possibilities occurred to me: 1) despite Mr. Kirby's affidavit, the government's response was already done and could have been filed immediately if Judge Niedermeier denied the delay, 2) the government was absolutely sure that Judge Niedermeier would grant any motion it put before him or, 3) the judge had given secret off-the-record assurances that he would rule in favor of the delay. As it was, the judge had waited nearly a week to rule on a motion for a delay of ten days. Whatever the precise truth of the matter was, it looked like I was in for a rough ride.

Actually I had no delusions about the judge's impartiality from the beginning. He had been an assistant U.S. attorney in Burlington, Vermont and I thought it foolish to assume that because he had moved down the hall and changed the sign on his office that he was suddenly free of partiality toward his former co-workers. Although AUSA Gary Shattuck was based in Rutland, some seventy-five miles to the south, David Kirby was in Burlington and must have run into the judge frequently in the Federal Building out of the eye of the general public. My initial skepticism regarding Judge Niedermeier prevented any disappointment later when his sympathies became obvious.

73

In due time I received the government's opposition to my motion[90], and Tony LaRosa had astutely anticipated the arguments. As expected, the government was squawking that I was abusing the writ by filing a second 2255 when I couldn't meet the "cause and prejudice" test. It argued that a number of eminent attorneys (including new federal judge William Sessions) had missed the jury instruction error, and for that reason it wasn't ineffective assistance when Gibson missed it. I therefore couldn't show a legitimate cause for not bringing up the issue earlier. Tony LaRosa cleverly countered that either Gibson should have picked up the defective instruction, or that the defect was so subtle that it wasn't obvious until the Birbal decision. The government could take its pick, but one way or the other I could show a cause.

Although the government was arguing that I couldn't show prejudice either, it didn't seem to be a problem since the Second Circuit had already ruled in Birbal (quoting the U.S. Supreme Court) that "where a jury instruction on reasonable doubt is constitutionally deficient, prejudice may be presumed, and we need not assess whether the instruction affected

210

the outcome of the trial." A few days after receiving the government's response, my reply[91] went out, and it was filed with the court on January 8, 1996. Then I waited - and waited.

I assumed that the government wanted to leave me in jail as long as possible, and would drag things out if it could. The government had asked the United States Supreme Court to review the Second Circuit's decision in Birbal, the case upon which my motion was based, and may have also wanted to delay things until that was decided, but any hope that Birbal would be overturned was no more than wishful thinking. The Supreme Court only heard cases it wanted to hear, and the odds of getting before that court were slim. Out of about 10,000 applications a year, the court usually granted somewhat less than 100, and criminal cases were only a portion of those. Further the cases the court considered were usually of constitutional magnitude or were to resolve conflicts between the circuits. The Second Circuit's Birbal decision was firmly grounded in recent Supreme Court precedent, and simply wasn't likely to rise to the level that would interest that court. (Inexplicably, the Court waited until 1997 to deny review of Birbal, but the denial ended any faint hope the government might have had on that score.)

Habeas corpus motions were, in theory, emergency motions and were supposed to be given preferential treatment. Thirty days came and went, and then another thirty days. At that point I felt I had to do something to prod Judge Billings into action, so I filed a motion for bail on February 25, 1996.

According to the relevant rules and law, the question of bail turned on whether I was presenting a substantial question of law likely to result in a reversal of my convictions and whether I could show exceptional circumstances. The first prong seemed easy enough as my jury instruction was virtually identical to Birbal's, but the second was problematic as it could be argued that my situation was the norm: a prisoner claiming he was entitled to relief, awaiting a decision from the court. From the beginning I had no delusions that bail would be granted, with my main purpose only to needle the court, but I received an unanticipated benefit when Judge Niedermeier tipped his hand regarding where he intended to go. His statement that "this time the result might be different" than Birbal told me all I needed to know about what his eventual recommendation would be.

The government, it seemed, wanted to reargue the entire Birbal case in a more sympathetic forum. It was now claiming that I hadn't even presented a substantial question in that there was overwhelming evidence of my guilt, and that the instructions were for the most part correct. This was exactly contrary to the Second Circuit's opinion in Birbal, and was inviting the District Court to put itself in the position of my trial jury, something both the Circuit and the U.S. Supreme Court had said was an "utterly meaningless" exercise.

The government's attempts to distinguish my case from Birbal's initially seemed irrelevant, but now took on a new importance. The government had claimed that in my case, unlike Birbal's, there had been overwhelming evidence of guilt. It had also claimed that, although I received the same jury instruction as Birbal, Judge Billings in my case gave corrective instructions mitigating the effects of his error. I suspected that these assertions were false, both from my acquaintance with Birbal and his case, and the fact that Judge Billings used what amounted to a canned jury charge. The various elements were all prepared in advance and pulled together to suit the circumstances of individual cases, with the reasonable doubt instruction used in all criminal cases and the conspiracy instruction used in virtually all. The problem was how to show clearly and concisely that my case was the same as Birbal's and that the government was trying to mislead the court.

At my request my father approached the attorney for Birbal's codefendant, who obligingly and promptly sent me the entire jury charge for Birbal's trial as well as the appeal briefs for both Birbal and the government. The documents were much better than I expected, showing beyond any doubt that the government was misrepresenting the record to the court, and that it was recycling arguments that had already been rejected by the Second Circuit. Since the authors of the Birbal brief, David Kirby and Gary Shattuck, were the same Asst. U.S. Attorneys involved in my case, there could also be no doubt that their actions were knowing and deliberate. In theory this was an extremely serious matter, and could have and should have resulted in a least a temporary revocation of their privileges to practice in federal court, effectively ending their careers. In practice it would turn out that the court had no interest in prosecutorial misconduct, but for the moment I was once again giddy with excitement, sure that I would eventually win.

While the court was in no hurry to decide my new trial motion, Judge Niedermeier wasted no time denying the bail motion, ruling just four days after the government's opposition was filed. Not surprising, his order quoted almost verbatim from the government's filings, and it was plain to see that he was going to ignore the Birbal decision entirely. Under the circumstances, I thought the best course would be to wait for Judge Niedermeier's report on the new trial motion, whenever that might be, and then show that he had been tricked by the government's lies. Meanwhile, I would appeal the bail decision to the Circuit.

Upon filing notice of appeal I received a letter from Gary Shattuck informing me that the proper appeal was to the District Court, not the Second Circuit, and I consequently appealed there. My appeal[92] pointed out that although the government was now claiming that I had failed to present a substantial question of law, David Kirby, in his affidavit in support of a delay, had stated that my "petition raise[d] substantial issues" and "[i]t raise[d] significant issues for that case and others in this District..." I went on to state: "This facial contradiction in the respective pleadings constitutes a fraud on the Court and, as such, should not be afforded further consideration relating to this bail proceeding." I further pointed out that extraordinary circumstances then existed due to the court's failure to rule in the five months that had passed since my motion was filed.

I need not have bothered filing any appeal of Judge Niedermeier conclusions in that Judge J. Garvan Murtha - not Judge Billings - adopted Niedermeier's report and denied my bail[93] before my objections had even arrived in Vermont. When the objections did arrive they were denied as "moot", again by Judge Murtha,[94] who may not have bothered to read them.

Under the circumstances I feared that my new trial motion might be a victim of the same shenanigans, and wrote to Judge Murtha[95] stating that I hadn't had a copy of the local rules at the time (the Vermont rules were unavailable at the Fort Dix library) and had assumed that my motion would be handled in the same manner as Judge Billings had handled the previous one: "That matter was never given to a magistrate, but was decided by Judge Billings in just over a month." I also wrote that the court clerk had since sent me the rules, that the mail was often delayed at Fort Dix, and that I intended to file something in connection with Magistrate Niedermeier's report on my motion "regardless of his findings".

At the time I gave Judge Murtha the benefit of the doubt concerning his integrity, but took advantage of the letter to mention the previous jury tampering and Gibson's default on that motion so that Judge Murtha would know that there had been some serious irregularities in my case. Finally, to set the stage for what I knew was coming, I closed with, "Hopefully, this Court will not tolerate further fraud or misrepresentation by the Government without taking disciplinary action against the attorney(s) involved."

As I waited for the Second Circuit's decision on my bail appeal, I began to research my options in the District Court. In theory the common law writ of mandamus was available from the Circuit to force a judge to do his duty, but in practice mandamus was not favored until about 14 months of inaction had passed. My research also indicated that judges were absolutely immune for their judicial acts, that is, their rulings, but vulnerable for ministerial acts like, I thought, leaving my motion on the bottom of the pile while deciding newer matters. Something was certainly wrong as I had asked several Vermont inmates at Fort Dix how long it had taken Magistrate Niedermeier to rule on their 2255s, and the consensus was about 30 days. Later I tried to get official information by writing the court clerk, but he was uncooperative. However, my mother had become friendly with one of the deputy clerks during her several calls to the court obtaining documents for me, and the deputy was incredulous that there had been no opinion in six months.

At this point I asked my father to try and determine what Judge Niedermeier had been up to in my case and others, and he went to the court in Burlington on May 13th. The clerks weren't particularly helpful, but directed Dad to a computer, of which he had only a rudimentary knowledge. Under the circumstances I was fortunate that Dad was willing and able to go at all, since just six week before he had had the lower lobe of his left lung removed. There had been a spot there for some years that seemed to stay the same, but the doctors decided that perhaps it had something to do with Dad's persistent respiratory problems, and that it was time to remove it. During the tests prior to the operation, it was discovered that Dad also had a form of leukemia, which had to be cured before the surgery. The operation went well enough, and he expected to make a full recovery, but no one had bothered to tell him that the removed piece of lung was malignant. No post-op cancer treatment followed, and Dad continued blithely along for three years until he was diagnosed as terminal.

74

Between the bail appeal and my father's fledgling investigation, perhaps Judge Niedermeier decided that further delay might have consequences. The government's brief for the bail appeal was due July 8th, and without Niedermeier's report the Circuit would have to delve into the merits of my 2255 motion, perhaps reaching a conclusion different than what Niedermeier was clearly planning. Or maybe it was that the court only wanted to hold up my motion until the Anti-Terrorism and Effective Death Penalty Act (AEDPA) passed Congress with its more stringent

214

requirements for habeas corpus appeals. It was signed into law on April 24th. For whatever reason or combination of reasons, Judge Niedermeier got out his report and recommendation on June 3rd. There were no surprises; he quoted liberally from the government's brief and bought all the arguments.

Meanwhile the Vermont court's Appeals Coordinator, Christine Barber, had been playing games of her own with my bail appeal. Somehow the appeals court got the idea, ostensibly from Vermont, that the appeal was for my new-trial (2255) motion, not the denial of bail, and that Judge Murtha, not Judge Billings, was my trial judge. Ms. Barber also decided not to send the full record to the Second Circuit, omitting the government's motion for a delay with David Kirby's affidavit stating that my motion "raise[d] substantial issues". I immediately wrote to Judge Murtha[96] protesting. I ended with: "While some may see this as coincidence, I see it as part of the same chicanery that has haunted my case from the outset. I expect that some action will be taken immediately."

While I didn't hear from Judge Murtha, Ms. Barber did subsequently send the rest of the record to the Circuit, and wrote[97] to inform me that "[a]t first glance, the two [documents] in question appear to involve only the §2255 motion, so they were not included." This was not to be the last "oversight" on the part of the clerk's office in Vermont, but at the time Ms. Barber's machinations were only a slight distraction.

The moment I had been waiting for had finally arrived and it took less than a week to prepare my objections to Magistrate Niedermeier's report and recommendation.[98] The essence of my objections were that, "It does not seem as if the Magistrate has read either [my] motion or United States v. Birbal ... [T]he Magistrate has been misled by a clear misrepresentation of the record by the Government, and has reached an erroneous conclusion...[His] Report and Recommendation is fatally flawed and should be disregarded in its entirety."[99] I included portions of the Kirby/Shattuck appeal brief in Birbal as exhibits and cited a few cases indicating that they should be disciplined for perpetrating a fraud on the court.

While the legal arguments concerning the jury instruction itself might have been technical and complicated, the new matter was not. A fundamental tenet of American jurisprudence was that everyone was equal before the law, meaning that if Birbal had been denied a fair trial and was entitled to another, then so was I. But the government had created a false distinction between my case and his by lying, and had fundamentally perverted the proceeding. Of course Judge Billings would have known immediately that the government was lying, just as the rule of 2255 procedure contemplated, but he was mysteriously missing in action.

Following the rules, I sent copies of my objections to the court clerk, the government (via Gary Shattuck) and the Magistrate at the address:

Hon. Jerome J. Niedermeier.
U.S. Magistrate Judge
Federal Building
Burlington, VT 05402

The letter to Niedermeier was returned to me at Fort Dix with delivery "Attempted: Not Known". I immediately wrote to Judge Murtha asking that, considering the circumstances, he deliver the letter for me.[100] I added, "I think it a sad commentary on the competence of government employees that they would fail to recognize the name of a federal Magistrate Judge that I'm told has worked in the Burlington Federal Building for 20 years."

Apparently Judge Murtha didn't have a sense of humor as just a week after I filed my objections he "AFFIRMED, APPROVED and ADOPTED" Niedermeier's report and dismissed my new-trial motion without mentioning the government's fraud. Murtha added, "It is further certified that any appeal taken in forma pauperis from this Order would not be taken in good faith because such an appeal would be frivolous."[101]

"Frivolous??!!" exclaimed a shocked Tony LaRosa after reading the order. "Well, one thing's for sure. You've got nothing coming in Vermont."

And indeed I didn't. By declaring any appeal frivolous Judge Murtha denied me in forma pauperis status, meaning that I would have to pay the $150.00 appeal fee. It also meant that no lawyer would touch the appeal. My father spoke with one of the Birbal appeal attorneys who was interested until he saw the word "frivolous". An attorney could be disciplined for pursuing a frivolous appeal, and this one wasn't taking any chances, nor were any others. Eventually Judge Murtha would pull this trick enough times to cause some consternation among the lawyers practicing in his court, although this was of little help to me at the time.

Working in the Fort Dix law library I had seen plenty of truly frivolous filings. Often, however, litigants and the courts themselves employed the word "frivolous" to ridicule arguments they didn't want to address, and used the word in the sense of "silly or unimportant". If something were frivolous, nothing further needed to be said about it.

216

And so it was with the Second Circuit. Magistrate Niedermeier's report was dated May 31, 1996 (Friday), but not officially recorded as filed by the court clerk until Monday, June 3rd. I didn't get it until Wednesday, the 5th. However, Mr. Niedermeier apparently gave the U.S. Attorney's office a copy on Friday as the government's brief in the Circuit stated that it was filed on May 31st. The effect was that the government sent Niedermeier's report to the Circuit (on June 7th) before I could object and point out the falsehoods that had "misled" the judge. Although I had asked for expedited consideration of my bail appeal under Rule 9, the Circuit was dragging its feet, but upon receiving the government's filing it immediately threw out my bail appeal as "so lacking in merit as to be frivolous."[102]

75

In spite of the Circuit's ruling on the bail matter it was the only show in town, and I appealed Judge Murtha's denial of my new-trial motion to that court. Unfortunately, since my motion was first filed, Congress had given criminal appellants another hoop to jump through, requiring that they apply for a Certificate of Appealability as a prerequisite - with the same court that had just denied the motion. This was nonsensical in that it was asking a judge to certify that the ruling he had just made needed review by a higher court. Some judges issued the certificates virtually automatically, apparently believing that one had a right to appeal regardless of what Congress said, but Judge Murtha took the opposite approach denying my application as "moot", ostensibly because he had declared any appeal to be "frivolous". However, I never received any notice from the clerk that the certificate had been denied and continued to wait for the ruling.

I didn't need any further proof to conclude that no one was minding the store in Vermont. Despite the court rules Judge Billings had not heard my motion, nor had he disqualified himself. Despite his active participation in court business, he had shrunk silently into the background in my case, allowing Judge Murtha to step in, and Judge Murtha had allowed two Assistant U.S. Attorneys to lie in his court without consequences. Moreover, since the jury tampering had come to light I had had little confidence in the integrity of the court clerk and now had even less following the file-culling incident during the bail appeal.

I concluded that if I did nothing, I could expect more of the same, and decided to take on the corruption in the court beginning with the fraud perpetrated by AUSAs Gary Shattuck and David Kirby. To that end I wrote all the judges of the district - Murtha, Billings, Sessions and Niedermeier - advising them that "[a]t this point every judge in the District of Vermont is aware that Assistant United States Attorneys David Kirby and Gary Shattuck have made fraudulent arguments and have misrepresented material facts to this Court", and that Local Rule No. 1(d)(5)(A) mandated that in cases of alleged attorney misconduct "the judge shall refer the matter to [special] counsel for investigation and the prosecution of a formal disciplinary proceeding or the formulation of such other recommendation as may be appropriate." Suspecting that the court would do nothing, I ended with: "If the District of Vermont is not going to follow its own rules, I would like to be advised of same before filing my appeal of my § 2255 motion with the Second Circuit."[103] I never received any response.

Neither had I received any response after 30 days to my motion for a certificate of appealability. Fed up with the games in the Vermont federal court, I wrote the Circuit saying, in essence, "let's consider the application denied by the district court and get on with it." I included a memorandum of law indicating why I thought the Circuit should give me the certificate and why I thought I should be exempt from the requirement, as my new-trial motion had been filed before the law had been passed.

Three months after I had applied to Judge Murtha for the certificate of appealability, my father made a routine inquiry and obtained the most recent copy of my docket sheet from the District Court, which showed my application had been denied as "moot" by Judge Murtha the day after it had been filed.[104] Although the docket sheet showed "Cy to parties" I had received nothing. I immediately wrote to court clerk Richard Wasko on October 22nd (with copies to Judge Murtha and the Second Circuit) stating that I viewed the "situation as extremely serious" and asked for a "copy of Judge Murtha's ruling, an affidavit from whichever of the clerks sent me the ruling, and a copy of the letter of transmittal for use in a prospective action against the mail room here at FCI Fort Dix." Chief Deputy Clerk Marge Krahn replied on October 25th that she couldn't send Judge Murtha's order as the file had already gone to the Circuit, they didn't use letters of transmittal and they wouldn't produce any affidavits

Of course, I actually believed that the omission had been deliberately orchestrated in Vermont, not the Fort Dix mailroom, with the idea of having the Circuit see Judge Murtha's declaration that my appeal was frivolous with nothing from me in rebuttal. My file from Vermont had been sent to the Circuit on August 21st, but my application directly to the Circuit had gone out the next day, effectively foiling the plan.

218

(Ultimately, the Circuit would decide I didn't need the certificate after all, since my motion had been filed before the law had passed, but that was a year and a half later.)

In the meantime, after considering the matter for six months, the Circuit granted the certificate "for the limited purpose of adjudicating on appeal whether the district court erred by denying appellant's motion to set aside the conviction and sentence pursuant to 28 U.S.C. § 2255 on the ground that trial counsel was ineffective for failing to object to the reasonable doubt jury instruction."[105] A month later the court appointed me free counsel for the appeal, Monica R. Jacobson, Esq., of New York City.

It was just as well I had Monica as barely two months before I had lost my friend and mentor, Tony LaRosa. Tony had sent the warden at Fort Dix a package with proof that the prison's staff attorney had committed perjury in connection with one of Tony's pending legal matters, and a short time later the attorney left the BOP. Subsequently, and without warning, Tony was transferred to Allenwood Camp in central Pennsylvania. Although he objected strenuously at the time, fearful that the transfer was an excuse to interfere with his legal work, it turned out that he went to a much better place. We later heard that the departed staff attorney had found new employment as the clerk for a federal judge in Philly.

76

I waited a month after I had written Vermont's federal judges about David Kirby's and Gary Shattuck's lying to the court and had heard nothing, but there was no question that something should have been done. Vermont's Local Rules were plain enough that "the judge shall refer the matter to counsel for investigation", and there was quite a body of law indicating the same. The Ninth Circuit, for example, had said, "[F.R.C.P.] Rule 11 prescribes that where the signing attorney has misrepresented the record the court 'shall impose' 'an appropriate sanction' upon the attorney. The imposition of sanctions is mandatory."[106]

Under the circumstances I thought I had everything to gain and nothing to lose by pursuing the matter, either to take out two sleazy Asst. U.S. Attorneys or to demonstrate the depth of the corruption in Vermont's federal court. Had I still been married I might not have gone forward for fear that some harm might have befallen Katrina or Lindsay from a group that seemed to be without scruples and above the law, but as it was, I had lost contact with both of them, and had already lost most of what I had in my previous life. All that remained was a long time left to serve in prison.

On August 1, 1996 I filed a formal complaint with Judge Murtha (with copies to Judges Billings, Sessions and Niedermeier) reiterating my allegations of fraud in connection with the government's opposition to my new trial motion, but adding a section on the government's use of counterfeit documents, and adding David Gibson as a respondent. Considering what Judge Murtha had done so far, I was afraid that if I merely repeated the fraud allegations they would be dismissed as "moot". The charges were well documented, and the complaint contained 48 pages of exhibits.

The essence of the new argument was that invoices for chemicals from Alfa Products, purportedly representing transactions I had made, were defective on their faces, showing as they did M. Keefe and D. Harotunian to be the buyers. A company representative had testified for the government at trial as to how the documents were generated, and nothing he said could account for anyone but the actual buyer being shown as the buyer. It followed that either these records were not generated in the normal course of business, as the witness had testified, or that Gary Shattuck had substituted counterfeit documents for the actual business documents. I had specifically instructed David Gibson to bring this to the attention to the court, and he had not done so, allowing me to be sentenced on documents he knew were false. Furthermore, Gibson had stipulated to the admission of these same documents without my knowledge or permission after I had refused to do so.

I, according to the government, surreptitiously placed one of the chemical orders (Trial Exhibits 9 and 9A) through Vermont Solar Engineering, a company in Rutland, Vermont owned by Allan and Beverly Hobson. They denied any knowledge of the order. However, David Kirby argued to the jury:

> Interesting enough, though, his [my] deception caught him up in a couple of places and provided some interesting evidence of his guilt ... The first of these is when he ordered chemicals using the Hobson letterhead, obviously to try to avoid detection that he was ordering precursor chemicals. He had his own company. He didn't have to borrow somebody else's letterhead. He didn't have to steal the Hobson's paper and use their rubber stamp ... The defendant ordered chemicals through Hobson's company because only five days earlier he had ordered another

precursor chemical, phenyl nitrile [sic]. And I submit to you he wanted to avoid looking like he was ordering a whole bunch of chemicals at once.[107]

As I stated in the complaint, "[w]hile making that statement, Mr. Kirby was surely aware that, according to the government's own exhibit 9A, the chemicals were apparently sold to" M. Keefe in Danvers, MA, not to anyone in Vermont.

My evidence of misrepresentation regarding the new trial motion was irrefutable in that it was a comparison of two contradictory documents authored by the same two men, Shattuck and Kirby. For instance, they had tried to distinguish my case from Birbal's by stating that, unlike Birbal, the evidence in my case was "overwhelming". The argument was that, unlike Birbal, the evidence in my case was so strong that that the erroneous jury instruction was irrelevant. However, previously in their appeal brief in the Birbal case they had characterized the evidence against him as "truly overwhelming". Faced with this obvious contradiction, Mr. Shattuck replied:

> Bloomer's other claimed misrepresentation -- that somehow we had made a misrepresentation when we argued that the evidence in his case was overwhelming when the Court of Appeals had found that the evidence in the Birbal case was not overwhelming -- is nonsensical. Apparently he is claiming that if the Court of Appeals finds the evidence not overwhelming in one case, we are barred in another case from raising the claim that the evidence **in that case** is overwhelming. This obviously is ridiculous."

What was truly ridiculous was that Shattuck had the gall to so completely and obviously misstate my allegation. Furthermore, I had made no such reference to the Court of Appeals in my complaint, and that Court had made no finding about whether the evidence against Birbal was overwhelming or not, a fact that could have been readily confirmed by reading the complaint and the Birbal decision.

While he expressly denied any conspiracy with David Gibson, Mr. Shattuck nonetheless gave a vigorous defense of his performance, although Mr. Gibson apparently never responded himself to my complaint. Shattuck stated:

221

David Gibson ably, carefully and articulately defended Robert Bloomer. It is offensive that Robert Bloomer should now slander a man that had worked so hard on his behalf.

and again in his affidavit:

I also state that in associating with attorney Gibson throughout these proceedings, it is my belief that he zealously, aggressively, and competently represented his client at all times, in pretrial, trial, and post-trial proceedings.

As to the mysterious chemical buyers Keefe and Harotunian, Shattuck wrote:

The logic of his claim escapes us. Just because an extraneous name appears on a document does not necessarily mean the document is counterfeit. Indeed, there may well be some obvious explanation for those names appearing on the documents, such as, these people were in the billing department of Morton Thiokol and the invoices were supposed to go to them for billing purposes.

Perhaps most significantly, Shattuck stated in a footnote in his affidavit:

The actual exhibits introduced at trial are available for the court's inspection, as it directs. These exhibits include both originals and, where originals could not be obtained, copies of letters and chemical order invoices. Exhibits 1A, 2A, 3A and 4A are photostatic copies and the remaining exhibits are originals.

The question was, photostatic copies of what? The difference between originals and copies was highly significant, as I had alleged 1A, 2A and 3A to be counterfeit. In addition Shattuck had represented to the trial court that what he was submitting were originals[108], and the Federal Rules of Evidence made it much more difficult to admit documents that were not.

Materials that I had obtained from the U.S. Attorney's office through the Freedom of Information Act indicated that the source of the copies bearing the names of Keefe and Harotunian was the Drug Enforcement Administration. This posed yet another ethical and legal

222

problem as the stipulation regarding these documents signed by David Gibson and David Kirby provided that all the invoices "c[a]me from the files of Alfa Products...". Not surprisingly, Mr. Shattuck characterized my complaint as "frivolous".

In an interesting display of chutzpah, Shattuck included a thinly veiled threat to ask for sanctions against me under Rule 11, which concerned making false statements to the court. My response was: "I would welcome the opportunity to defend my allegations, and I would especially welcome any forum that gave me the opportunity to examine under oath Kirby, Shattuck, Gibson, [Morton Thiokol records provider Vincent] Ronayne and perhaps others about the matters alleged in the instant Complaint." I also suggested that the government could remove any doubts about the authenticity of the chemical invoices by revealing the identities of Keefe and Harotunian, who were surely known to the government at that time. I heard nothing further on that point - ever.

I filed the reply with Judge Murtha[109] pointing out the further misrepresentations in the government's response, and the fact that Gary Shattuck had made contradictory statements regarding the invoices, meaning necessarily that he must have been lying one time or the other. I ended my cover letter with the statement: "I have other matters to bring before the District Court, but I would have some doubts about the impartiality of any forum that disregarded its own rules and permitted US. Attorneys to make gross misrepresentations with impunity."

In my reply I had also amended the complaint to include U.S. Attorney Charles Tetzlaff for allowing Shattuck to further misrepresent material facts. I had written to Tetzlaff on three different occasions[110] in conjunction with my bail motion, my opposition to the magistrate's report, and the present complaint asking that David Kirby and Gary Shattuck be removed from my case for repeated misrepresentations. Each time Tetzlaff had refused, in effect condoning lying as a tactic of the U.S. Attorney's office, and the lying continued.

Judge Murtha saw nothing improper in any of my allegations, and sent me a letter of dismissal dated September 9, 1996. He found "no basis for [my] allegations that documents introduced at [my] trial were altered or counterfeited." As to my allegations of misrepresentation of material facts, he concluded "[my] contentions concerning the Section 2255 proceedings appear to be without merit and have already been dealt with by this court." And indeed they had, by ignoring them.

In defense of his actions, Murtha misquoted the rule as: "Local Rule 1(d)(5)(A) allows a judge of this Court to refer a complaint of misconduct to counsel for investigation providing the allegations are substantial." The rule actually said:

> When misconduct or allegations of misconduct which, if substantiated, would warrant discipline on the part of an attorney admitted to practice before this court shall come to the attention of a judge of this court...the judge shall refer the matter to counsel for investigation...

When I showed Tony LaRosa the letter from Judge Murtha he shook his head in disbelief. "They're just freewheeling up there now," he said.

Since Judge Murtha had decided a legal question, ignoring the court rules in the process, I considered the matter appealable and filed a notice of appeal, which Judge Murtha instructed the clerk not to docket. Neither did the complaint itself appear anywhere on the official record anyplace I was aware of. I wrote the Second Circuit in connection with the status of the appeal, but never heard anything in response.

77

I tried several avenues to discover the identities of M. Keefe and D. Harotunian, as I believed that they had some kind of tie to the government, either as legitimate agents or as cooperators in one capacity of another. Had I been able to show this, there would have been no question that the documents were not only fakes, but also some kind of government concoction.

Unfortunately, none of my efforts were completely successful. I asked U.S. Attorney Tetzlaff directly, but he refused to tell me. After I had reestablished my friendship with Mark Malmros following the death of his father, he did an internet search for me, an impossibility for anyone in prison. While Keefe was too common a name to return any useful results, it turned out that Harotunian was very unusual, with only a few telephone listings for the country.

During his search Mark found a 1990 legal case, U.S. v. Harotunian[111], which was easy for me to check at Fort Dix. The Harotunian in the case was one Dennis Harotunian, who had embezzled eleven million dollars while he "was comptroller and administrative manager for the Aesar Group, a New Hampshire-based division of Johnson Matthey Company". Johnson Matthey had purchased Alfa Products from Morton Thiokol, and it seemed unlikely that there was more than one D. Harotunian involved with the company. What I believed to be a relevant fact was that the government had moved for a downward sentencing departure "to reward Harotunian for his substantial assistance in tracking down other suspected criminals."[112]

Harotunian pled guilty in August of 1989, just a year before the raid on my house, and the chemical orders bearing his name were part of the probable cause. The published case didn't lay out exactly what "substantial assistance" Harotunian had provided, but did note that "his disposition of the [stolen] funds remains very much a mystery" with millions unaccounted for. Apparently Harotunian's assistance was sufficiently valuable that the government wasn't looking too hard for the money. (Even with this information I was unable to get anything more from the DEA through the Freedom of Information Act.)

Several years later Associated Press reporter Dave Gram was planning to run a series of articles about the abuses in my case, and told me that he had contacted Dennis Harotunian by telephone through his mother in Massachusetts. (Most of the story was suppressed by someone Gram described as his "boss", ostensibly Vermont bureau chief Chris Graff, later fired by the AP.) While Gram believed that Dennis Harotunian's phone number had been given in confidence, he did confirm the mother's address, and I wrote to her asking that she forward my letter to Dennis inquiring as to how his name came to be on the chemical orders.

The response was angry, complaining that an AP reporter had bothered him and his mother. His explanation for the orders was ridiculous, but strangely reminiscent of the process Gary Shattuck had suggested to Judge Murtha. Harotunian said he (and apparently Mr. Keefe) had worked in Alfa's accounting department and "all invoices paid by cash or check were sent to the accounting department for processing...Further review indicates a check was enclosed for each order, so that explains why my name ended up on the invoices."

I replied:

> ...My exact questions are these: For a given order, whether prepaid or not, why would a separate invoice be generated by Alfa's computer showing you as the buyer with an address in Danvers, Massachusetts? And why would this spurious invoice be retained by the company as its official record of the transaction when a different document was sent to the actual buyer?
>
> This is certainly a very odd situation. First, Alfa created what appears to be a superfluous document. Surely there was a better way to route invoices to the

accounting department. Second, vital information was destroyed in the process, i.e. the identity and address of the actual buyer. The invoice, by having distinct SOLD TO and SHIP TO boxes, certainly contemplated that there would be instances where the billing address and shipping address would be different. However, the billing address was deleted from the official record. Should there have been a dispute or inquiry concerning an order, you were shown to be the buyer. This makes no sense at all..."

I never heard anything from Harotunian in response - or from anyone else.

78

While the court's actions concerning my jury selection, new-trial motion and subsequent complaint were certainly troubling, they were not the only indicators of a deep-seated rot in Vermont's federal court. I had learned as far back as 1994 that Dr. Brown had probably not been paid for his services at resentencing in January of that year. My father had paid him through David Gibson for my original sentencing in 1992, but shortly thereafter Gibson had filed papers in the District Court showing me to be destitute. I was subsequently found in forma pauperis (indigent) by Judge Billings, and had proceeded on appeal with the Second Circuit paying Gibson's fees. When my case was remanded for resentencing, I had assumed that the court would continue to pay.

Again David Gibson hired Dr. Brown on my behalf with my Dad paying his $1500 retainer through Gibson. What had happened after that was somewhat of a mystery, and consequently I wrote to Dr. Brown on August 15, 1995 to determine the status of his fee. His address had changed in the meantime and it took a month to get his response, which was that, aside from the retainer, he had not been paid. Furthermore, he had called David Gibson's office several times, but had been unable to speak with Mr. Gibson. Likewise Dr. Brown's letters to Gibson with his invoices had gone unanswered.

Considering my in forma pauperis status, I wrote the federal court clerk in Rutland[113] (where my trial and sentencing had taken place) to determine: (1) if "any request [was] ever made of the court to pay Dr. Brown"; (2) "the status of the request(s)" and (3) how "may we resolve this matter?" I heard nothing. Dad wrote David Gibson[114] also asking about Dr. Brown, and also heard nothing.

Dad wrote the court clerk himself[115] on my behalf, received a call from someone in response, and subsequently sent a copy of Dr. Brown's bill to the clerk. Apparently the clerk responded eventually by letter, but this was during the period of my father's serious health problems and I never received a copy from his office. I decided to follow up myself and wrote the clerk again on May 6, 1996 enclosing a copy of my original (unanswered) letter with additional requests for: (1) the "procedures by which attorneys apply for and receive payments for representing defendants in forma pauperis", (2) the "procedure by which attorneys procure payment for expert witnesses who appear on behalf of defendant in forma pauperis", (3) "[a]ny applications for payment from attorney David Gibson for his representation of myself, or for expert witnesses", and (4) "[r]ecords of any payments to Mr. Gibson, or denials thereof...". I sent a copy to David Gibson.

A couple of weeks went by with no answer, so I wrote again[116], this time specifically to the head clerk, Richard Wasko, in Burlington. I noted that I had received nothing in response to my previous requests, and that "I [had] developed evidence of perjury on the part of an expert witness that testified for the government in my case, and I anticipate the need for my own expert to aid me in evaluating and possibly developing this evidence for presentation to the court...Lacking the cooperation of my former attorney, Mr. David Gibson, I need the documents I have requested to know how to proceed in this matter. If I do not hear from you on the very near future, I will take such action as I consider appropriate" - lawyer-speak for "I'll sue you". This time I sent copies to judges Billings, Murtha, and Sessions as well as Gibson, Dr. Brown, and my father.

Clerk Wasko must have been extremely busy, as the reply[117] came from Marge Krahn, Chief Deputy Clerk. It was short but not too sweet:

> ...As I believe our financial administrator has already
> notified you, no forms requesting payment have been
> received, so no payments have been made to Dr. Brown.
> Normally, sometime after the testimony is given the
> defense attorney submits a form requesting that the judge
> authorize payment for the expert services.

I sent Ms. Krahn a copy of my previous letter, noting that she had not been fully responsive, and ended with:

> Certainly there is something very odd about the matter of
> Dr. Brown's payment as evidenced by your reluctance and

Mr. Gibson's refusal to answer simple and direct questions. This is my final request before bringing an action against you, Mr. Wasko, and whoever else in the clerk's office that is impeding my progress and my access to the courts. It may be that the only way to get to the bottom of this is through in-depth civil discovery.

Again copies went to Gibson and the judges. This time I got some answers[118], although very curious ones.

> Ms. Krahn "had the financial administrator check further into [my] case and any possible attorney or expert witness payments. Before the government can pay any attorney or witness fees under the Criminal Justice Act (CJA), the defendant must have been granted in forma pauperis status by the judge in his/her case. To do that, the defendant must file a financial affidavit, which the judge reviews. Based upon the information in the affidavit, the judge either grants or denies in forma pauperis status to the defendant. There is no record that you were ever granted in forma pauperis status at the district level. Your docket shows that your attorney, Mr. Gibson, was retained by you, not appointed by the court, and therefore <u>was being paid by you</u>. Pursuant to this information, the answers to your questions are that we have no record of any applications for payment made by Mr. Gibson, or payments made to him...it also follows that there could have been no applications for, or payments to, Dr. Brown."

This made no sense because what my docket sheet showed was that, following my original sentencing, Mr. Gibson had filed a motion with Judge Billings to proceed in forma pauperis on appeal along with a financial affidavit showing me to be in debt.[119] The docket sheet showed nothing regarding Billings' disposition of the motion, and neither did the motion itself, obtained from the court clerk. (Sometimes the judges issued so-called endorsed orders, where they wrote "granted" or "denied" or equivalent language in the margin of the motion and signed it.) However it was my belief, later confirmed, that the Circuit had paid Gibson's fees on appeal.

Likewise following my resentencing, Gibson had filed another motion with Judge Billings to proceed in forma pauperis on appeal, making reference to the previously filed financial affidavit and the court's finding that I had been unable to pay a fine. Although the docket sheet showed no disposition, the a copy of the motion itself, supplied by the court clerk, had "SO ORDERED" typed at the end of the motion above Judge Billings's signature.[120]

Marge Krahn's answer was all the more perplexing considering the document I had obtained not even two months before from the U.S. Attorney's Office as a part of its Freedom of Information disclosure. Following my resentencing David Gibson had written Judge Billings[121] (with a copy to AUSA David Kirby) "inquiring as to whether [his] services following the remand of [my] case from the Second Circuit would be appropriate to be compensated as assigned counsel. If so, perhaps the clerk's office could forward the appropriate forms and information to me in that regard."

This seemed to be exactly what Ms. Krahn had described as the procedure, but the court had no record of it. It was time for me to write Mr. Gibson, noting that "it is long past time to clear this up. I ask for nothing less than a complete and candid explanation of what has transpired concerning the payments to both yourself and to Dr. Brown."[122] Copies went to judges Billings, Sessions and Murtha. No one ever responded.

(However, when I finally obtained more documents from my client file in 2007, I discovered a letter from Judge Billings to David Gibson dated March 7, 1994 wherein the judge replied to Gibson's inquiry:

> ...Enclosed please find CJA form No. 23, which is the financial affidavit which must be filled out before you can be appointed as assigned counsel. If you will have your client fill out the form and then return it to me, I will be in a position to appoint you as counsel.

Gibson never sent me the form, or filed the CJA 23 with the court, leaving my Dad to pay his bill on my behalf, and Dr. Brown unpaid.)

79

At this point I was deeply concerned that if I eventually won my appeal I would be facing retrial in Judge Murtha's kangaroo court, where the primary objective seemed to be protecting crooked judges, clerks and lawyers. It was, therefore, imperative to remove him from my case and I decided to wind up the court any way I could

Determined to press the matter, I looked around for a way back into court where I could file a motion to disqualify all Vermont's federal court judges for bias and corruption, and it came unexpectedly from the Executive Office of United States Attorneys (EOUSA). On November 5, 1996 the EOUSA returned two of my chemistry books that had been seized in August of 1990, books that had never been inventoried and had never been used as evidence, and this seemed to be a good excuse to demand an accounting from the government for the rest of my missing property.

My initial Freedom of Information request to the EOUSA hadn't produced a single document, or an acknowledgment that they had my books, but the intervention of Senator James Jeffords pried some materials loose. Jeffords had voted with the Clinton administration more than any other Republican senator, and was frequently lobbied by the administration. When Attorney General Janet Reno called asking a favor, Jeffords asked for a favor of his own - a release of my files. A disclosure of several thousand pages had been made on April 17th, and now some months later the chemistry books arrived in response to my appeal for more information.

It seemed ridiculous that the government could hold my property for so long, especially considering Judge Valente's order from five years before that the government return any property not necessary or material to the investigation, and on November 22, 1996, I filed a motion with the federal court asking that "the government be ordered either to return any of [my] property still in its possession, or to produce a detailed list thereof and the legal authority for retaining same."[123] Along with it I filed a motion to recuse all of Vermont's federal judges: Sessions for participation in the criminal case as Spencer's attorney, Billings for his toleration of or complicity in the jury tampering, Billings and Murtha for failure to follow the rules of 2255 procedure and all of them (including Niedermeier) for failure to follow the rules of the court regarding charges of attorney misconduct.[124] A week later I filed a formal misconduct complaint with the Second Circuit making the same charges.[125] The jury tampering, in particular, was laid out in considerable detail.

The complaint was dismissed in February of 1997 on the basis that the allegations were better handled through a motion to recuse. The court also said, "To the extent Complainant alleges bias on the ground that the Judges failed to comply with statutes, or violated the district court's local rules, through a ruling (Judge D) or by inaction (Judges A, B, and C),

230

Complainant raises matters directly related to the merits of judicial determinations" which, according to the Circuit, were not proper subjects for a judicial misconduct complaint. Jon O. Newman, Chief Judge of the Second Circuit, signed the dismissal.

A week later I tried to amend the complaint, as it had come to my attention that the District Court was revising its Local Rules to change the section that a part of my complaints had relied on, the section requiring the appointment of counsel to investigate allegations of misconduct. The appointment was now to be discretionary, and I considered this to be compelling evidence that the judges knew very well what the rule required and deliberately refused to follow it. My amendment was rejected by the Circuit as too late - the matter had been decided.

Judge Murtha denied the return of property motion on the basis that the criminal matter was concluded, and the proper procedure was to bring a separate civil action. He also denied the motion to recuse because the "fact that this Court has made determinations unfavorable to the petitioner is insufficient to demonstrate objectively that the Court's impartiality might be reasonably be questioned". Although I had no illusions that the Second Circuit would do anything at that point, I nonetheless appealed to enlighten as many judges on that court as I could about the problems in Vermont.

The Vermont judges couldn't represent themselves, so they were defended by the U.S. Attorney's office, surely an unholy alliance. The government moved to dismiss the appeal on the basis that nothing was pending in the District Court, and that the question of recusal was not "ripe" for decision. I pulled no punches in my opposition stating, "Considering the facts in the light least favorable to Judge Murtha, he participated in a scheme wherein the government was allowed to perpetrate a fraud upon the court, and when the scheme was exposed, tried to protect the principals." The Second Circuit could have dismissed the appeal on the ripeness or jurisdictional issues, but went further and, in effect, exonerated the judges. The order bore the now-familiar notation, "any appeal from this order would be frivolous".[126]

80

United States Attorneys had to be lawyers, and lawyers were licensed and regulated by the states, but Attorney General Janet Reno had declared U.S. Attorneys to be exempt from any state disciplinary process. I had read somewhere that the Justice Department had its own disciplinary arm to investigate misconduct by United States Attorneys and, suspecting that it didn't work very well, decided to find out for sure by filing a complaint on December 30, 1996. I sent a copy of the complaint I had originally filed with Judge Murtha, but added a new allegation that U.S. Attorney Tetzlaff had refused to divulge the identities of the mysterious chemical buyers Keefe and Harotunian,[127] and there was no question that he should have done so. The Local Rules of the Vermont federal court specified that Vermont's Code of Professional Responsibility (code of ethics) applied in that court, and the Code provided that a "public prosecutor ... shall make timely disclosure ... to the defendant ... of the existence of evidence, known to the prosecutor ... that tends to negate the guilt of the accused, mitigate the degree of the offense, or reduce the punishment."

The case that had brought my attention to the Office of Professional Responsibility was a lost, high profile drug case in Florida, after which a U.S. Attorney had become despondent and had gone to a strip club to unwind. It was alleged that, after becoming thoroughly intoxicated, he had bitten a topless dancer. The OPR had dutifully sent a team to investigate which predictably found it necessary to interview all the dancers, although only one had been allegedly bitten. The U.S. Attorney resigned, and that was the end of it.

Since my case lacked exotic dancers, I doubted that the OPR would show the same investigative zeal with my allegations of lying to the court, and it didn't. Barely a week after receiving my complaint, the OPR dismissed it with the determination that "the proper forum in which to raise your claims is the court", knowing at the time that the court had already thrown out the complaint.

I was perfectly willing to raise more claims in court, but first wrote Asst. U.S. Attorney Gregory Waples, who represented the government in my appeal of Vermont's judges' refusal to step down. Since he was now handling my case, I asked him also for the identities of Keefe and Harotunian. His reply was that he had not "generally been 'assigned' to [my] case, and [was] not in a position to respond..."[128] which was probably true.

Nevertheless, on March 20, 1997 I filed another complaint with Judge Murtha (with copies to Sessions, Billings and Niedermeier) against Tetzlaff and Waples, laying out the importance of the mystery buyers, the chemicals' relationship to my sentence and the prosecutors' duty to provide exculpatory information. I certainly didn't expect much of the judges, but I did want to make them aware of what was being covered up. If there had been an innocuous explanation for the Keefe and Harotunian invoices the government would surely have provided it, if for no other reason than to

232

trivialize my complaint - a fact that could not have been lost on the court. Less than a week after receiving the complaint Judge Murtha again misquoted the Local Rule of the court in his letter of dismissal.

Although I knew it was futile in the short term, I thought I'd poke at Charlie Tetzlaff one more time, both to point out the magnitude of the misconduct on the parts of his subordinates and to show him that the government's case wasn't as rock solid as it might appear on the surface. In that regard I wrote to Tetzlaff directly on August 26, 1997 asking for the inquest testimony of Sharon Stickney. I included a copy of the affidavit she had given to Ed Lucas proving that her testimony would have been exculpatory, and also pointed out the discrepancy between the indictment showing methamphetamine sales to Stickney by Spencer in 1988, and the government's admission (on appeal) that I had sold no drugs in 1988. The obvious conclusion was that someone else was supplying Spencer with methamphetamine, contrary to his testimony that he'd gotten it all from me. If Stickney had received a large amount of meth from Spencer in 1988, the evidence would have been all the more compelling. I again cited Tetzlaff's obligation to produce exculpatory evidence.

It came as no surprise that Tetzlaff refused, ending his letter:

> I am also denying your request because it constitutes yet another of the many allegations you have made, none of which have proven credible, concerning misconduct by court personnel, judges and attorneys. This office seeks to address reasonable requests. We will not expend time on vague, unsubstantiated allegations. I view this most recent letter as falling within this area.

81

I hadn't forgotten about David Gibson, and he was the key to two other unresolved issues, the jury matter and the non-payment of Dr. Edward Brown. The jury, in particular, was a big weapon in my fight to get out of jail, especially since the violations were probably criminal. While no one in Vermont appeared willing to do anything, that didn't rule out an investigation by a higher court, the FBI, or even a special prosecutor out of Washington.

I had written to David Gibson twice in 1996[129] asking for all the materials that he had in support of the new-trial motion including the jury lists and reports of the private detectives. Receiving no response to the first request, I was more blunt in the second stating " I think you have a special responsibility to me in this matter in that you defaulted on the [jury tampering] motion and abandoned me in spite of the fact that I had just received a sentence increase of more than 5 years with your representation." Again, there was no response from Gibson.

I subsequently wrote to court clerk Richard Wasko asking for the jury materials. While Wasko did supply me with the jury lists, he informed me that many of the temporary juror excusals, like the ones used to rig my jury, were "handled informally, and no written record even exists."[130] He also stated that he didn't know what Judge Billings had done regarding Gibson's request to be paid by the court, and suggested that the Second Circuit might have information regarding my in forma pauperis status.

I wrote that court for information relating that David Gibson had represented me on appeal, but would not respond to me about the finances of the case, a definite violation of the Code of Professional Responsibility. Case Manager Frank Perez forwarded my letter to Gibson, ordering him to respond. I wrote back twice advising that I had received nothing from Gibson, and both times another order went out. Gibson never answered, and as far as I know the court never did anything about his refusal to respond.

It took a few months to get everything together and obtain a satisfactory affidavit from Dr. Brown, and then it was time to move ahead on that issue. On March 31, 1997 I filed a motion with the district court[131] to pay Dr. Brown under either 18 U.S.C. § 3006A (allowing the court to pick up the tab for indigent defendants) or Federal Rule of Evidence 706. I pointed out that the record was contradictory, documents that could reasonably be expected to be part of the court records didn't seem to exist, that Gibson had been uncooperative, and the only way to get to the bottom of it was to hold a hearing.

Along with the payment motion I filed a second motion to recuse all the judges[132] incorporating by reference the first one, but adding that I intended to call as witnesses various court clerks and Judge Billings himself, as apparently only he knew what he did with Gibson's request to be paid by the court. (Judge Billings' response to Gibson's letter containing the financial forms was never a part of the court record, and was unknown to me until 2007.)

Vermont was a very small district with only two judges (Murtha and Sessions) and one senior judge (Billings) and it was inconceivable to me that Chief Judge Murtha would fail to make inquiries after my motion was filed, especially considering that I had already made several complaints and still had a few political connections, even if they hadn't

234

been too effective to date. However if Murtha were going to decide my motion, any such investigation would have been improper as he would have then have had "extrajudicial knowledge", that is, personal knowledge of relevant facts outside the record. Judge Murtha waited three months, then typed "DENIED" in the margins of my motions and signed them on June 30, 1997. Of course, there was no hearing where I could have conducted my own investigation. I again appealed to the Second Circuit.

82

Without waiting to hear from Judge Murtha about Dr. Brown's payment, I filed a formal complaint against David Gibson with the Vermont Professional Conduct Board, the entity charged with investigating and prosecuting ethical violations by Vermont attorneys. There was no question that Gibson had a duty to send me materials from my own file and to respond to financial questions, and it later turned out that there were disciplinary cases covering these very subjects, but they were unavailable at Fort Dix. However my father had sent me a copy of the Code of Responsibility, the legal code of ethics, and that was sufficient to frame my charges, which were:

> 1. Mr. Gibson failed to represent his client zealously when he defaulted on the jury tampering motion and failed to appeal.
> 2. Gibson failed to conduct himself in an honest and professional manner with Dr. Brown, and
> 3. Mr. Gibson abandoned his client by refusing to provide materials I had requested regarding the jury matter and errors in my trial transcript.

The charges were fully developed with appropriate exhibits in support. I was to wait more than two years for action on the complaint, although others that had been filed after mine were decided.

It was not that I expected anything different, or even fair treatment. The Professional Conduct Board had been criticized as unfair by a number of lawyers, but matters finally came to a head in late 1996 when it was learned that two chairpersons of the Board had dismissed complaints against an attorney with whom both had a business relationship. The Supreme Court, which had the ultimate supervisory authority for the Board, appointed a special bar prosecutor to investigate complaints of lax enforcement and conflict of interest by former members of the Board, and hired experts from the American Bar Association to examine its operations. Vermont Bar Association President Joan Wing formed another committee to conduct its own probe, but not everyone was pleased with its makeup. Barre lawyer Oreste Valsangiacomo, Jr. commented to the *Rutland Herald/Times Argus* (December 8, 1996), "This committee must first determine the truth before reform and justice can be attained. However, some of the committee members are, in fact, part of the many problems that exist within the Professional Conduct Board and should not be evaluating their own conduct."

I didn't need any outside investigation to realize that the lawyer disciplinary process was rigged. While I was trying to appeal the complaint filed with Judge Murtha against Gibson, Shattuck and Kirby, I read in the newspaper that David Gibson was on the Judicial Conduct Board. This seemed to be a conflict of interest on its face considering that Gibson's brother, Ernest W. Gibson, III, was a justice of the Supreme Court and that the Court made the appointments to the Board. There also seemed to be an appearance of impropriety with David Gibson judging the ethical conduct of judges while he was himself the subject of an unresolved ethics complaint. In that regard I wrote the court including my complaint, the government's response, my reply, and Judge Murtha's letter of dismissal "so that an informed decision can be made as to whether Mr. [David] Gibson should sit in judgment of others at this time."[133]

Barely a month later I received a letter from Robert Keiner, Esq., Chair of the Professional Conduct Board dismissing my complaint against Gibson, Shattuck and Kirby - except I hadn't filed any complaint nor would I have until the various investigations into the Board had been completed. I later learned that the complaint had been secretly filed by Larry Abbott, Deputy Clerk of the Supreme Court "per direction of the Court".[134] Although it was filed in my name, I was never notified until it had been dismissed.

I assumed that the dismissal was to benefit David Gibson, whose brother was conveniently on the Supreme Court, but later learned that the situation was even more convoluted. Judge Murtha had served on the Professional Conduct Board with Robert Keiner in the two years preceding his appointment to the federal bench, and therefore was well known to the Board and to the Court. Under the circumstances it was unlikely that the Board was going to find any violations where Judge Murtha had declared there weren't any, regardless of how compelling the evidence was.

At that time, the chair of the Professional Conduct Board served as the gatekeeper of the system, deciding himself which complaints the full Board would consider and which would be dismissed on his personal authority, a system that made the Board notoriously easy to corrupt.

236

However, the chair was supposed to step aside in cases where a judge, similarly situated, would have to recuse under the Code of Judicial Ethics.

Following the receipt of Keiner's letter of dismissal I wrote him back protesting that he should have been disqualified from participating in any part of the process. Keiner had been the attorney for my ex-wife, Mary Ann, during our bitter divorce and his former law partner was none other than William Sessions, who had represented my cooperating codefendant in the federal criminal case. Inasmuch as my non-complaint involved misconduct during the criminal case, that alone should have been enough. I also pointed out that either Keiner didn't have all the documents related to the complaint or hadn't bothered to read them as my complaint before Judge Murtha had been amended to include U.S. Attorney Tetzlaff. (I later learned that Larry Abbot, ostensibly "per direction of the Court", withheld some of the materials I had sent to the Supreme Court.) Copies of my letter to Keiner went to Frederic Allen, Chief Justice of the Court, the other 14 members of the Professional Conduct Board, and Joan Wing, President of the Vermont Bar Association. No one ever responded. Neither was my complaint reinstated so that I could submit all the relevant materials.

Considering that the Board was under investigation for rigging the lawyer disciplinary process in favor of insiders, it was a little surprising that Mr. Keiner, with the complicity of the Supreme Court, would be continuing the very practices that were the subject of the investigation. It was all the more surprising considering that barely ten years before three Justices of the Court, a majority, had been charged by the Judicial Conduct Board with numerous ethical violations including trying to influence an inquiry into the activities of lower court judge Jane Wheel. The charges were eventually dropped against David Gibson's brother, Ernest Gibson, III and Thomas Hayes, perhaps in part because Hayes had died in the meantime from lung cancer. Justice William Hill received a public reprimand and was suspended from judicial duties, although by then he had retired.

At the time former Governor Philip Hoff, a lawyer himself, remarked that the public already was suspicious of the legal profession and this had had a negative impact on the public's views.[135] The public might have been even more suspicious had it realized that the eventual reforms of the Professional Conduct Board adopted by the Supreme Court were mostly window dressing. Even Robert Keiner, who served at the pleasure of the Supreme Court, continued as the chair. There was, however, one ominous change: the Board's hired investigators, aka Disciplinary Counsel, could now dismiss complaints themselves without the overt involvement of any corrupt Board members.

83

My appointed appeal attorney, Monica Jacobson, sent me a draft of her proposed appeal, and then a copy of the appeal brief, which I thought very well done. I called Monica's office on July 17, 1997 for an update and discovered that a copy of the government's brief had been mailed out to me that very day, and I expected to have it a day later. When it hadn't arrived in a week I went to the mailroom to inspect the legal mail log, which showed nothing from Monica for the period July 15 through July 23. I had Monica try to fax a copy to my father's office, but a problem with one or both of the fax machines prevented the entire document from transmitting despite numerous tries. Finally I received the government's brief at mail call on July 28th. Although Monica had properly marked the envelope, it had not been handled as legal mail by the Fort Dix mailroom.

July 28th was exactly the same day as Monica's reply brief had gone out, precluding me from participating in any way, which was way too convenient to have been coincidental. The postmark on Monica's envelope was the 18th, meaning she had sent it as she had said, and she was not responsible for the delay.

As I read the government's brief, I got cold chills, and saw immediately why my mail hadn't been delivered on time. The government was not only using the same lies that had "tricked" Magistrate Niedermeier, the lies were now embellished and stated with greater force. I immediately wrote to U.S. Attorney Tetzlaff protesting, and demanding that he correct the record. He replied, "The record before the Court of Appeals needs no correction."[136]

It turned out that Monica did an outstanding job for me throughout her representation, although at the time I was not prepared to trust anyone. My main concern was that Shattuck and Kirby were once again lying, this time to the Appeals Court, meaning either that the government lied all the time without consequences, or that it had been given permission to lie in my case. In either event, given the direction things were headed, I saw the probable result as the denial of my appeal as "meritless" or even "frivolous" on the basis that my case was clearly distinguishable from the Birbal case. At that point any allegations of fraud or misrepresentation of facts would be dismissed as the ranting of a bitter convict who had lost his case. I figured that the only thing to do was to strike first and, giving

Monica the benefit of the doubt, I sent her no advance notice of what I was going to do for fear she might suffer unknown - but serious - consequences.

On September 23rd I wrote to Jon O. Newman, Chief Judge of the Second Circuit, "I wish to bring to your attention the wild-west atmosphere in the District of Vermont with hopes that something can be done about it. I have tried repeatedly to bring instances of misconduct and criminality before what I believed to be the proper authorities without any success whatsoever. The system doesn't work." The letter was 14 pages, single spaced, and I went on to describe the jury tampering, the strange matter of Dr. Brown's non-payment, the related lack of court documents, the District Court's refusal to follow its own rules and it's toleration of governmental misrepresentation. Finally I expressed some puzzlement as to why David Kirby would be repeating lies when he was certain to be caught. I continued that it seemed certain "neither Kirby nor [U.S. Attorney] Tetzlaff believed that the Second Circuit would impose any sanctions for their behavior", and "[f]or that reason, I have grave doubts that my appeal will be considered impartially."

Although I had addressed my letter to Jon Newman, he had been replaced as Chief Judge by Ralph Winter. A little less than a month went by, and then I received a reply from Senior Deputy Clerk Kathleen Brouwer on behalf of Judge Winter that my arguments had "no legal significance", but "you may wish to include them in your briefs in your pending appeals, or in whatever other submissions are permitted by the Rules." She returned my original letter, including the manila envelope, and I immediately noticed something very interesting. There were at least three sets of staple holes in my letter, indicating that it had been destapled and copied on at least two occasions. Perhaps someone, although he or she wouldn't admit it, was finally listening.

84

On the same day I wrote to Judge Newman, I also filed a judicial conduct complaint against Judge Billings with the Second Circuit regarding the jury tampering, which included as exhibits the affidavits from the jurors, and letters I had written to Judge Billings and U.S. Attorney Tetzlaff regarding any investigations that might have been made. Billings claimed that "the clerk followed all procedures"[137] and according to Tetzlaff, "This office did not conduct any investigation into the subject matter...as it was deemed to be without merit."[138]

I was beginning to learn the tricks, and made it very clear that my complaint was not about any of Judge Billings' rulings but rather his failure to perform ministerial duties required of him by law as the Chief Judge for the District of Vermont. I alleged that Billings had allowed the clerk to contravene his order as to where the jurors were to be selected, failed to perform an adequate (or any) investigation into the jury tampering, and permitted the continuation of an informal system of juror excusals without written records despite knowledge that it had been abused.

I also figured to tweak the Circuit a bit by stating the obvious: it was likely that Billings was involved personally. He had failed to step aside in a matter for which he bore the ultimate supervisory responsibility, and had allowed the offending clerk to remain at his post, a post he held solely at the pleasure of the judge. Moreover, David Gibson had refused to answer any of my inquiries for some time, and had sent nothing from my client file about the jury despite two requests. As I observed to the Circuit, "something considerably more than the wrath of a corrupt deputy clerk must have caused Mr. Gibson to default on his [jury tampering] motion and abandon his client. That something could only have been Judge Billings."[139]

The system in the Circuit for handling complaints was much like that of the Vermont Professional Conduct Board. Where Chairman Robert Keiner was the gatekeeper in Vermont, Chief Judge Winter was the gatekeeper in the Circuit, and complaints could be dismissed without submitting them to a higher authority. However while Keiner's decisions were final, Winter's could be appealed to the Judicial Council of the Second Circuit, which consisted of all the judges of the appeals court plus the chief judges from the districts that comprised the circuit. An appeal was necessary as Judge Winter dismissed my complaint as "unsupported and directly related to the merits of judicial rulings".[140]

85

As my complaints were pending in the Circuit, my oral argument date for my appeal was pushed back. First arguments were scheduled for November 5, then November 24, then finally to January 26, 1998. While those matters were certainly important, problems at Fort Dix were of more immediate concern. I had been led to believe that in the spring of 1997 my security level problems were over, and that an application was being submitted for a gate pass, which would allow me to work outside the prison in one of the BOP's support facilities or on the base itself doing

240

grounds keeping, and supposedly there was a desperate need for such inmates. I preferred a transfer to a camp like Allenwood but, considering my father's uncertain medical condition, decided to take whatever was offered. At the time I was also told that a 125-bed prison camp would be opening at the former Fort Devens in Massachusetts, which would have been highly desirable due to its proximity to Vermont. Since the BOP had a stated policy of trying to locate inmates as close as possible to home, an eventual transfer to that facility seemed inevitable.

An inquiry during the summer by Senator Jeffords' office indicated that it would be a long time before any inmates transferred to Fort Devens, meaning that my case manager had lied to me, and she had also lied about submitting an application for a gate pass. The false statements, plus the likely deliberate mishandling of my legal mail coupled with continuing threats to confiscate my tightly boxed legal papers as a "fire hazard" prompted an angry confrontation with my unit manager. Shortly thereafter I was informed that my security level was minimum-out, and that a transfer request to Allenwood camp had been submitted to the regional office.

While I didn't believe it at the time, the Allenwood transfer request had actually been made by Associate Warden Keith Hayes. However on November 18th I was transferred, not to Allenwood, but to the West Side institution of Fort Dix to work in the outside cadre. By that time the security nightmare of having hundreds of inmates pass in and out the gate every workday had been restricted to the West Side only, and an entire housing unit had been devoted to the cadre.

A week after arriving at Fort Dix West I was informed by my case manager, an unpleasant woman named Doty, that my gate pass had been denied, but she would pursue a redesignation to Allenwood, my preferred destination. After hanging around in limbo for a month I was told that my transfer was off, my security level had been raised, and that I had a new case manager, another unpleasant character named Langehennig. (The inmates referred to him as "Lanahan", perhaps for the same reason that most called the institution at Fairton, New Jersey, "Farrington".)

A day later I was abruptly told by my counselor that I could no longer stay in the cadre housing unit, and I had to be out in three hours. Either I could find myself a new room in one of the five low-security units or he would do it for me. Since I had no idea where any vacancies might be, I took an assigned room and wound up in a much better place - an all-Latino 12-man room with the exception of a lone Haitian.

At that point I thought it possible that Doty or Langehennig might have submitted my name for some highly undesirable detail like night shift in the kitchen, and moved quickly to get a job in the law library, where I really needed to be at that point. Fort Dix West was much more tightly controlled than the East Side, and the only way I could have near constant access to legal resources and a typewriter was to work in the library. Fortunately, I had done a good job for Miss O on the East Side, and she gave me a recommendation. I started January 7, 1998.

While I much preferred my quarters in low-security to the pettiness and constant snitching of the cadre unit, I nonetheless had to straighten out my security level problems before any new family emergency arose back in Vermont. My new case manager was much more professional than the mean-spirited Doty and Langehennig, and I obtained numerous documents from my central file, including absolute proof that Doty had used false information to raise my security level.

It was very difficult for an inmate to prevail against a prison, and I had to be careful to frame the matter just right. There was a successful court case, Sellers, where an inmate had successfully sued over a violation of the federal Privacy Act, a part of which required that determinations be made on the basis of accurate information. The only question left in Sellers was how much the prison had to pay him, a situation that struck fear into even the most callous prison administrator.

Two written requests to my unit manager to have my record corrected were denied, but the language I used was right out of the Sellers case and the manager surely realized where things were headed. A short time later a friend from the cadre unit saw me on the compound. He had overheard the warden and an associate warden talking in the mess hall and thought they were talking about me. "We've got a serious legal problem with Doty," the warden had said.

About a week later my name appeared on the Change Sheet showing that my job had been changed from the library to the outside garage, where I had originally applied for employment after being assigned to the cadre. A day later (March 17, 1998) I reported to the gate at work call in the morning, my name was read, and out I went with the garage crew. The same day my name was posted in my housing unit for a quarters change back to the cadre unit, and a day after that I was put back in my old room. It had taken four months to the day to get back where I'd started.

86

Oral argument for my appeal had finally taken place on January 26, 1998. I didn't trust anyone but family, and my brother, Tom, also a lawyer, had offered to attend the proceedings and report back. He said Monica was very sharp, quickly answering questions posed by the three-judge panel hearing the arguments with Judge Cardamone (who eventually wrote the opinion) looking at Monica and nodding during parts of her presentation. Asst. U.S. Attorney David Kirby (Chief, Criminal Division), on the other hand was visibly agitated in spite of his extensive experience, laughing nervously at inappropriate moments. According to Monica, Kirby argued that Judge Billings' instruction really didn't make any difference because juries knew the proper legal standards from watching television.

After the arguments, there was nothing to do on that front except wait for the decision, but time passed quickly in the garage. After nearly six years in prison the freedom was odd at first, and the glow from that softened the less palatable aspects of the prison experience. The work wasn't very demanding, consisting mainly of performing routine maintenance on the prison's fleet of over 50 vehicles, and repairing the golf carts that were used and frequently abused by the guards.

About two months into the job my boss sent me to a safe driving course offered on the base to mostly soldiers, and a day later I had a base driver's license. After a while I was routinely issued keys to a nice 1995 Ford pickup to run errands and deliver papers. The base was huge, and theoretically garage personnel were restricted to a portion of it, although some abused the privilege and took jaunts far from the designated area. After all the problems I'd had with my security level, I wasn't about to jeopardize it with prohibited travel, but as it was I made frequent trips some distance from the garage to the fuel depot to fill up various vehicles including the warden's car.

Although life was now better, it was still prison and I began to wonder why I had heard nothing from the Circuit six months after oral arguments. Monica began to call the clerk every week to see if there had been a decision, but never received an answer in the affirmative. She asked the clerk what might be causing the delay and, although he professed not to know, said, "There's something special about this case."

There also seemed to be something special about my appeal of the Billings complaint, aka petition for review, as I had heard nothing in seven months, so I wrote the clerk myself to inquire.[141] The response was, "[O]ur records indicate that a petition for review was never received for filing in this case...the time has expired in which to submit a petition for review...The complaint has been dismissed, the case is closed and the Rules do not provide for any further relief in this matter."[142]

This was certainly an interesting state of affairs as I had filed the appeal on time. I didn't trust the Circuit at that point and thought it might try some kind of trick, so I mailed the notice of appeal along with a change of address form giving my new address at Fort Dix West. I also mailed my father a copy with a dated cover letter. The Circuit subsequently sent me mail at my new address, necessarily meaning it had received the notice of appeal.

I again wrote to Chief Judge Winter stating, "...the unrefuted evidence shows that the deputy clerk [in Vermont] rigged the jury pool for my trial. Assuming that Judge Billings is completely exonerated after a thorough investigation, there will remain a problem with the clerk...If I have used the wrong vehicle to initiate an investigation of this matter, please advise me of the correct procedure."[143] I never heard anything in response.

My father wrote twice to the Circuit inquiring about what had happened and stated that in 50 years of practice he had never heard of an appeal being dismissed permanently due to a postal error "or worse". According to Senior Deputy Clerk Kathleen Brouwer[144], the solution was to "file a proper lawsuit against the prison authorities", but the bottom line was, as previously stated by Deputy Clerk Madsen, "...the case is closed...".

The clerks, and the judges directing them, must have hoped that this brush-off would be effective, but Tony LaRosa had taught me well, and I had in the back of my mind that there was an exception for prisoners. It turned out that the U.S. Supreme Court had recognized the difficulties of prison litigation and the propensity of prison officials to tamper with the mail, and had crafted a remedy, probably not intending that the remedy would apply with equal effect to corrupt court personnel. This was subsequently codified in Federal Rule of Appellate Procedure 21(a)(2)(C) which provided that "A paper filed by an inmate confined in an institution is timely filed if deposited in the institution's internal mail system on or before the last day for filing." The required proof was a notarized declaration by the inmate.

I wrote back to the clerk saying that apparently Mr. Madsen was unaware, not only of the court's rules, but also recent court decisions wherein the Circuit had reinstated appeals after the inmates had complied with the requirements of the rule. I enclosed my declaration and asked that my appeal be docketed immediately. Two weeks later I received a one-sentence letter from Kathleen Brouwer: "In response to your letter dated July 7, 1998, I enclose a copy of my response dated June 29, 1998, to Robert A. Bloomer, Esq." In other words, sue the prison system.

244

Just a week before, the court had issued its opinion on the matter of Dr. Brown's payment. It decided that it had no jurisdiction to review Judge Murtha's decision to deny Dr. Brown's payment, and that I had "failed to show any bias or partiality by the judges that [I] sought to recuse."[145]

87

In this atmosphere, I puzzled over how to proceed with my jury tampering allegations, wondering if anyone at all would be interested. By this time, a large number of people in the system were aware of not only the jury issue, but the U.S. Attorney's unethical tactics, Judge Murtha's cover-up of same, and the Vermont Supreme Court's perversion of the lawyer disciplinary process.

I had begun to write Vermont's Congressional delegation (Sens. Patrick Leahy and James Jeffords, Rep. Bernard Sanders) after receiving Magistrate Niedermeier's report relying on the government's misrepresentations of fact as I thought they should know that, for all intents and purposes, the system in Vermont had broken down. The U.S. Attorney and the judges were all political appointees, ostensibly recommended by Sen. Leahy as the senior senator of the president's party, although since Vermont's representatives worked together more closely than most there was likely a consensus. Sen. Jeffords was a former Vermont Attorney General and Sen. Leahy had been a longtime State's Attorney in Chittenden County, so both certainly knew how the courts were supposed to work even if Rep. Sanders did not.

Sen. Jeffords had met with my father several times and was well aware of my situation but, although Jeffords had been helpful in obtaining documents and solving some prison difficulties, he did nothing about the corruption. Rep. Sanders wrote that, due to the separation of powers he could do nothing, and Sen. Leahy never replied at all.

Regarding the Vermont Supreme Court situation, I had written twice to Bar Association President Joan Wing, who had forwarded my initial letter to the chairman of her professional conduct investigating committee, Peter Hall. (Hall was a former Asst. U.S. Attorney, at the time in private practice, who went on to become U.S. Attorney and later served as a federal appellate judge on the Second Circuit.) I had also written to several other lawyers, one of whom wrote back that I hadn't told him anything new, but dealings with the Conduct Board were "scary", and he wasn't going to get involved.

I sent numerous letters to the *Rutland Herald* regarding all my allegations and to a lesser extent the *Burlington Free Press*, and even the *New York Times*, and never received a reply. I was particularly intrigued that the *Herald*, my hometown newspaper noted for bombastic editorials about the role of the press, had not bothered to follow up on any of the proof I had sent, but had found the ink to carry articles about big pumpkins and sunflower arranging contests.

After conferring with my brother, Tom, during a visit I decided that I should ask the U.S. Supreme Court for a writ mandamus, an old common law writ issued by a superior court to command an inferior court to do its job. I also thought that perhaps I could use the corruption in the system against itself.

While I was at Ray Brook another inmate from the Carolinas had told me that a certain U.S. Senator wanted to replace the corrupt local government in a seaside town with similarly corrupt operatives from his own political party. The instrument of this momentous change was to be the local U.S. attorney, and the star witness was to be my acquaintance. That particular scheme fell apart when the star witness had a change of heart and tipped off the targets of the investigation such that they were able to cover their tracks. However, I thought that an equally unscrupulous congressman or senator might want to install his own brand of judges on the appellate court, and for that reason might pursue an investigation into the Second Circuit's cover-up of the illegalities in Vermont with the goal of creating a few vacancies. There were already some vacancies, as the Republicans in Congress were refusing to approve President Clinton's nominees for the various federal courts, prompting Chief Judge Winter of the Second Circuit to declare a judicial emergency in the spring of 1998 due to the shortage of judges. A few more vacancies would be good, I thought, including Judge Winter. After filing for the writ of mandamus, I planned to send copies to about everyone in Congress.

88

As I was preparing to implement my plan, there was good news at Fort Dix: my case manager was soliciting applications for transfer to the new Federal Medical Center at the former Fort Devens, Massachusetts. The medical center itself had not yet opened, but an inmate work cadre was needed and was going to be housed in a temporary camp facility until a permanent camp could be built. I immediately submitted my request, and a week later was summoned to pack up. Four days after that, I was awakened at 3:15 a.m., and finally about a dozen of us left Fort Dix by prison bus at 6:30, shackled hand and foot.

The trip wasn't much fun. Theoretically we were the cream of the inmate crop, going as we were to open a new, minimum-security institution, and all of us were eligible for a furlough transfer, that is, an unsupervised trip by commercial bus. However, it turned out that we were to be the shakedown group for the Medical Center itself, an administrative or high security level facility, so we were treated as desperados. It was very disconcerting to watch a guard load a 12-gauge shotgun before boarding the bus, and the whole trip I imagined being accidentally shot by one Fort Dix's poorly-trained finest.

We stopped at FCI Otisville, some 70 miles north of New York City, to pick up a half-dozen more inmates and finally arrived at Devens at 3:30 in the afternoon. The entire staff of the new institution turned out to meet its first arrivals, and we were given the full in-processing treatment. All our personal property was thoroughly searched, and everything not on the FMC Devens approved list, including extra underwear and the small fans we had purchased at the Fort Dix commissary, was either sent home or thrown out. After enduring about two hours of this nitpicking nonsense, we were escorted to our new home - a dozen old house trailers left over from Hurricane Andrew relief that had been brought from Florida and set up on part of the old military golf course.

89

The Devens medical center had, in theory, been completed some time before and an open house had been held for the public. Then a team of volunteer guards had been brought in and, under the direction of an experienced welder, steel bars were retrofitted everywhere, even in the windows of the dining hall - windows thirty feet off the floor that led only to the roof. Wherever the bars were welded in, fresh paint was burned off, and when bars were welded over windows the hot spatter melted into the glass. The laundry was an incredible fortress, as if they were expecting a visit from John Dillinger, but all there was to steal was prison-issue clothing. There had been no bars of any sort at the Ray Brook or Fort Dix laundries, and no problems I was ever aware of.

Another Devens afterthought was the belated installation of three hundred security cameras, which required ripping holes in the new ceilings to run the necessary cable. Also ripped out were the floor tiles. A visiting team from the regional office decided that tiles were too good for inmates despite their near-universal presence in other institutions, and only bare concrete would do. The institution was already reputedly behind schedule and over budget, and this last minute madness made it imperative to bring in an inmate team to help out, even if it meant housing them in old trailers. My initial job was helping two electricians finish up the camera project.

Devens camp was superior to Fort Dix in every respect, in particular the tranquility. Gone were the constant din, confusion and bright lights that obscured the stars at night, and visiting was much better, too. My mother had almost been strip-searched at Fort Dix when her artificial hip set off the metal detector, but Devens visitors were treated courteously, and processed efficiently. And it was much closer to Rutland enabling people I hadn't seen for years to visit. Although some inmates made completely unjustified complaints about the food, it was far better than Fort Dix, and on Thanksgiving we were given a tremendous feast at the main institution with guards serving the inmates.

I'd barely settled in when I received word in early December that I'd won my appeal - sort of. The Second Circuit said I appeared to have established my claim, but "our cases emphasize that generally an assertedly ineffective attorney should have an opportunity to he heard and to present evidence before being declared ineffective. This issue must therefore be remanded to the district court for such a hearing."[146] Actually, such a hearing was rather rare, and both my attorney and I were puzzled as to the reason for it especially since, according to Monica, the court had decided another ineffective assistance case the same day on the record without a remand.

David Gibson's only defense could have been that his failure to object was a tactical decision but, as Monica put it, "...what possible tactical reason was there to ignore the obvious defects in the reasonable doubt instruction...?"[147] While I was angry at the time that this unnecessary remand would leave me in jail another few months, it turned out that the Circuit did me a favor. Once the federal district court gave Mr. Gibson a full and fair hearing and ruled on his ineffectiveness, the matter could not be relitigated before Gibson's cronies in the Vermont state court system, where I expected to bring my malpractice claim.

In the meantime, Gary Shattuck immediately filed for an "enlargement of time", that is, a delay, as he wanted to ask for a rehearing of the appeal but first had to get permission from the Justice Department in Washington. Such a rehearing was very unlikely, especially considering the judicial emergency declared by Judge Winter, and Shattuck's move was either an act of desperation or a ruse to keep me in jail for a few more weeks. In either event, the government never moved for a rehearing, and

248

the final order or mandate issued February 8, 1999, more than two months after the decision.

90

As I was waiting for the Circuit's decision, I decided to find out what had happened in the other cases that relied on Judge Billings' erroneous instruction, which the government had thoughtfully listed in its opposition to my motion in the District Court. I had known two of the defendants during my time in Ray Brook, Alan Harwood and Frederick McKee, knew that they had received tremendous sentences for an LSD drug conspiracy, and figured that they would have filed something regarding the instruction. My father was able to obtain the relevant documents and sent them to me.

Sure enough, Asst. U.S. Attorney Gary Shattuck was using the same misrepresentations of the record that had worked before in my case and, since Magistrate Niedermeier and Judge Murtha had already bought into the hoax, it was not surprising that they did so again. This time, however, Niedermeier might have wanted to hedge his bets because his analysis was a little different. In ruling on McKee's motion the Magistrate found counsel's performance was deficient for not appealing an obviously defective jury instruction. All that was left was to show that the outcome of the proceeding would have been different, but at this point Niedermeier's opinion jumped the tracks.

Since the relevant facts were the same in McKee as they were in Birbal, it was inescapable that, had McKee's lawyer appealed the jury instruction issue, McKee's convictions would have been reversed. Instead of dealing with the obvious, Niedermeier focused on the fraudulent amelioration argument, reanalyzed the entire question of the jury instruction that had already been settled by the Second Circuit, and concluded that McKee wasn't entitled to a new trial.[148] Judge Murtha performed his own lengthy analysis, closely following the magistrate, and arrived at the same nonsensical result.[149]

Codefendant Alan Harwood's motion, also alleging ineffective assistance of counsel, was shot down in a short opinion relying on McKee. Knowing very well that six months before the Circuit had granted me permission to appeal the ineffective assistance issue, Judge Murtha nonetheless wrote, "...[Harwood's] grounds for relief do not present issues which are debatable among jurists of reason ... or which deserve further proceedings...any appeal taken in forma pauperis from this Order would not be taken in good faith because such an appeal would be frivolous."[150]

249

As disheartening as the results must have been for McKee and Harwood, they were good news for me. In McKee, Judge Murtha had found that counsel's performance was deficient for failing to appeal the defective instruction, and the Circuit said in my case that, "if on remand the district court [Judge Murtha] concludes that Bloomer's previous counsel's performance was deficient, Bloomer will succeed on his ineffective assistance claim." With this in mind I wrote to David Gibson on December 28, 1998 advising him that "At this point, I doubt that anything you might say [on remand] could change the outcome in that Judge Murtha has already ruled in other cases that counsel was ineffective...I am advising you now of the situation to give you sufficient time to decide if you wish to be heard before the mandate [from the Circuit] issues. I ask that you make your intentions known to the Court promptly so that I do not languish needlessly in prison." Gibson never responded.

Considering the stakes, I thought it wise to let Judge Murtha know I was aware of his finding in McKee and, after consultation with Monica, filed a pro se memorandum of law on January 7th citing McKee and suggesting that "the question of counsel's ineffectiveness is moot and that this Court could, for reasons of judicial economy, reverse [my] conviction without further proceedings." Technically, Judge Murtha had no jurisdiction as my case remained in the Second Circuit until the mandate issued. He noted as much a few days later, but I had made my point.

The mandate came down February 8th, but two weeks later I had heard nothing from Judge Murtha, and decided to move things along by filing a motion for bail noting that, "It is unconscionable that Bloomer should remain incarcerated awaiting a proceeding in the District Court where the result - a reversal of his conviction - is a virtual certainty."[151] A couple of days after I had sent the bail motion, Judge Murtha issued a Notice of Hearing and Order setting the date for March 30th. The next day, another Notice of Hearing issued "to take evidence on petitioner's claim of ineffective assistance of counsel",[152] but that's not what the Circuit had ordered. The Circuit's instructions to the District Court were explicit: "...first hear Bloomer's former counsel, and then [] make a finding in the first instance as to Bloomer's claim of ineffective assistance...".

It was a little difficult to figure out what Judge Murtha might have up his sleeve, but his order had made it clear enough that I was not to be released from prison following the hearing. The U.S. Marshals were directed to "return the defendant to the [Federal Bureau of Prisons] facility upon completion of the proceedings".[153] At the suggestion of my brother, I

250

filed a Motion to Amend pointing out that the Order didn't follow Circuit's mandate. Judge Murtha denied the motion the next day.

I had planned to have my appeal attorney, Monica, appointed to represent me at the hearing, but she couldn't make it on the 30th, which would have meant yet another delay. I didn't trust any lawyer in the state of Vermont, and decided to represent myself, which wasn't particularly daring. I knew my case as well as anyone, and the Circuit had preordained the result of the hearing. If Judge Murtha were determined to go his own way in defiance of the Circuit, then he would do so regardless of whether I had counsel or not.

Dad became a little apprehensive about the hearing, and called David Gibson on March 4th to see if Gibson intended to testify. At that time he thought not, but promised to call back in a few days. When he didn't, Dad tried to call from the 8th to the 12th, but Gibson would neither accept nor return calls. Dad was upset, but my mother was incensed and drafted a very nasty letter to Gibson. Dad toned it down a bit, left in some thinly veiled threats, and sent it out on the 15th. Gibson replied by fax on the 16th that he wasn't sure whether he needed to be present, he didn't "intend to state anything against [my] interests", and he was unfamiliar with the previous Second Circuit decision, Delibac, criticizing Judge Billings' jury instructions. Without that knowledge, Gibson could not have performed effectively, as the Birbal case had relied on Delibac.

I was hoping that I would remain at Devens until the last minute, but the day after Gibson's fax two U.S. Marshals brought me to the Cheshire County Jail in New Hampshire, just across the river from Judge Murtha's court in Brattleboro, Vermont. Luckily, most of my preparation for the hearing was done, because Cheshire was at least as unprofessional an institution as the state prison in Rutland, and perhaps worse. My legal papers were confiscated immediately and not returned for five days despite several protests and, when they finally were returned all the staples had been removed for "security reasons".

After two unpleasant weeks at Cheshire, two marshals brought me the ten miles or so to the federal courthouse in Brattleboro, Vermont and, after changing from prison garb into a suit, I appeared before Judge Murtha. I had never seen the judge before, but I had most certainly seen his clerk, Austin Burbank, the man who had been responsible for my trial jury. Dutifully taking down the proceedings was court reporter William Currie, III, the same reporter Judge Murtha knew had mistranscribed my trial. I had written or sent copies to Judge Murtha on several occasions about the activities of those two, so he was very well aware of the message their presence was sending.

251

My brother Rick, an attorney, sat at the defense table with me to give advice if necessary. Asst. U.S. Attorney David Kirby and I made brief statements to the court, and I offered Gibson's letter to my father as an exhibit. No one knew exactly what to do, but Gibson took the witness stand and stated that he was available if anyone wanted to question him. I had no questions and, after some small talk with David Kirby, Gibson could only offer that he had simply missed the bad instruction. Judge Murtha than reversed my convictions from the bench and ordered a new trial in ninety days.

The government opposed my bail, although it had no legal justification to do so. In the end it made no difference as Judge Murtha announced that in the month since my bail motion had been filed, he hadn't had the opportunity to read the three pages of my previous release conditions, and that I would be remanded to Cheshire until U.S. Probation could interview me. I was then removed to the basement holding cell of the court, where I changed back into my prison outfit and was shackled for the return trip. At that point, David Kirby and Gary Shattuck arrived and proposed a deal. If I would agree to a trial in 180 days instead of 90 they would drop their opposition to my bail.

I didn't trust that pair at all, and refused to discuss the matter without consulting with my brother. Luckily, the government attorneys hadn't waited too long to make their pitch, and my brother was located on the front steps leaving the courthouse with my parents. Rick couldn't see any downside for me, and I agreed to the delay. We then returned to Judge Murtha's courtroom, where it turned out that nothing further was required than the recommendation of David Kirby, and I was released on the prior conditions, a copy of which just happened to be available. I had no home to return to, and planned to stay with my parents in Rutland temporarily until my life stabilized. I was still representing myself and, with retrial coming up, had to hit the ground running.

91

Unfortunately, my driver's license had lapsed during the time I was in prison for failure to mail in the requisite renewal fee. Fortunately, a friend knew one of the Department of Motor Vehicles examiners, and I was able to take the tests and get my license the day after my release, a process that otherwise might have taken weeks. The next day my brother, Rick, and I drove from Rutland to Burlington, some seventy miles away, to meet with my new case worker in U.S. Probation. We then headed southeast to Vermont Law School so that Rick could introduce me to the

252

law library there, the closest one to Rutland with federal resources, and then we drove the thirty-five miles back to Rutland.

It was tempting to consider another trial in that the government's drug case against me had been substantially weakened and an aggressive defense could be mounted. However, within a few minutes of my release in Judge Murtha's courtroom, Rick began to warn me of the dangers of going back to trial. After subsequent discussions, we agreed that I could not be allowed to win. If I were acquitted at trial, I would sue, at the very least, the court clerk, Judge Billings, the Vermont State Police Laboratory, numerous police officers and perhaps the court reporter and some United States attorneys. What was at stake was the integrity of the courts, the police and prosecutors, and I simply was not going to be allowed to wreck the whole system. However as long as I had even one conviction, all these people were immune. The legal reasoning was that in order to maintain a civil claim I had to show damages but, since my imprisonment was punishment for my crime, other people could not have been responsible, no matter what they had done.

Since the drug case wouldn't fly easily by itself, Rick and I expected that the tactic would be to paint me as a really evil and dangerous person, a person who should be jailed on general principles even if the drug evidence was weak. In order to paint this picture, the government would have to rely on a tried and true method, prison snitches, and I could easily see a dozen or more denizens of Ray Brook and Fort Dix testifying that I had confessed to the most heinous acts as well as a huge methamphetamine conspiracy. In return, the witnesses would receive breathtaking sentence reductions.

While one or two of these questionable witnesses could have probably been discredited effectively, a large number created a much greater difficulty. The jury either would have to believe that they were telling the truth, or that the U.S. Attorney's office was vicious enough to orchestrate such a conspiracy. Having seen others convicted by false prison snitch testimony, I preferred not bet my life on which version the jury would choose.

As far as receiving a fair trial, Judge Murtha had made his sympathies abundantly clear. The same clerk who had influenced my first jury had been placed by Murtha in a position to influence the second, and Circuit had remanded my case to a judge it had ample reason to believe was at least biased against me, if not corrupt. The message was clear enough: "Plead guilty to something."

Not surprisingly, David Gibson was urging the same course. He had taken the liberty of discussing my situation with well-known criminal lawyer Thomas Zonay and, two days after I had been released, wrote my father that "...Tom thinks that it might be an auspicious time to explore the possibility of an agreement for entry of a plea with a sentence to be agreed upon for time served only."

Curiously, although no one acknowledged any problems with jury selection procedures in Vermont someone, probably the Circuit, had been trying to clean up the mess or at least sweep it under the carpet. In 1998 my mother had been called for federal jury duty for the first time in her life, although in the past lawyers' wives generally received an automatic excusal. And when I reviewed the Vermont Local Rules, I noticed that several changes had been made regarding juries. A letter to the clerk asking if the previous practices were still in effect elicited a response from Jury Administrator Kathleen Carter: "To answer your question of whether we use an informal system of juror excusals the answer is no. I formally respond to every juror's request for excusal in writing so we both have written documentation regarding the request."[154] Considering that the guilty parties in my jury selection had not been disciplined, I hoped that I would not have to personally determine if the changes had been effective.

92

While a satisfactory plea agreement was a theoretical possibility, in the meantime I had to prepare for trial, and the better prepared I was, the stronger negotiating position I would have. Fortunately, during the time I'd been incarcerated the internet had taken off, my mother had purchased a computer, and had opened an internet account. Many legal resources were online, which saved numerous research trips to Vermont Law School. Nonetheless, most of my time was consumed with legal work.

The first order of business was to get a lawyer for retrial. I wasn't experienced enough to represent myself in a complex trial and, since I planned to testify in my own defense, figured I couldn't effectively question myself. As David Gibson so amply proved, paying an attorney was no guarantee of either loyalty or competence, but that was academic since I had no money left. However, since Gibson had shown himself incapable of adequately cross-examining the government's experts, I thought I would be better off doing that myself. Two weeks after I was released from prison I filed a motion with Judge Murtha for the appointment of co-counsel[155], which was denied. I was required to choose - either appointed counsel or pro se.

I filed a motion for reconsideration, citing Second Circuit cases and three instances where Gibson had bungled his cross-examination so badly that the courts had reached erroneous conclusions. This time Judge Murtha granted my motion, but limited any participation on my part to the government's chemical experts. The next day the court coincidentally, or not so coincidentally, appointed counsel in the person of Thomas Zonay, the attorney with whom David Gibson had recently consulted about a plea agreement.

<h1 style="text-align:center">93</h1>

A week before the appointment of Tom Zonay, I had moved to the family camp at Lake Bomoseen, an ideal place to acclimate myself to normal life after seven years in prison, and to continue my legal work without distractions. It was going to take Mr. Zonay some time to read my trial transcript, filings with the court and other materials to come up to speed on the case, and in the meantime I went ahead researching three matters I thought would be important.

The first was that I wanted Asst. U.S. Attorneys David Kirby and Gary Shattuck named as defense witnesses, which would have removed them from the case and required the new prosecutor to spend a very substantial amount of time preparing for trial. While such a move was not favored, there was ample legal precedent, and only Shattuck and Kirby could explain where they had obtained the Alfa Products chemical orders and how the names of Keefe and Harotunian came to appear on them.

Second, I prepared an elaborate discovery motion for the grand jury and inquest testimony of numerous witnesses that, according to the indictment, had purchased methamphetamine from my codefendant, Robert Spencer, in 1988. Since the government had conceded that I sold no meth in 1988, it had to have come from somewhere that no one had yet revealed, and the more that had been sold in that year, the bigger the problem.

Lastly, I wanted to challenge the search warrant application, and spent a tremendous amount of time documenting the inaccuracies or outright falsehoods in Det. LaMoria's affidavit. The first time around, it was always very difficult to challenge a federal warrant because all the protections and inferences were in favor of the government, and discovery was specifically not allowed. However, the second time around I had obtained information that was not available for the suppression hearing, and I thought a very persuasive argument could be made. Also, the second time around I knew how the hearing should be conducted, and I was not relying on David Gibson.

Although I was working on trial issues, the emphasis from the beginning was on reaching a plea deal. Mr. Zonay applied to the court for an investigator, which was approved, and Guy Paradee was hired. Since he had done the investigation for my father on my trial jurors, I was not unhappy with the choice. Guy did perform some work at the direction of Tom Zonay, but I was never quite sure what it was, and it definitely didn't include an interview with Mark Malmros, my partner in the medical research project. We had filed a motion to change my release conditions to permit me to visit my brother, Tom, in New York and to permit me to have contact with Mark, who had visited me numerous times in prison and was eager to testify for the defense, but in a month's time Judge Murtha never ruled on it. No discovery motions were ever filed.

I had indicated to Mr. Zonay that the only acceptable plea agreement would be for time served, no fine, and no supervised release. Whether or not the conditions of supervised release were violated was pretty much in the discretion of the judge, as was the penalty, which could include jail. Given the circumstances of my case, it didn't take too much imagination to figure that Judge Murtha would send me back to prison for a few years if he got the opportunity, and that the opportunity might arise very soon after the agreement. Under Federal Rule of Criminal Procedure 11(e)(1)(C) (since revised) an agreement between myself and the government could be submitted to Judge Murtha, but his only options would be to accept it or reject it in it's entirety, a much different situation than generally occurred where the judge could determine the sentence himself and was not bound by any agreement.

Given Mr. Zonay's knowledge of the government's previous treachery in my case, I was astounded to receive a proposed plea agreement on July 20th containing the following conditions:

> 10. If the United States determines, in its sole discretion, that the defendant has committed any offense after the date of this agreement, or violated any condition of release, the United States' obligations under...this agreement will be void and the United States will have the right to recommend that the Court impose any sentence authorized by law and will have the right to prosecute the defendant for any other offenses...the defendant understands and agrees that, under such circumstances, he will have no right to withdraw his previously entered plea of guilty.

256

Again, it didn't take too much imagination to see where things were headed. I immediately sent Mr. Zonay a fax indicating that the proposal was "completely unacceptable, and not representative of what I understood the agreement to be." I ended with, "We either have a deal or we don't. I would like an answer today. If the government is going to continue to play these kinds of games, I will need to gear up for trial immediately." This apparently got the ball rolling, as the government quickly came up with a satisfactory agreement.

I was to plead guilty to Count 3 of the indictment: maintaining a place for the purpose of manufacturing, distributing and using methamphetamine. In return I was to get time served, no supervised release, and a mandatory special assessment of $50.00, against which I had already paid $300.00. Count 3 was chosen because it was the only count not requiring supervised release. The government insisted on adding language to the plea agreement that I would bring no civil or administrative claims (including ethical violations) against the United States, the State of Vermont or any of their agencies, employees, or agents involved in the investigation and prosecution of my case.

We all appeared in court before Judge Murtha on August 2, 1999. After the requisite formalities, he accepted the agreement, but not without one last trick. The procedure for a guilty plea was for the judge to read down the agreement, and for the defendant to acknowledge and accept each provision. During the process, Judge Murtha asked, "...do you understand that the maximum penalty for a plea -- in connection with a plea of guilty on this charge is not more than 20 years of imprisonment or a fine of not more than -- $500,000 or both..."[156] I don't know what might have happened if I had perfunctorily agreed, but my brother had anticipated just such a stunt, and I replied that those were the statutory maximums. Mr. Zonay jumped immediately to his feet, pointing out that my plea was a Rule 11 agreement, and the judge had no discretion except to accept or reject it. The statutory maximums, although listed in the agreement, were irrelevant as the agreement specified the sentence as time served and no fine. Judge Murtha claimed that he was just reading from the agreement, but obviously he was not. Of course the error could have been inadvertent, but given Judge Murtha's previous behavior it also could have been deliberate. Luckily, I didn't have the opportunity to find out for sure with a twenty-year sentence.

After the proceeding I walked out of the courthouse, free at last, sort of. There are a number of disabilities for felons, including that they not have "constructive possession" of a firearm. In a state like Vermont, where virtually all the natives have guns, I would have to be careful. At least my Dad was able to see me free from prison and free of the court system before he died of cancer a scant four months after my plea.

94

The big loose end left by my plea agreement was David Gibson, and I sued him for malpractice before the end of 1999. Although the case was in state court instead of federal court, I wondered if the same network of insiders, unethical lawyers and corrupt judges that had dogged me from the beginning would prevent me from ever getting any satisfaction from Mr. Gibson.

There was not much reason for optimism. Both of my complaints against Gibson with the Vermont Professional Conduct Board had been dismissed by the Board's gatekeepers without submitting them to the full panel, and the Vermont Supreme Court had been directly involved in the secret submission of the defective first complaint, apparently to orchestrate a preemptive dismissal. When I finally figured out what had happened, that Court would not allow me to reopen the complaint with all of my proof.

As to the second complaint alleging that Gibson had failed to respond to his client, failed to turn over the client file on demand, and failed to act in a professional manner regarding the fees owed to Dr. Edward Brown, the response was incompetent and insulting. The letter from Disciplinary Counsel Michael Kennedy began: "This office has completed its review of the complaint that you filed against Attorney Lorenz. For the reasons stated below, your complaint has been dismissed."[157] I had never been represented by, nor filed a complaint against, any "Attorney Lorenz".

The Vermont Supreme Court oversaw the Professional Conduct Board and, unlike many states, came up for periodic retention reviews by the Legislature. Shortly before leaving Devens, I sent a package of materials to each member of the Judicial Retention Committee about my experiences with the Board, and the Supreme Court's rigging of the process. According to my cousin, Sen. John Bloomer, Jr., a member of the Committee, the subject of the Conduct Board never came up, although there had been a considerable scandal only a couple of years before and lingering complaints from lawyers. All of the Justices were retained.

The sadistic Teri Ames of U.S. Probation, who had recommended a sentence for me of 30 to life, didn't seem to have mellowed with age. As reported in the *Addison Independent* on October 4, 2012:

A former prosecutor with the Addison County State's Attorney's Office pleaded innocent to charges of grossly negligent operation of a motor vehicle and reckless endangerment. The charges stemmed from a Sept. 8 incident in which she allegedly drove up Middlebury's Seminary Street for around 200 feet while her 8-year-old daughter was holding onto and running alongside the vehicle.

Teri Ames, 48, is accused of the misdemeanor charges...

[A police affidavit stated] "The child eventually let go on her own and Ms. Ames never stopped to check her welfare."

Ms. Ames attorney (the quintessential insider, Robert P. Keiner) filed a motion to dismiss, which was denied, and a motion to reconsider, which was also denied. In an amazing display of judicial independence, Judge Brian Grearson was unwilling to do the necessary dirty work, requiring the prosecutor to dismiss all the charges himself.[158] Once again, the system had taken care of its own.

One of the few bright spots in an otherwise sordid history was an article by Associated Press reporter Dave Gram that appeared in the *Sunday Herald/Times Argus* on May 21, 2000. Gram told me that this was to be part one of three-part series on my case, but the other two would "never see the light of day" because they had been squashed by his "boss", ostensibly Chris Graff. It looked to me like Graff had become yet another insider, too cozy with those in the system. Perhaps my opinion was shared by his superiors at the AP, as Graff was fired after putting a piece authored by Vermont U.S. Senator Patrick Leahy on the AP wire. According to *Seven Days*[159], "Politicians from [Republican] Jim Douglas to [Democrat] Pat Leahy said it is a huge loss and complete surprise."

As it was, Mr. Gram had read my plea agreement and realized immediately that something serious was wrong in that the U.S. attorneys were using the agreement to shield themselves from ethics charges. According to his article, "Two law professors said the prosecutors' actions could warrant criminal charges under the federal bribery or extortion laws." U.S. Attorney Tetzlaff, interviewed for the article, justified the ethics provisions in the agreement: "We had spent considerable time and resources in matters that we felt were frankly a waste of time and frivolous. And we wanted to stop that."

The U.S. Attorney's office was often a stepping-stone to another position in the federal government, assuming that one did not become embroiled in a major scandal, and so it was with Mr. Tetzlaff. Not even a year after Gram's article, Tetzlaff was appointed general counsel to the United States Sentencing Commission, where he could ostensibly ride out the rest of his career in well-paid obscurity. (However, at this writing Mr. Tetzlaff is back in Vermont in private practice.)

Assistant U.S. Attorney Gary Shattuck, on the other hand, found himself in the limelight. Someone must have thought that Vermont-style prosecutorial tactics were worthy of export, as Shattuck was sent on a U.N. mission to Kosovo "helping to rebuild the shattered province's justice system."[160] As the ghastly ethnic violence continued, one of Shattuck's contributions, a tune-up of Kosovo's drug laws, must have been appreciated. Apparently someone considered the program a success, as Shattuck was subsequently sent to Iraq. In spite of his efforts, that country descended into chaos, but Shattuck may have learned some techniques there that could be applied to Vermont. One of his activities was to accompany a U.S. military group for the scheduled delivery of a load of cash to an Iraqi judge. Following his Iraq adventure, perhaps Mr. Shattuck concluded that someone with considerable influence wanted him out of the U.S. Attorney's Office. In any event, he wisely retired before receiving another assignment to a war zone.

David Kirby, likewise, left the office although he had a supervisory position, and had filled in as acting U.S. Attorney until a full-time appointment could be made. Given his considerable guaranteed income and the comfortable nature of his federal job, there was again speculation as to why he would want to trade that for the uncertainties of private practice well past the midpoint of his career.

Shortly after the Gram article appeared I wrote to U.S. Senator James Jeffords[161], reminding him off all the abuses that had occurred in Vermont, abuses of which he was well aware because of my father's frequent contacts and the several letters I had previously written to him. I concluded:

> I submit that the same standard should apply to everyone.
> Either a completely independent special prosecutor should
> be appointed to investigate the entire criminal justice
> system in Vermont or everyone involved in these incidents
> should be allowed to walk away with no criminal record.
> I can only walk away with a presidential pardon, as the
> president is the only person who can expunge a federal
> criminal conviction. In that regard I note that according to
> the Rutland Herald you voted according to the wishes of

president Clinton more than any other Republican senator. For that reason I believe that any request for a presidential pardon sponsored by yourself would receive careful scrutiny. Please advise me as to what, if anything, you intend to do about this matter.

I never heard from the Senator. A short time later my mother received a fundraising letter from Jeffords, which she sent back along with a copy of my letter and an inquiry as to what Jeffords' answer was. She never heard anything either. Considering that President Clinton granted nearly 400 pardons, some to highly controversial characters like fugitive financier Marc Rich and Clinton crony Susan McDougal*, a Jeffords-sponsored pardon request might well have been granted.

In a considerable irony, Judge Murtha clearly understood the corrosive effects of dishonesty. During a sentencing lecture to a disgraced microbiologist who had faked his scientific data, Murtha noted that his actions could have led to dangerous results and could have undermined the public's confidence in the work of credible scientists. "It could have caused some serious problems for people," the judge said.[162] Micro-biologists were one matter, but Judge Murtha's own court appeared to be another. As to public confidence in the latter, the judge, along with most of the rest of the legal community, just didn't seem to care.

---

* Susan McDougal was an instant favorite in the prison community for her steadfast refusal to testify about the Clintons, even though it meant a jail term for her.

END NOTES

All transcripts are from the case *U.S. v. Robert A. Bloomer, Jr.*, United States District Court, District of Vermont, Docket No. 91-00082 unless otherwise noted.

Paper refers to a numbered document on the docket sheet of the above case.

Civil Trial refers to *Bloomer v. Gibson*, Rutland [Vermont] Superior Court, Docket #S0651-99RcC

Gibson Deposition refers to the deposition Mr. Gibson gave in the above case on August 24, 2000

[1] Affidavit of Raymond LaMoria, Jr. dated August 10, 1990,
[2] Investigation Report of Det. Sgt. James W. Baker, Vermont State Police Case #2001-90-01448 dated 10/23/90
[3] Id.
[4] Transcript of probable cause hearing, August 10, 1990, District Court of Vermont, Judge Paul F. Hudson presiding, page 7.
[5] *Rutland Herald*, September 5, 1990
[6] Vermont Supreme Court Docket # 92-074
[7] Investigation Report of Trooper Russell Penka, Vermont State Police Case #2001-90-01448 undated
[8] Sharon Stickney affidavit before Edward Lucas signed November 23, 1991
[9] Trial Transcript IV-43; 84-85
[10] Transcript of probable cause hearing, supra, page 5
[11] Penka report, supra.
[12] Baker report, supra.
[13] Suppression Hearing, Transcript page 36.
[14] Federal Bureau of Prisons Program Statement 5720.07 Chapter 5, page 1.
[15] Civil Trial Exhibit 105
[16] Paper 29.
[17] Paper 31.
[18] Gibson letter dated March 16, 1992.
[19] Trial Transcript I-61
[20] Trial Transcript I-26.
[21] Trial Transcript IV-24.
[22] LaMoria Affidavit, page 3.
[23] Paper 1
[24] Counts 9, 10, 12, 14, 15. 16, 17, 18, 19, 20.
[25] Counts 9, 10, 12, 14, 16, 17, 18.

[26] Trial Transcript III-14.
[27] Id.
[28] Trial Transcript IV-44-50
[29] Trial Transcript II-152.
[30] Trial Transcript II-153.
[31] Trial Transcript II-155.
[32] Trial Transcript IX-4.
[33] Trial Transcript IX-14.
[34] Paradee Investigative Report dated October 29, 1994.
[35] Grand Jury Testimony of Beverly Hobson April 18, 1991; Transcript p. 43
[36] Trial Transcript VIII-47
[37] Trial Transcript III-14.
[38] Trial Transcript II-177.
[39] Trial Transcript II-162.
[40] Trial Transcript II-178.
[41] Personal notes.
[42] Civil Trial Exhibit 12.
[43] Gibson billing statement dated December 18, 1992.
[44] Papers 68 and 70
[45] *Rutland Herald* February 5, 1993.
[46] Paper 72
[47] Paper 84.
[48] Civil Trial Exhibit 43
[49] Civil Trial Exhibit 44.
[50] Paper 80.
[51] *Rutland Sunday Herald*, April 11, 1993.
[52] Trial Transcript II-178
[53] Trial Transcript II-177.
[54] Trial transcript VII-139
[55] Trial transcript VII-139
[56] Trial transcript VI-36-37.
[57] *U.S. v. Spencer, 4 F3d 115 (1993)*
[58] Civil Trial Exhibit 95
[59] *U.S. v. Bogusz*, 43 F.3d 82 (3rd Cir. 1994)
[60] Paper 104
[61] *U.S. Dept. of Justice v. Landano*, 508 U.S. 165 (1993)
[62] Paper 107
[63] 28 U.S.C. §1861 et. seq.
[64] Resentence Transcript I, pp. 50-51
[65] Resentence Transcript II, page 8
[66] Paper 108
[67] Paper 113

[68] Gibson Deposition, Exhibit 55

[69] *Bloomer v. U.S, 162 F.3d 187 (2d Cir. 1998)*

[70] Gibson Deposition, Exhibit 55

[71] *U.S. v. Bloomer*, Second Circuit Court of Appeals Docket No. 94-1049, 2nd Cir. (1994)

[72] Civil Trial Exhibit 76

[73] On September 27, 1995

[74] On May 27, 1994

[75] *Bloomer v. Pollution Solutions and State of Vermont,* Rutland [Vermont] Superior Court Docket # S0497-93 RcC

[76] McMahon Deposition (taken May 27, 1994) Transcript, p. 19

[77] Id.

[78] Sentell letter of October 5, 1994

[79] On August 23, 1995

[80] On December 26, 1995

[81] 430 U.S. 817 (1977)

[82] 516 U.S. 804 (1996)

[83] 86 F3d 23 (2d Cir. 1995)

[84] 899 F.Supp.1257 (D.Vt. 1995)

[85] 2nd Circuit Court of Appeals Docket # 95-1664

[86] 2nd Circuit Court of Appeals Docket #96-1325

[87] *US v. Schneider*, 2nd Circuit Docket # 96-1048

[88] Paper 126

[89] Kirby affidavit, Paper 126

[90] Paper 128

[91] Paper 129

[92] Paper 136

[93] Paper 134

[94] Endorsed order to Paper 136

[95] On April 25, 1996

[96] On May 15, 1996

[97] On May 29, 1996

[98] Paper 139

[99] Paper 140

[100] On June 17, 1996

[101] Paper 141

[102] Mandate, 2nd Circuit Docket # 96-2309

[103] Letters of July 3, 1996

[104] Paper 144

[105] 2nd Circuit Court of Appeals Docket No. 96-2531

[106] *In Re Curl*, 803 F.2d 1004, 1007 (9th cir. 1986)

[107] Government's Closing Statement, Pp. 3-4

[108] Trial Transcript V-90
[109] On September 9, 1996
[110] April 6, 1996; June 11, 1996; August 1, 1996
[111] 920 F.2d 1040 (1st Cir. 1990)
[112] Id.
[113] On September 25, 1995
[114] On October 18, 1995
[115] On November 17, 1995
[116] On May 22, 1996
[117] On May 28, 1996
[118] On June 5, 1996
[119] Papers 80 and 81
[120] Paper 115
[121] On March 4, 1994
[122] On June 12, 1996
[123] Paper 146
[124] Paper 147
[125] 2nd Circuit Court of Appeals Docket Nos. 96-8543, 44,45,46
[126] 2nd Circuit Court of Appeals Docket No. 96-1800
[127] Tetzlaff letter of December 24, 1996
[128] Waples letter of March 3, 1997
[129] On May 28 and August 12, 1996
[130] Wasko letter August 21, 1996
[131] Paper 152
[132] Paper 151
[133] Letter of October 21, 1996
[134] Letter from Larry Abbott to Shelley Hill dated October 29, 1996
[135] *Time,* February 23, 1987
[136] Tetzlaff letter of letter of Sept. 9, 1997
[137] Billings letter of letter of June 12, 1997
[138] Tetzlaff letter of June 6, 1997
[139] 2nd Circuit Court of Appeals Docket No. 97-8529
[140] Id.
[141] On June 1, 1998
[142] Letter from 2nd Circuit clerk Bernard F. Madsen dated June 4, 1998
[143] Letter of June 18, 1998
[144] Letter of June 29, 1998
[145] *U.S. v. Bloomer*, 150 F.3d 146 (2d Cir. 1998)
[146] *Bloomer v. U.S.,* 162 F.3d 187 (2d. Cir. 1998)
[147] Jacobson letter of December 4, 1998
[148] United States District Court, District of Vermont, Docket No. 1:91-CR-68, Paper 87

[149] Id. Paper 91
[150] Id., Paper 94
[151] Paper 162
[152] Paper 161
[153] Paper 160
[154] Letter of April 7, 1999
[155] Paper 168
[156] Plea and Sentence Hearing of August 2, 1999; Transcript p. 6
[157] Letter from Michael Kennedy dated January 18, 2000; PCB File No. 98.13
[158] *State v. Ames*, Vermont Superior Court, Chittenden Criminal Division, Docket No. 368-10-12
[159] *Seven Days*, March 22, 2006
[160] *Rutland Herald,* May 13, 2000
[161] On June 19, 2000
[162] Rutland Herald February 1, 2007